THE CATHOLIC UNIVERSITY OF AMERICA
CANON LAW STUDIES
Number 53

COMPETENCE IN MATRIMONIAL PROCEDURE

A DISSERTATION

Submitted to the Faculty of Canon Law of the Catholic University of America in Partial Fulfilment of the Requirements for the Degree of

DOCTOR OF CANON LAW

BY THE
REVEREND THOMAS HENRY KAY, J.C.L.
Priest of the Diocese of Albany

THE CATHOLIC UNIVERSITY OF AMERICA
WASHINGTON, D. C.
1929

Nihil Obstat:

JACOBUS H. RYAN, Ph.D., S.T.D.,
Censor Deputatus.
Washingtonii, D. C., die XV Maii, 1929.

Imprimatur:

✠EDMUNDUS F. GIBBONS, D.D.,
Episcopus Albanensis.
Albaniae, die XVI Maii, 1929.

WASHINGTON TYPOGRAPHERS, INC.
WASHINGTON, D. C.

TABLE OF CONTENTS

PART II

Matrimonial Competence Within the Church
(*Canons 1962-1965; 1990-1992*)

FOREWORD

"Competence in Matrimonial Procedure" is presented as a dissertation in partial fulfilment of the requirements for a doctorate in Canon Law. The treatment does not pretend to be exhaustive. The question of the competence of the Church and State in matrimonial matters is itself an unlimited field for research, and the history of the relations of the ecclesiastical and secular authorities could not be adequately considered within the scope of this work. However, a summary sketch, affording an outline of the historical progress, has been given.

The limitations of the proper spheres of ecclesiastical and civil competence, and the adjustment of the necessary reciprocal relationship in the matter of marriage, have ever been problematic. The ecclesiastical regulation of matrimony is based fundamentally on the dogmatic teachings of the Church. The marriage between baptized persons is a Sacrament, and even where the sacramental character is lacking, marriage is, to the Church, a sacred relationship. The State, on the other hand, views and legislates for marriage from the standpoint of "practical social science and humanity." In the United States, there are as many marriage legislations as there are States. To the secular authorities marriage is a purely civil contract, unique indeed, yet one which is daily being robbed of its traditional sacredness. When fundamental principles are thus at variance, the practical consequences in marriage questions will be difficult to reconcile. Theory may be clear but the individual case demands particular study and prudent treatment, if no open clash of competence is to result.

Within the Church, the general limits of matrimonial competence are well known and understood. Her dogmatic concepts and the canonical principles outline the spheres of jurisdiction, and mark the limits of authority. For the universal Church, complete authority is found in the Roman Pontiff; for the particular diocese, in the Bishop. At Rome matrimonial causes are treated either personally by the Pope, or as is usual, through the Roman Curia.

In the diocese the Bishop assisted by the local curia is called upon to decide matrimonial questions. Procedure in the normal judicial process does not present much difficulty. But the most exact process will have been in vain if the sentence is given by a court not properly competent. Competence is sufficiency of authority in the ecclesiastical official to act in a given matter. A sentence borne by an absolutely incompetent judge or by a tribunal lacking the requisite number of members, or given for a party who has no juridical standing in court, would be invalid beyond the remedy of a sanation. An ecclesiastical judge, therefore, must look to his competence before he acts. This is reason enough for a consideration of matrimonial competence in the diocesan curia.

Much time and space have been devoted in the present work to a consideration of the documentary process. This brief form of procedure is of comparatively recent origin, and it offered a rather unexplored reach of canon law. The limits of administrative and judicial authority in processes are often obscure. From this study, however, has evolved the conviction that the documentary process is fundamentally judicial. And from this finding, the practical consequences have been drawn by the application of canonical principles.

One accepted principle with roots embedded in the Code, is that the Vicar General exercises administrative power while the Official possesses judicial authority. The view set forth in Chapter VI seems to be most firmly established by the particular response of the Pontifical Commission for the Authentic Interpretation of the Code given to the Paris Curia. Further, just before the publication of this work, a personal communication from Professor Franciscus Roberti brought the assurance that in his learned opinion the brief process is truly judicial.

Grateful acknowledgment is expressed to the members of the Faculty of Canon Law at the Catholic University for their direction and assistance throughout the course of studies: to Monseigneur E. Deschamps, of the Archdiocesan Curia of Paris, for his several kindnesses: to Professor Roberti for his assuring response: to the Rev. Norbert E. O'Connell, J. C. L., of Chicago: to the Rev. Daniel M. Dougherty, A. M., of New York: and to those who have most generously cooperated in the preparation of this monograph for the press.

PART I

Competence of the Church and State in Matrimonial Causes

***Canon 1960.*—Causae matrimoniales inter baptizatos iure proprio et exclusivo ad iudicem ecclesiasticum spectant.**

***Canon 1961.*—Causae de effectibus matrimonii mere civilibus, si principaliter agantur, pertinent ad civilem magistratum ad normam can. 1016; si incidenter et accessorie, possunt etiam a iudice ecclesiastico ex propria potestate cognosci ac definiri.**

In approaching an understanding of these canons of the Code which embody the Church's public law principles governing matrimonial causes, there is needed an appreciation of the unalterable dogmatic basis maintained throughout the centuries. An historical review of the relations between Church and State in the judgment of matrimonial questions will outline the legislations that have crystallized in these two canons. In speaking of the Church's competence in matrimonial matters, Pope Leo XIII appealed to "the great weight and crucial test of history from which it is plainly evident that legislative and judicial authority has been freely and constantly enjoyed by the Church, even in ages when some foolishly suppose that the head of the State either consented or connived at the Church's exercise of this power."[1] In the world there are two perfect societies, the Church and the State, the one entrusted with things spiritual, the other with temporal matters, both independent and supreme in their proper spheres.[2] In many concerns the two powers never conflict; but of the possible overlap of ecclesiastical and civil authority, a matter of great mutual concern has ever been the question of marriage. Christian marriage is a Sacrament of

[1] Leo XIII, ep. encycl., *Arcanum*, Feb. 10, 1880, §11—*Fontes*, n. 580.
[2] Leo XIII, ep. encycl., *Immortale Dei*, Nov. 1, 1885, §6—*Fontes*, n. 592.

the New Law[3] and the matrimonial contract is itself the Sacrament so that between baptized persons the contract cannot exist without the Sacrament and vice versa.[4] As judicial authority is the subsequent and the complement of legislative jurisdiction, the Council of Trent in the twelfth canon of the twenty-fourth session (*de matrimonio*) declared: "Si quis dixerit, causas matrimoniales non spectare ad iudices ecclesiasticos, A. S." Evidently the secular power has no competence, direct or indirect, in the judgment of the matrimonial causes of Christians because of the spiritual character of such questions,[5] apart from the discernment of the separable temporal effects of the conjugal bond. The Church, however, was never unmindful that the Sacrament of Matrimony, instituted for the preservation and increase of the human race, has a necessary relation to those circumstances of life which, though connected with marriage, belong properly to the civil order, and about which the State rightly makes its own enactments.[6]

---

[3] C. of Trent, sess. XXIV, *de matr.*, can. 1; sess. VII, *de sacr. in gen.*, can. 1.

[4] Pius IX, litt. ap., *Ad apostolicae*, Aug. 22, 1851, §2—*Fontes*, n. 511.

[5] Pius VI, const., *Auctorem fidei*, prop. 58-60—*Fontes*, n. 475; Pius IX, litt. ap. ad reg. Sardiniæ, Sept. 9, 1895—*Fontes*, n. 514.

[6] Leo XIII, ep. encycl., *Arcanum*, Feb. 10, 1880, §21—*Fontes*, n. 580. Cf. Canons 1016, 1961.

CHAPTER I

The Historical Development

Historically considered, the relation of the Church and State in the judgment of matrimonial causes may be surveyed under a fourfold division:

1. Roman times (to 476 A. D.).
2. From the fall of the Western Empire through the Middle Ages (476-1300).
3. The period of Nationalism (1300-1789).
4. Modern period (1789-1918).

Art. 1. Roman Times (to 476 A. D.)

When the young Church found itself entrusted with the Sacrament of Matrimony it could not but realize that the prevalent secular laws and notions were at marked variance with the matrimonial doctrine taught by its Divine Founder.[7] To the Roman mind marriage was a sacred private matter under State tutelage,[8] a notion which endured even in the days of Justinian.[9] The legal existence of the Church was not recognized in the early days much less the Church's proper and exclusive competence in the matrimonial causes of Christians which was to become more pronounced with each new piece of matrimonial legislation.[10] No open clashes occurred between the two authorities for the faithful submitted their cases to the ecclesiastical officials and due to the circumstances of the times the Christians avoided the secular forum presenting even the civil suits which arose between them to the discernment of an ecclesiastical

---

[7] St. Jerome, ep. ad Oceanum, §77—*Corp. Script. Eccl. Lat.*, vol. 55, p. 39; St. Augustine, *De Nuptiis et Concup.*, I, c. X—*Corp. Script. Eccl. Lat.*, vol. 42, p. 222. Cf. Esmein, *Le Mariage en Droit Canonique*, I, p. 7.

[8] Gaius, *Instit.*, I, §56 sq.

[9] Justinian, *Instit.*, I, tit. X; *Novell.*, 22, c. IV: 117, c. X: 134, c. XI. Cf. Mackenzie, *Roman Law*, p. 94.

[10] Duchesne, *The Early History of the Christian Church*, II, p. 517.

judge.[11] St. Paul affords evidence of this exercise of judicial power in both spiritual and temporal matters.[12] Matrimonial cases are noted among the causes considered in a judicial manner[13] by the Apostle of the Gentiles—an incestuous relationship[14] and a mixed marriage, the famous Pauline privilege.[15] This latter case shows the indirect authority over the infidel which the Church exercised in the matter of marriage. The Corinthians had proposed their questions to St. Paul and his answer came as a true judgment and not merely as a bit of fatherly advice.[16]

Documentary evidence of individual cases in this early age is scarce,[17] yet the fewness of the impediments in the early Church (the exercise of the judicial power is always subsequent upon legislative enactments) and the peculiar relationship then existing between Church and State, allow a presumption that any matrimonial causes which arose between Christians were treated by the Church exclusively. The faithful refrained from any negotiations in the secular tribunals of the first three centuries for any case.[18] As marriage was only contracted with the approval of the bishop is it likely in those days of faith that any Christian would think of deciding questions concerning his marriage without first consulting the bishop?[19]

---

[11] I Cor. V: 1; Prat, *The Theology of Saint Paul,* I, p. 103.

[12] I Cor. VI: 1 sq.

[13] Cappello, *Summa Iuris Publici Ecclesiastici,* p. 217; Perrone, *De Matrimonio Christiano,* II, pp. 15, 173; Cornelius à Lapide, *Commentaria* (super I Cor. V: 3.)

[14] I Cor. V: 5.

[15] I Cor. VII: 13.

[16] St. Augustine, *Enchiridion sive de Fide, Spe, et Charitate,* cap. 78—*MPL,* XL, 270: *Super Ps. 118,* sermon 24—*MPL,* XXXVII, 1570; Bellarmine, *De Matrimonio,* contr. VI, p. 859.

[17] C. of Ancyre (314), can. 24—Mansi, II, 522. C. of Vannes (465), can. 2—Mansi, VII, 953.

[18] *Didascalia,* II, §§45, 46-ed. Funk, I, p. 139.

[19] Ignatius M., *ep. ad Polycarp,* c. 5—Lightfoot, *Apostolic Fathers,* II, pp. 347, 573; Perrone, *De Matrimonio Christiano,* II, p. 8; Justin (Apologia, II, n. 2—*MPG,* VI, 443) relates the case of a convert who divorced her husband in a civil manner (*repudium*). This, apparently, was done to safeguard her civil rights and was considered as having no effect as to the bond of marriage. Cf. *Theologia Dogmatica, Polemica, Scholastica et Moralis,* RR. Patrum S. J., Vol. X, p. 531. Cf. Sands, "Phases of Relations Between Church and State,"—*The Catholic Historical Review,* VIII (1928), 131.

Once the Church's legal existence was recognized[20] and Christian emperors sat on the throne of Decius and Diocletian, ecclesiastical authority was openly exercised. Far from seeking to wrest the authority of the Sacrament of Matrimony from the Church many emperors respected the Church's claim[21] and styled themselves the guardians of the sacred canons.[22] The Justinian[23] and Theodosian Codes[24] adopted many ecclesiastical legislations on marriage; the Church in turn canonized some civil regulations; bishops passed upon the civil effects of matrimony[25] and were commissioned by the secular power to arbitrate purely civil cases.[26] The proper authority of the Church in matrimonial causes was recognized in the later days of the Roman Empire though it must be admitted that the exclusiveness of this power was disregarded at times.

Art. 2. From the Fall of the Western Empire Through the Middle Ages (476-1300)

Conditions created by the influx of new peoples to continental Europe provoked further matrimonial legislations in which the Church's proper and exclusive competence became more pronounced. European principalities generally recognized the prerogative of the ecclesiastical forum down almost to the nineteenth century though there are instances in medieval history where princes did not respect this right of the Church.[27] The medieval mind had its peculiar conception of the relation between Church and State.[28] Europe had adopted the Theodosian Code and consequently civil law paralleled the canon

---

[20] Edict of Milan (313); cf. Funk, *Manual of Church History,* I, p. 117.

[21] Leo XIII, ep. encycl., *Arcanum,* Feb. 10, 1880, §11—*Fontes,* n. 580. Cf. Vlaming, *Praelectiones Iuris Matrimonii,* I, nn. 42, 45.

[22] *Novell.,* 137, c. V. Perrone, *De Matrimonio Christiano,* II, p. 348.

[23] *Novell.,* 137.

[24] Cf. L. III, tit. 12, *Etsi licitum,* with C. of Neocesarea (314), c. 2—Mansi, II, 543.

[25] Jungmann, *Dissertationes in Historiam Ecclesiasticam,* III, p. 86.

[26] Justinian, *Code,* L. I, tit. IV, lex 7; Sherman, *Roman Law in the Modern World,* II, n. 903; Migne, *Encyclopedié Theologique,* vol. X, 673.

[27] Perrone, *De Matrimonio Christiano,* III, p. 347.

[28] Shahan, *Outline of Church History,* p. 28. Smith, *Church and State in the Middle Ages,* p. 57.

law in the matter of marriage.[29] Secular rulers followed the example of the later Roman Emperors[30] considering themselves the protectors of the sacred canons.[31] Canon law and ecclesiastical courts retained a stability amid the shiftings of politics and held sway in the legal field.[32] It was understood that the civil enactments on marriage respected civil rights alone and had no power to affect the bond substantially except where canonized by the ecclesiastical authorities.[33] As in Roman times, the bishops often acted as arbitrators in purely civil cases.

The actions of the papacy in royal marriage affairs attest the vigor with which the Church asserted her proper competence in matrimonial causes.[34] Some princes submitted their cases willingly while others were proceeded against by the Church on her own initiative. Pope Vigilius was consulted in the cause of Theodobert I, King of the Ostrogoths, whose marriage had been declared null on the grounds of affinity.[35] Charlemagne, strong secular arm of the Church that he was, fell under papal disapproval when he sought to disobey the ecclesiastical laws in a case which, it appears, was submitted to his bishops.[36] The celebrated divorce of Lothar II was handled entirely by ecclesiastical courts.[37] Gregory V judged the marriage of Robert of France.[38] The synod of Poitiers proceeded against Philip I and

---

[29] *Catholic Encyclopedia,* IX, p. 696—*Marriage;* Esmein, *Le Mariage en Droit Canonique,* I, p. 324.

[30] Devoti, *Ius Universum,* I, ch. XII, n. XV sq.

[31] Cf. e.g. the general tenor of the capitularia of Charlemagne—Mansi, 17 bis.

[32] Westermarck, *The History of Human Marriage,* III, p. 333; Esmein, *Le Mariage en Droit Canonique,* I, pp. 3, 25. Sands, "Phases of the Relations Between Church and State,"—*The Catholic Historical Review,* VIII (1928), 131.

[33] Perrone, *De Matrimonio Christiano,* III, pp. 352, 383.

[34] Jungmann, *Dissertationes in Historiam Ecclesiasticam,* V, pp. 249, 263; Roskovany, *Matrimonium in Ecclesia Catholica,* I, p. 65.

[35] Ep. ad Caesar. Arel.,—*MPL,* LXIX, 21.

[36] Mombert, *A History of Charles, the Great,* p. 80; Ep. of Stephen III—*MPL,* XCVIII, 256. *Theologia Dogmatica, Polemica, Scholastica et Moralis,* RR. Patrum S. J., vol. X, p. 549.

[37] Jungmann, *Dissertationes in Historiam Ecclesiasticam,* III, p. 233; c. IV, C. XXXIII, q. 2. Hincmar, *De Divortio Lotharii, Regis,*—*MPL,* CXXV, 629.

[38] C. of Paris (997)—Mansi, XIX, 223. C. of Rome (998) cans. 1, 2—Mansi, XIX, 223.

Betrada and the king found himself excommunicated for his contempt of ecclesiastical authority.[39]

Marriage causes were judged, as a rule, in provincial councils[40] and solely on the basis of canon law. The synod of Tribur denied recognition to secular marriage enactments.[41] In the Council of Mayence (813), with its triple division of bishops, abbots, and laymen, marriage cases were proposed before the bishops alone.[42] Bernard of Pavia taught that lay judges had no power in ecclesiastical cases, insisting that only an ecclesiastical judge was competent in affairs of divorce.[43] Gregory IX warned the King of Hungary, Andrew II, that secular judges must refrain from deciding matrimonial causes[44] and local synods vindicated the competence of the Church in this matter even under threat of censure.[45] In this they were but making more explicit the earlier enactments of the Church that lay persons were not competent judges in spiritual causes.[46] At times the aid of the secular magistrate was invoked to enforce the sentences of the ecclesiastical court.[47] Crimes against marriage were sometimes handed over to the secular court to save a repetition of the trial for the bishop based his punishment on the findings of the lay court.[48]

Churchmen judged even the separable civil effects aside from

---

[39] C. of Poitiers (1100)—Mansi, XX, 1117.

[40] C. of Agatha (506), can. 25—Mansi, VIII, 329. Cf. c. 1, C. XXXIII, q. 2; c. 10, C. XXXV, q. 6; Benedict XIV, *De Synodo Dioecesana,* L. IX, c. 9, n. 3.

[41] C. of Tribur (895), can. 39—Mansi, XVIII, 151. Cf. c. 1, X, *de spons. et matr.,* IV, I.

[42] Mansi XIV, 75. Cf. Perrone, *De Matrimonio Christiano,* II, p. 351; Devoti, *Ius Universum,* I, ch. XII, n. XV, in note.

[43] Bernard Pap., *Summa Decretalium,* L. II, tit, I, n. 5—in ed. Laspeyres, p. 33; L. IV, tit. 20, n. 3—in ed. Laspeyres, p. 188; *Catholic Encyclopedia,* V. p. 65—*Divorce.*

[44] Roskovany, *Matrimonium in Ecclesia Catholica,* I, p. 61.

[45] Synod of Bremen (1266), c. 8—Mansi, XXIII, 1159; C. of Bourges (1286), can. 1—Mansi, XXIV, 626.

[46] C. of Rheims (1148), can. 5—Mansi, XXI, 715: cf. c. 2, X, *de iudiciis,* II, 1; C. Lateran IV (1215), can. 40—Mansi, XXII, 1027: cf. c. 8, X, *de arbitriis,* I, 43.

[47] C. of Tours II (567), can. 15—Mansi, IX, 795.

[48] Hincmar, *De Divortio Lotharii, Regis,—MPL,* CXXV, 655; Esmein, *Le Mariage en Droit Canonique,* I, p. 21; Conventus of Attigny—Hartzheim, *Concilia Germaniæ,* II, p. 26; Westermarck. *The History of Human Marriage,* III, p. 333.

any question of the bond;[49] and when delegated judges failed to decide the question of dowry after declaring a marriage null, they were rebuked for not having decided the accessory question which came within their competence.[50] Honorius III made it clear to Louis of France that the question of legitimacy upon which the succession to the land of Campania rested was a matter for the ecclesiastical forum to decide.[51]

Despite the close intertwining of the ecclesiastical and civil courts in the Middle Ages and though the tribunal of the medieval ecclesiastical judge was approached in all sorts of temporal disputes, the exclusive and proper competence of the Church in matrimonial causes was rarely questioned.[52]

Art. 3. Period of Nationalism (1300-1789)

As the Middle Ages were passing into history a new spirit began to disquiet the great family of European principalities. It was the vigorous spirit of nationalism. New political theories filled the secular world, ebbed and flowed, until like a mighty tidal wave the French Revolution turned them in a definite direction. This era of national formations, extending over some five hundred momentous years in the world's history, can be divided by that general council which defended the Church against religious nationalism, or Protestantism. For convenience the period of nationalism will be treated under the years:

(a) Prior to the Council of Trent (1300-1563);

(b) From the Council of Trent to the French Revolution (1563-1789).

(a) *Time Prior to the Council of Trent (1300-1563)*—The relations between the secular and ecclesiastical forums had been friendly and understanding for the most part. With the advent of the fourteenth century the State began to encroach upon the exclusive matrimonial competence of the Church. The action of Louis of Bavaria (1342), at a time marked by grave political

---

[49] De Urrutigoyti, *Tractatus de Competentiis Iurisdictionis* q. XVI, n. 13.

[50] C. 3, X, *de donat. inter vir.*, IV, 20.

[51] C. 3, X, *de ordine cognit.*, II, 10. Bouix, *De Iudiciis Ecclesiasticis,* I, p. 74.

[52] Cf. Pollock-Maitland, *History of English Law,* I, p. 106; II, p. 365.

disturbances and the removal of the papal court to Avignon,[53] stands as a determined departure from the traditional obedience of princes. This monarch dissolved the bond of marriage between John of Bohemia and Margaret that Margaret might be married to his son, Louis of Brandenburgh.[54] This high handed action was strongly condemned and caused a general stir that attested the common acknowledgment of the Church's competence in such matters.[55]

Local councils contested the aggressiveness of the civil forum insisting that the recognition of matrimonial causes belonged to the ecclesiastical judge and threatened with excommunication seculars who presumed to treat these cases.[56] Royalty, however, did not follow the example of Louis but continued to submit their marital differences to the Church's judgment. Henry IV of France had his union with Margaret passed upon by the ecclesiastical tribunal and dissolved by Clement VIII.[57] The divorce case of Henry VIII, which shook Christendom, was submitted in the beginning to the proper ecclesiastical courts and throughout the proceedings care was taken to impress all that the affair had ecclesiastical sanction and was not a mere civil matter.[58]

Hitherto the Church's jurisdiction had never been seriously questioned on doctrinal grounds. The individual violations had been disobediences arising from princes' whims or political schemings. Now the false winds of doctrine began to blow and the Reformers denied not one but both bases for the exclusive competence of the Church in matrimonial cases by teaching that the Church was not a perfect society and that marriage was not a Sacrament. Luther in his *Babylonian Captivity*,[59] Calvin,[60]

---

[53] Funk, *Manual of Church History*, II, p. 6.

[54] Roskovany, *Matrimonium in Ecclesia Catholica*, I, p. 2.

[55] Cf. Hefele, *Conciliengeschichte*, VI, p. 664.

[56] C. of Merciac (1326), c. 10—Mansi, XXV, 779; C. of Wurzburg (1407)—Roskovany, *Matrimonium in Ecclesia Catholica*, I, p. 70; C. of Mayence (1549), cap. 76—Mansi, XXXII, 1399; C. of Cologne II (1549), tit. 6, cap. 3—Mansi, XXXII, 1357.

[57] *Theologia Dogmatica, Polemica, Scholastica et Moralis*, RR. Patrum S. J., vol. X, p. 501.

[58] Funk, *Manual of Church History*, II, p. 117.

[59] Cf. Grisar, *Luther*, II, p. 27.

[60] *Institutiones Christianae Religionis*, L, IV, tit, 19, nn. 34-37, p. 473 sq.

and other reformers defended the authority of the State in matrimonial causes.[61] In Verona, the noble counter-reformer, Bishop Giberti, is found drawing matrimonial cases more closely under episcopal scrutiny.[62].

The trend of French civil legislation caused anxiety among churchmen. The famous Edict of Blois (1556) of Henry II asserting the power of the civil forum, was variously interpreted as in accord with or contrary to Catholic doctrine.[63] Austria, too, showed signs of departing from the path of obedience and yet at this period Ferdinand I admonished the Ruthenians of his land that marriage cases belonged to the ecclesiastical courts.[64] Meeting at a time when secular authority, conscious of its power, considered nothing beyond its competence and when heresy was seeking to rob matrimony of its sacred character, the Council of Trent formulated the doctrine on the competence of Church and State in matrimonial causes in practically the same manner as the Code defines it today.

(b) *From the Council of Trent to the French Revolution (1563-1789)*—The Council of Trent, treating Matrimony in the twenty-fourth session (November 11, 1653), dogmatically defined Christian marriage as a Sacrament[65] and declared that matrimonial causes belonged to ecclesiastical judges.[66] Though this twelfth canon reproduced in dogmatic definition the rulings of many earlier synods, it did not quiet the proponents of the power of the secular authorities in matrimonial causes. The words of the canon were subjected to keen distinctions. Post-Tridentine times found two avenues of thought favoring the power of the princes. One opinion held that the contract and the Sacrament of Marriage were separable,[67] another group

---

[61] Cf. Perrone, *De Matrimonio Christiano,* II, p. 7. Balmez, *European Civilization,* p. 139.

[62] Tit. VII, cap. 5, *Const. M. Giberti Eppi Veronensis* (1542)—Roskovany, *Matrimonium in Ecclesia Catholica,* I, p. 79.

[63] Roskovany, *Matrimonium in Ecclesia Catholica,* I, p. 3; Benedict XIV, *De Synodo Dioecesana,* L. IX, c. IX, n. 5.

[64] Rescript of Ferdinand I (1552)—Roskovany, *Matrimonium in Ecclesia Catholica,* I, p. 81.

[65] C. of Trent, sess. XXIV, *de matr.,* can. 1.

[66] C. of Trent, sess. XXIV, *de matr.,* can. 12. Cf. Roskovany, *Matrimonium in Ecclesia Catholica,* I, p. 47; Richter, *Canones et Decreta Concilii Tridentini,* p. 214 sq.

[67] E.g. The regalists as Launoy, Nuytz. Cf. *Syllabus errorum,* prop. 66—Denzinger-Bannwart, *Enchiridion,* n. 1766.

injected into the word "Ecclesia" of the twenty-fourth session the notion that secular jurisdiction was also understood in view of their doctrine that the Church's matrimonial competence had been derived originally from the secular authority.[68] Among the historians of the Council of Trent, Sarpi places matrimonial authority in the hands of the State,[69] while Pallavicini refutes that interpretation in his account of the council.[70] Heresy and nationalism joined forces and provided opposition in the succeeding centuries to the proper and exclusive competence of the Church in matrimonial causes.[71] Generally, the marriages of Catholics were left to the Church and to the guidance of canon law[72] but mixed marriages ever proved a sore point in the relations of the two powers.[73]

The doctrines of the Council of Trent were reechoed throughout Europe by local councils.[74] Some synods in explaining the twelfth canon of the Council of Trent made it explicit that accessory causes came within the competence of the Church.[75] That the purely civil effects of matrimony were causes for the civil judge was commonly understood though the Archbishop of Gran complained (1658) that the state was overstepping the bounds of competence in judging such matters as dowry and paraphernalia.[76] When a question of inheritance (1732), en-

---

[68] Cf. Pius IV, *Auctorem fidei,* Aug. 28, 1794, §59—*Fontes,* n. 475; Syllabus errorum, prop. 68, 69—Denzinger-Bannwart, *Enchiridion,* nn. 1768, 1769; Roskovany, *Matrimonium in Ecclesia Catholica,* I, p. 5.

[69] *Histoire du Concile de Trent,* L. VIII, p. 763.

[70] *Istoria del Concilio di Trento,* L. XXII, c. 8; L. XXIII, c. 9.

[71] Cf. Lehr, *Traite Elementaire de Droit Civil Germanique,* II, p. 256.

[72] *Special Report, Marriage and Divorce, Dept. of Commerce and Labor, Bureau of Census,* pp. 338, 358, 366, 376.

[73] "Le 41e des articles secrets de l'Édit de Nantes attribuait aux juges royaux la connaissance des mariages entre deux personnes de la Religion réformée. Si l'une des parties était religionnaire et l'autre catholique, c'était le tribunal du dédendeur qui était compétent, c'est-à-dire, selons les cas, tantôt l'officialité et tantôt le juge royal."—Esmein, *Le Mariage en Droit Canonique,* I, p. 44.

[74] E.g. C. of Cambray (1565), tit. 15, c. I—Mansi, XXXIII, 1413; C. of Salzburg (1569), const. 49, cap. 5—Mansi, XXXVI-A, 270; C. of Tours (1593), cap. 19—Mansi, XXXIV-A, 850; C. of Narbonne (1609), cap. 42—Mansi, XXXIV-B, 1524.

[75] C. of Constance (1609), P. 1, tit. 16, n. 43—Roskovany, *Matrimonium in Ecclesia Catholica,* I, p. 90; C. of Osnabrück (1628), P. 1, cap. 20, n. 13—Hartzheim, *Concilia Germaniæ,* IX, 475.

[76] Roskovany, *Matrimonium in Ecclesia Catholica,* I, p. 97.

tered before a civil magistrate, finally resolved itself to a question of the validity of the union, the Sacred Congregation of the Council, when questioned, asserted the exclusive competence of the Church to judge the validity of the marriage both in law and fact.[77] Benedict XIV in his work *De Synodo Diocesana* upheld the definition of the Council of Trent and explained it by distinguishing three classes of matrimonial causes: questions of the bond itself, the inseparable effects, and the separable (civil) effects. In this last class the secular forum was properly competent.[78]

Regalism was gaining its point in France.[79] Though the twelfth article of the Edict of 1606 (in the reign of Henry IV) admitted the Church's competence in matrimonial causes,[80] subsequent civil enactments undermined that authority. The French clergy (1629), seeing that the reissuance by Louis XIII of the Edict of Blois (1556) might be construed as contradicting the Council of Trent, petitioned the king to make it clear that this was not intended.[81] The request was heeded. Yet the marriage case of Gaston, duke of Orleans, and Margaret presented an example of the conflict. The cause was heard before both the civil and the ecclesiastical courts. The French bishops inclining toward royal favor adjudged the marriage invalid on the grounds that royal consent, required by civil law, had not been obtained.[82] The Pope reversed the decision[83] and later made it clear that canon, not civil law, was the norm in matrimonial causes.[84]

In the Empire a movement was growing to bring matrimonial cases under the complete control of the secular power. Since the

---

[77] Roskovany, *Matrimonium in Ecclesia Catholica,* III, p. 207.

[78] L. IX, c. 9, nn. 3, 4. Cf. *Instruction to the Bishops of Sardinia,* Jan. 6, 1742—*Raccolta di Concordati,* pp. 369, 372.

[79] Cf. Billuart, *Summa Sancti Thomae,* vol. XIX, p. 569 sq. for examples of French Matrimonial edicts in the years 1579-1736.

[80] Esmein, *Le Mariage en Droit Canonique,* I, p. 44. Vlaming, *Praelectiones Iuris Matrimonii,* I, n. 42.

[81] Roskovany, *Matrimonium in Ecclesia Catholica,* I, p. 94. Perrone, *De Matrimonio Christiano,* II, p. 178. Benedict XIV, *De Synodo Dioecesana,* L. IX, c. 2, n. 5.

[82] *Theologia Dogmatica, Polemica, Scholastica et Moralis,* RR. PP. S. J., X, p. 506.

[83] Perrone, *De Matrimonio Christiano,* II, p. 177.

[84] Roskovany, *Matrimonium in Ecclesia Catholica,* I, p. 95.

days of the pro-king Stephen the bishops had handled matrimonial cases. This condition remained undisturbed through the pacification of Vienna (1606).[85] However, the Cardinal of Waitzen complained of the encroachments of the civil power (1731)[86] and the Bishop of Nitrava objected to the judgment of matrimonial cases in which one party was a non-Catholic, according to non-Catholic principles. This had been prescribed in the fifth point of the Act of the Commission of Pest.[87] To stay the tide the King's curia requested (1770) that all matrimonial causes be left entirely to the ecclesiastical forum but secular authority gained control when Joseph II in 1783 boldly issued the royal edict *Ehepatent* revolutionizing the matrimonial law of the Empire and affecting Austria, Hungary, and Belgium.[88] This marked the first serious affront to the Church's proper competence in matrimonial cases for when the Archbishop of Vienna remarked that the new law apparently affected only the civil aspects of marriage,[89] the secular authorities retorted that the civil judges were to judge matrimony considered even as a Sacrament.[90] This stand incensed the episcopacy of the Empire and days of bitter feeling ensued.[91] A case occurring in 1786 shows the resultant conditions. The civil court had dissolved the marriage of a Protestant woman and a Catholic man. A week later the Bishop of Vesprim regretting the incident passed on the evidence adduced in the secular court and declared that the marriage had been invalidly contracted.[92] The royal edict passed into the Josephine Code October 1, 1786.[93] The same condition was brought about in France by the royal

---

85 Roskovany, *Matrimonium in Ecclesia Catholica,* I, p. 119.

86 Roskovany, *Matrimonium in Ecclesia Catholica,* I, p. 122.

87 "Matrimonium porro causas fundamento positivarum Regni legum iudiciis dioecesanis Episcoporum ita substerni, ut hi illas iuxta principia Augustanae et Helveticae Confessionis diiudicent, admissa inde ad Archiepiscopum appellatione."—Roskovany, *Matrimonium in Ecclesia Catholica,* I, p. 124.

88 Roskovany, *Matrimonium in Ecclesia Catholica,* I, p. 5; II, p. 496. *Special Report, Marriage and Divorce, Dept. of Commerce and Labor, Bureau of Census,* p. 329.

89 Roskovany, *Matrimonium in Ecclesia Catholica,* I, p. 191.

90 Roskovany, *Matrimonium in Ecclesia Catholica,* I, pp. 6, 192, 200.

91 Roskovany, *Matrimonium in Ecclesia Catholica,* I, pp. 5, 122. sq.

92 Roskovany, *Matrimonium in Ecclesia Catholica,* I, p. 248.

93 *Special Report, Marriage and Divorce, Dept. of Commerce and Labor, Bureau of Census,* p. 338.

edict of 1787.[94] In the South a concordat with Naples insured the exclusive power of the Church over the conjugal bond,[95] but conditions were changing in Europe. With the political and philosophical upheaval attending the French Revolution marriage was further secularized. The opening of the new century saw the modern State, after successfully abolishing the special claims of royalty, trying to wrest every vestige of matrimonial competence from the Church.[96] Marriage had no sacredness in the new thought. The Church, ever conscious of its exclusive and proper competence in the matter of the Sacraments and over the persons of the baptized, held to the doctrines of the Council of Trent while the world swept into the era of civil marriage and civil divorce.

Art. 4. Modern Period (1789-Code)

The acceptance of matrimony as a purely civil contract and, consequently, the absolute competence of the secular authorities in matrimonial causes became the established principle of the nineteenth century.[97] Mindful of the Europe of the Middle Ages one writer in marking the transition notes: "the secularization of marriage by the state was only the result and expression of the common worldliness or turning to worldliness of that which was previously supramundane, conceived as the majestic autonomy of the divine." [98] The conflict, which was to resolve itself into the present day attitude of total indifference, armed neutrality, or polite toleration between Church and State in matrimonial matters, was on. The challenge of Pius VI sounded in his letter to the bishop of Motulense [99] and his condemnation of the fifty-eighth and fifty-ninth articles of the Synod of Pistoia[100] was carried out by his successor, Pius VII (1800-1823), who faced a critical period in the relationship of the two societies in matrimonial affairs. Pius VII denied the compe-

---

[94] De Smet, *De Sponsalibus et Matrimonio,* n. 451.
[95] *Raccolta di Concordati,* p. 353.
[96] Esmein, *Le Mariage en Droit Canonique,* I, p. 3.
[97] Cf. French Constitution of 1791, tit. II, art. 7.
[98] Bernhart, "Marriage as a Sacrament,"—*The Book of Marriage* (Keyserling), p. 472.
[99] Roskovany, *Monumenta Catholica,* I, p. 370.
[100] Const., *Auctorem Fidei,* Aug. 28, 1794—*Fontes,* n. 475.

tence of the secular court to dissolve a marriage even where one party was a non-Catholic.[101] The provisions of the Austrian[102] and Napoleonic Codes[103] requiring parental consent, he declared, did not invalidate the marriages of minors. Conditions in Austria[104] forced the pope to reprimand the Archbishop of Prague and order him to reverse a decision after that prelate had adjudged a matrimonial cause as a delegate of the secular power.[105] In a later period the declarations of Pius IX[106] and Leo XIII[107] placed it beyond all doubt that the contract and the Sacrament of matrimony were inseparable. They insisted, too, on the teaching of the Council of Trent that judgment belonged properly to the ecclesiastical judges.

The common question in this era concerned the participation of Catholics in civil divorce suits either as parties or as officials. As early as 1817 the Holy Office declared that civil legislators and judges seriously violated the divine law when they dealt with divorce. Catholic judges were considered unworthy of absolution unless they promised to avoid such cases.[108] When the civil "Court for Divorce and Matrimonial Causes" was established in England in 1859,[109] the Third Provincial Council of Westminster (1859) issued a warning to Catholics that they had no part in it.[110] The reply to a query from the Bishop of Southwark gave more explicit instructions in the matter. Lawyers could defend the marriage in civil court provided the principles of the natural and ecclesiastical laws were upheld. A Catholic advocate could not appear for the plaintiff in a

---

101 *Breve ad Arch. Moguntin.*, Oct. 8, 1803—*Fontes*, n. 477.

102 Letter to Vic. Capit. of Trent—Roskovany, *Matrimonium in Ecclesia Catholica*, II, p. 14.

103 Cf. De Smet, *De Sponsalibus et Matrimonio*, n. 519.

104 Cf. Funk, *Manual of Church History*, II, pp. 221, 223: Pius VII, Instr. to papal nuntio at Poland—Roskovany, *Monumenta Catholica*, II, p. 152.

105 Roskovany, *Matrimonium in Ecclesia Catholica*, II, pp. 2, 17.

106 Alloc., *Acerbissimum*, Sept. 27, 1852—*Fontes*, n. 515; litt. ap. ad reg. Sardiniae, Sept. 9, 1852—*Fontes*, n. 514.

107 Ep. ency., *Arcanum*, Feb. 10, 1880—*Fontes*, n. 580; ep. ency., *Immortale Dei*, Nov. 1, 1885, §11—*Fontes*, n. 592.

108 S. C. S. Off., Instr. (*ad Praef. Miss. Martinicae, etc.*), July 6, 1817—*Fontes*, n. 855.

109 Westermarck, *A History of Human Marriage*, III, p. 337.

110 "Numquam igitur vobis licet hoc tribunal adire ad ea obtinenda, quae cum S. Matris vestrae Ecclesiae doctrina apertissime pugnant."—Roskovany, *Matrimonium in Ecclesia Catholica*, IV, p. 13.

divorce action nor could a Catholic act the role of judge or juror in such a case. Yet under certain conditions Catholics could act as officials in cases for limited divorce, or separation.[111] The same question arose in Canada when a civil divorce court was established. Catholics were forbidden to take any formal part in this court. They could testify if subpoenaed.[112] Further difficulty arose when the Canadian Parliament sought to extend the competence of this court. Then it was revealed that Catholic legislators could neither approve the measure nor appoint judges for such a tribunal.[113] The Swiss bishops were confronted with the same problem in 1878.[114] Considering the condition of affairs in France, the Holy Office tolerated the retention by Catholic lawyers and magistrates of their offices in divorce courts provided these officials openly professed the Catholic doctrine of marriage, acknowledged the competence of the ecclesiastical judges, and had the mind never to pass sentence, aid, defend, or abet what was contrary to the divine or ecclesiastical laws. In doubtful cases they were to consult the Ordinary and be guided by his judgment. Should need arise the problem was to be submitted to the Sacred Penitentiary.[115] This decree did not settle all doubts and a further response on May 27, 1886, showed that the earlier instruction was not fulfilled when a judge allowed a divorce where the marriage was valid in the eyes of the Church even though the magistrate considered the case merely civilly and intended only civil effects. Nor could a mayor, accepting a court decision, allow a divorce in such a case.[116] The response of 1886 was particular, being applicable only in France.[117] In individual cases, these rulings of the Holy Office were applied by the Sacred Penitentiary.[118]

---

[111] S. C. S. Off., Dec. 19, 1860—*Coll.*, n. 2272. Cf. *NRT*, XVIII (1896), 484.

[112] C. of Quebec (1868), decr. 12—Roskovany, *Matrimonium in Ecclesia Catholica*, IV, p. 10. Wernz-Vidal, *Ius Canonicum*, I, n. 712, note 19.

[113] S. C. S. Off., June 2, 1870—*Coll.*, n. 1353.

[114] Cf. Query of the bishop of St. Gall (Dec. 9, 1877)—Roskovany, *Matrimonium in Ecclesia Catholica*, IV, p. 64, and the response of the Holy Office (Apr. 3, 1878)—*Coll.*, n. 1491. Cf. *AfkK*, XLI, 178.

[115] S. C. S. Off., June 25, 1885—*Fontes*, n. 1093.

[116] Denzinger-Bannwart, *Enchiridion*, n. 1865.

[117] Cappello, *De Sacramentis*, III, n. 836-6°.

[118] Cf. Cappello, *De Sacramentis*, III, n. 836-8°, 9°.

Catholics generally abstained from presenting their causes to the civil courts. They were dissuaded from doing it even for the civil safeguards though a reply of the Sacred Penitentiary in 1898 apparently tolerated approaching the civil court to insure the civil safeguarding of rights.[119] In the nineteenth century local councils and synods repeated the Church's doctrine on divorce,[120] threatening censures for those who took part in civil divorce proceedings.[121] In the United States the Second (1866) and Third (1894) Plenary Councils of Baltimore insisted on the exclusive power of the Church in matrimonial causes.[122] Though upholding her competence the Church allowed that judgments in the purely civil effects of the matrimonial bond were the concern of the secular forum.[123]

While some states did not respect the proper and exclusive competence of ecclesiastical judges in matrimonial causes they did phrase their legislations so as to allow only limited divorce, or separation, for Catholics.[124] Frequently this was but a mere deference of words.[125] During the nineteenth century the Church entered into a series of concordats in which some understanding was reached in regard to the judgment of matrimonial causes. The tenor of these agreements is the same as canons 1960 and 1961: there is either the general acknowledgment that all causes affecting the Sacraments are ecclesiastical causes;[126] or more explicitly that all matrimonial causes were to be submitted to ecclesiastical judges excepting the competence of the secular forum in the purely civil effects of the bond.[127] Concordats since the Code make no express mention of matrimonial causes but in general terms assure the Church freedom and

---

[119] Cappello, *De Sacramentis,* III, n. 835.

[120] *E.g.* C. of Tuam (1858), cap. 16—*Coll. Lacen.,* III, 887.

[121] *E.g.* C. of Quebec (1854), decr. 13—Roskovany, *Matrimonium in Ecclesia Catholica,* IV, p. 8.

[122] *Acta et Decreta Balt. II,* cap. nn. 326, 327, p. 171. *Acta et Decreta Balt. III,* nn. 123, 124, p. 63.

[123] Leo XIII, ep. encycl., *Arcanum,* Feb. 10, 1880, §21—*Fontes,* n. 580.

[124] *E.g.* Ireland—*Special Report, Marriage and Divorce, Dept. of Commerce and Labor,* p. 373.

[125] *E.g.* Germany—*Special Report, Marriage and Divorce, Dept. of Commerce and Labor,* p. 366.

[126] V. g., Spain (1851), art. 14; Costa Rica (1852), art. 13; Haiti (1860), art. 10—*Raccolta di Concordati,* pp. 772, 805, 932.

[127] V. g. Baden (1859), art. 5; Ecuador (1862), art. 8; Montenegro (1886), art. 10—*Raccolta di Concordati,* pp. 883, 987, 1049.

liberty.[128] The recent pact with Italy is rumored to contain a definite agreement in regard to matrimonial competence between Church and State.

But civil marriage had come to stay. Civil authorities claimed complete competence in judging matrimonial causes affairs whether civil legislation made a civil form of marriage obligatory or accepted a religious ceremony. The result is, as the present conditions indicate, a tolerant dualism in matrimonial concerns. The State is either indifferent to the sacred and sacramental character of marriage (an outgrowth of the notion that the contract and the Sacrament are really separable) or denies the spiritual aspect though tolerating the ecclesiastical courts so long as the secular authority is not openly gainsayed (an outgrowth of the heretical doctrine that matrimony is not a Sacrament). The Church on the other hand, while insisting on her matrimonial doctrines, must tolerate the encroachments of the State and endeavor to avoid any open clash with the existing civil matrimonial legislation. The entire matter of the competence of the Church and the State in matrimonial causes has returned to the pristine condition of the relation of Church and State in the early Roman Empire.

---

[128] Lettonia—*AAS,* XIV (1922), 577; Bavaria—*AAS,* XVII (1925), 41. Poland—*AAS,* XVII (1925), 274. Lithuania—*AAS,* XIX (1927), 129. Cf. *Apollinaris,* I (1928), 151.

CHAPTER II

The Canonical Aspect

Art. 1. Definitions and Distinctions

"God has placed the care of the human race into the hands of two powers, the ecclesiastical and civil, the one charged with things spiritual, the other with human affairs. Each in its kind is supreme; each has certain bounds within which it is contained, limits which are defined by the nature and the special object of each power. There is, so to speak, an orbit traced within which the action is exercised by its own native right. But as each of these powers has authority over the same subjects, it might happen that one and the same matter—considered differently, but still remaining one and the same thing—may belong to the jurisdiction and determination of both. Therefore, God who foresees all things and who is the author of these two powers, has marked out the course of each in the proper relation to the other." So wrote Pope Leo XIII in discussing the relations of Church and State in the matter of marriage.[1] The world forgets that the church as well as the State is a perfect society.[2] To the Church as a perfect society belongs the innate right to make laws, pass judgment upon these laws, and to enforce the same laws and judgments. This is according to the present commonly accepted theoretical division of the authority of a perfect society into legislative, judicial, and executive branches.[3] Whatever theory of government may be accepted there must be the recognition that the judicial power, or the authority to declare the application of the law and to

---

[1] Ep. encycl., *Immortale Dei,* Nov. 1, 1885, §6—*Fontes,* n. 592.

[2] "Ecclesia non est vera perfectaque societas plane libera, nec pollet suis propriis et constantibus iuribus sibi a divino suo fundatore collatis, sed civilis potestatis est definire quae sint Ecclesiae iura ac limites, intra quos eadem iura exercere queat." *Syllabus errorum,* prop. 19—*Fontes,* n. 543. Cf. Cappello, *Summa Iuris Publici Ecclesiastici,* p. 107 sq.

[3] Cavagnis, *Institutiones Iuris Publici Ecclesiastici,* I, n. 95.

define the effects of law in relation to the actions of the subjects, is an essential element of government. Judicial authority is the complement of legislative power. Only the society that made the law can give a proper interpretation and application of it.[4] For example, it is manifestly absurd that an American court should consider itself competent to interpret the laws of France or any other nation.

Just as long as the Church concerns itself with things spiritual and the State with temporalities there is no conflict in competence. But when a question has both a civil and a religious aspect which places it in the class of mixed matter, then both Church and State will claim competence and, if an understanding is not reached, a clash in the matter of competence may result. Marriage presents such a mixed matter for it is the concern of both Church and State. Whether the State has been friendly or hostile, the Church has had to deal with this problem of matrimonial competence in every age as has been seen in the historical survey.

Marriage by its very nature, even apart from any consideration of the sacramental character, falls into the class of mixed matter.[5] When the character of a Sacrament is added in the marriages of the baptized, or in the expression of the schools, when the natural contract is super-naturalized, the marriage comes more within the scope of the Church[6] though remaining at the same time a matter of great concern for the State, of which the family is the foundation.[7]

Of the contracts known to man the most unique is that union of a man and woman designated as marriage. Marriage from a purely natural standpoint is defined as a "legitimate contract."[8] This imports that marriage is subject to some laws.

[4] Cappello, *Summa Iuris Publici Ecclesiastici*, p. 74; Bouix, *De Iudiciis*, I, p. 29.

[5] "Igitur cum matrimonium sit sua vi, sus natura, sua sponte sacrum, consentaneum est, ut regatur ac temperetur non principum imperio, sed divina auctoritate Ecclesiae, quae rerum sacrarum sola habet magisterium." Leo XIII, Ep. encycl., *Arcanum*, Feb. 10, 1880, §11—*Fontes*, n. 580. Cf. Coronata, *Ius Publicum Ecclesiasticum*, n. 87.

[6] Cf. Canon 1013 §2.

[7] Leo XIII, Ep. encycl., *Arcanum*, Feb. 10, 1880, §10—*Fontes*, n. 580.

[8] Coniunctio maris et feminae consortium omnis vitae divini et humani iuris communicatio. Dig. I, *de ritu nupt.*, XXIII, 2; Matrimonium est contractus legitimus et individuus maris atque feminae ad generandam et educandam prolem.—Wernz-Vidal, *Ius Canonicum*, V, n. 21.

It is surely regulated by the divine natural and positive laws. States, too, have their laws on "Domestic Relations" and the Church has its numerous canons on matrimony. The marriage of Christians is a peculiar contract in that the matrimonial contract is itself the Sacrament[9] and between baptized persons the contract cannot exist without the Sacrament and vice versa.[10] The marriages of the baptized therefore fall within both the spiritual and temporal order and come under ecclesiastical and secular supervision. The Church's judicial competence follows from the Church's legislative competence which is defined in the other places in the Code.[11] In ascertaining the respective competence of each society in the judgment of matrimonial causes sharp distinctions must be remembered and while the theory can be clearly set forth, the practice is fraught with difficulties.[12] Where distinctions are to be drawn definition and division are prerequisites. An appreciation of canons 1960 and 1961 may be facilitated by a consideration of:

§1. The effects of matrimony;
§2. Matrimonial causes;
§3. Mixed causes and caused of mixed forum;
§4. Proper and exclusive jurisdiction;
§5. Causes entered principally, incidentally, and accessorily.

§1. *The effects of matrimony*—The basic effect of matrimonial consent is the conjugal bond, perpetual and exclusive by nature,[13] and enduring until legitimately severed.[14] From this bond, as from a true and lawful cause, depend spiritual and temporal effects. In the spiritual order the sacramental con-

---

[9] Canon 1012 §1.

[10] Canon 1012 §2. *Syllabus errorum,* prop. 66—*Fontes,* n. 543.

[11] Canon 1016.—Baptizatorum matrimonium regitur iure non solum divino, sed etiam canonico, salva competentia civilis potestatis circa mere civiles eiusdem matrimonii effectus.

Canon 1038.—§1. Supremae tantum auctoritatis ecclesiasticae est authentice declarare quandonam ius divinum matrimonium impediat vel dirimat.

§2. Eidem supremae auctoritati privative ius est alia impedimenta matrimonium impedientia vel dirimentia pro baptizatis constituendi per modum legis sive universalis sive particularis.

[12] Wernz, *Ius Decretalium,* IV, pars I, p. 3, note 1.

[13] Canon 1110.

[14] Canons 1118, 1119. Schmalzgrueber, *Ius Ecclesiasticum Universum,* lib. IV, tit. 1, n. 314.

tract increases sanctifying grace, the supernatural habits and gifts, and bestows the right to the actual graces pertaining to the married state.[15] Among the temporal effects there are some which are inseparable and necessarily inherent in the matrimonial contract—the mutual rights and duties of the marital relationship[16] and the legitimacy of offspring:[17] while other temporal consequences of the bond are accidental, being separable from the contract itself—matters affecting succession, dowry, and privileges.[18]

Such is the traditional division of matrimonial effects. In this division the terms "separable effects" and "merely civil effects" are used interchangeably and explained by examples.[19] In view of the necessity of considering marriage today as under dual control (for secular authority claims complete jurisdiction over the marriages of all its citizens)[20] a further distinction may be ventured. It is a division of the separable temporal effects of matrimony into those (a) purely canonical:[21] (b) purely political: (c) civil. The division is based on the diverse origin and nature of these effects. The distinction would make it clear that civil effects include all those questions that are commonly cited as effects *"mere civile."*[22] These would include causes in which both the ecclesiastical and secular forum are competent but in which the secular court is to be preferred when this matter is the principal issue. Cases of the purely canonical effects are exclusively and properly questions for the ecclesiastical court while questions of purely political effects are not only properly but exclusively within the scope of the secular tribunal. This latter group would include questions of citizenship, suffrage, civic obligations, etc., or what the State politically grants as matrimonial effects.[23]

---

[15] Canon 1110.

[16] Canon 1111.

[17] Canons 1114-1117.

[18] Schmalzgrueber, *Ius Ecclesiasticum Universum,* lib. IV, tit. 18, nn. 6, 7.

[19] Cf. Cappello, *De Sacramentis,* III, n. 71.

[20] Cf. Leo XIII, ep. encycl., *Immortale Dei,* Nov. 1, 1885, §11—*Fontes,* n. 592.

[21] Canon 1112. Cf. canons 93 §1; 98 §4; 1229 §2; 1561.

[22] Cf. canons 1016, 1961.

[23] *E.g.* a separate civil domicile for married women was provided in a New York State legislation for 1929.

An outline of the effects may be helpful. The Sacrament of Matrimony gives rise to:

A. The conjugal bond—exclusive, perpetual, indissoluble;
B. The dependent effects of the bond:
   1. Spiritual (supernatural)—habitual grace, the supernatural habits and gifts, and actual graces;
   2. Temporal (natural):
      a. Inseparable (intrinsic or essential);[24]
      b. Separable (extrinsic or accidental):[25]
         1°. Purely canonical (*causa eccl. fori*);
         2°. Purely political (*causa secularis fori*);
         3°. Civil (i. e., the *mere civile* of canons 1016 and 1961, or *causa mixti fori*).

§2. *Matrimonial causes*—Should a dispute develop which concerns the nature, qualities, or contract of marriage: the nuptial blessing: the validity, rights, obligations, dissolution and reintegration of matrimony: the legitimacy of children: matrimonial impediments and dispensations: or any matrimonial matter: such a controversy is considered in itself a matrimonial question.[26] The submitting of the question to the authoritative judgment of a public official[27] puts it in the class of matrimonial *causes*. The term "case" is a generic term while "cause" specifically implies a matter of judicial character.[28] Materially, any dispute in a matrimonial matter has the possibility of developing into a matrimonial cause. Canon 1960 simply states that matrimonial causes without distinction are to be referred to ecclesiastical judges.[29] Authors, however, are wont to distinguish a strict and a broad use of the term "matrimonial causes." By this they seek to show that matrimonial causes in the strict sense of the term, or those questions concerned with the bond itself, the spiritual effects, or inseparable

---

[24] Sometimes termed *civil*.

[25] Sometimes termed *merely civil*.

[26] "Questio est ipsa res ipsumve ius controversum quod in iudicium nondum est deducta sed deduci potest."—Vlaming, *Praelectiones Iuris Matrimonii*, II, n. 785.

[27] Cf. can. 1552.

[28] C. 10, X, *de verb. signif.*, V, 40. "Causa est res, seu ius deductum in iudicium"—Vives, *Compendium Iuris Canonici*, p. 409.

[29] Cf. Pius VI, *litt. ad Ep. Motulen.*, Sept. 16, 1788—Feije, *De Impedimentis et Dispensationibus Matrimonialibus*, n. 12.

temporal effects of the bond, are matters for the ecclesiastical forum exclusively. Matrimonial causes in the broad sense, or questions of the separable temporal effects, are causes in which the secular tribunal may be competent.

A matrimonial cause in the strict sense deals with the validity or nullity, and the inseparable effects of the marriage tie—all that is intrinsic to the contract: while under the wider meaning come all the other possible matrimonial disputes—the matters extrinsic to the bond.[30] More specifically matrimonial causes in the proper sense embrace any and all disputes as to the validity or invalidity of the bond due to the existence of diriment impediments, lack of consent, or defect in required form, the declaration of the fact of consummation or non-consummation of the marriage,[31] perpetual separation,[32] the verifications of the conditions for the solution of a *"matrimonium legitimum"* [33] by virtue of the Pauline privilege,[34] the rights and obligations necessarily inherent in the marriage contract,[35] and the legitimacy of offspring.[36] Practically, the matrimonial causes brought to ecclesiastical authorities today are reducible to three classes, *viz.*, (1) validity or nullity of the contract; (2) declaration of the fact of non-consummation; (3) perpetual separation.[37]

Questions concerning the validity, liceity, and effects of espousals (sponsalia), formerly more extensive and important than now, come under the class of matrimonial causes[38] being classed as spiritual causes and consequently belonging exclusively to the ecclesiastical forum.[39] Action for damages resulting from the severance of betrothal is allowed[40] but judicial

[30] Schmalzgrueber, *Ius Ecclesiasticum Universum,* IV, tit. 18, n. 6; Benedict XIV, *De Synodo Dioecesana,* IX, c. 9, nn. 3, 4; Bouix, *De Iudiciis Ecclesiasticis,* I, p. 82; Aertnys-Damen, *Theologia Moralis,* II, n. 635.

[31] Cf. cans. 1119, 1015 §2, 1970 sq.

[32] Cf. can. 1130. Wernz-Vidal, *Ius Canonicum,* VI, n. 27 e.

[33] Can. 1015 §3.

[34] Cf. Cans. 1120-1127.

[35] Can. 1111.

[36] Cans. 1114-1117, 1051.

[37] Vermeersch-Creusen, *Epitome,* III, n. 276.

[38] Schmalzgrueber, *Ius Ecclesiasticum Universum,* IV, tit. 18, n. 6.

[39] Cf. Can. 1553 §1—n. 1; ". . . pro utroque foro . . ."—can. 1017 §1; Pius VI, *Auctorem Fidei,* Aug. 28, 1794, n. 58—*Fontes,* n. 475.

[40] Can. 1017 §3.

action to demand the fulfillment of the contract is wisely denied[41] by positive law.[42] The dissolution of espousals does not require the intervention of a judge.[43]

Matrimonial causes in the broad sense include questions of the separable effects of the marriage bond. These generally concern matters of dowry, inheritance, etc.

Crimes against marriage,—abortion,[44] rape and abduction,[45] bigamy,[46] adultery and concubinage,—[47] are to be classed as criminal rather than matrimonial causes and though the ecclesiastical forum is competent[48] it is more satisfactory to leave these cases to the civil magistrate as the Code advises.[49] The denunciation of matrimonial impediments is not *per se* included under the heading of matrimonial causes.[50] The establishment of the freedom to marry prior to the ceremony is *per se* more a matter of administrative investigation than of trial:[51] yet a judicial process may be necessary if there had been a previous marriage.[52] The permission to pass to a second union on the presumed death of the former spouse is a question which can be decided either judicially or extrajudicially.[53] Perpetual separation can be effected judicially or on private authority[54] while temporary separation likewise can be effected extrajudicially (by a decree of the Ordinary) or on private authority.[55]

§3. *Mixed causes and causes of Mixed Forum*—The term forum, recalling the much pictured market place of Rome, may

---

[41] Zitelli, *Iuris Ecclesiastici*, p. 398.

[42] Can. 1017 §3: cf. can. 1667. Pontif. Comm. Inter. Cod., June 2-3, 1918—*AAS*, X (1918), 345.

[43] Wernz-Vidal, *Ius Canonicum*, V, n. 102.

[44] Can. 2350 §1.

[45] Can. 2353.

[46] Can. 2356.

[47] Can. 2357 §2.

[48] Can. 2198.

[49] Canons 1933 §3, 2223 §3-3°; Gasparri, *De Matrimonio*, n. 1454.

[50] Vermeersch-Creusen, *Epitome*, III, n. 276. Cf. *AfkK*, CV (1925), 113.

[51] Canon 1019. Cf. *ETL*, I (1924), 35.

[52] Canon 1069 §2. Cf. *AfkK*, CV (1925), 117.

[53] Cf. cannon 1053. Cappello, *De Sacramentis*, III, n. 434; Wernz-Vidal, *Ius Canonicum*, V, n. 255, III; S. C. S. Off., April 27, 1887—*AAS*, II (1909), 198; Aertnys-Damen, *Theologia Moralis*, II, n. 721.

[54] Canon 1130.

[55] Canon 1131 §1.

designate the place where a judgment is held,[56] the judge or court exercising the judicial authority, the territory within which the tribunal has authority, or the very judicial power itself.[57] Throughout this discussion the term forum will be used to denote the proper court of trial in respect to the authority of the tribunal or judge.

By pertaining simultaneously to the spiritual and temporal welfare of mankind matrimonial causes are generically mixed causes[58] (*causa mixta*), or matters in which there are both ecclesiastical and secular juridical elements. Wherefore Church and State are competent not under the same but under *different* aspects for the respective elements have distinct juridical complexion or status, or beget rights that are quite distinct.[59] The specific point at issue determines whether the matrimonial cause (*causa mixta*) belongs strictly to the ecclesiastical forum, pertains to a secular magistrate, or is on the borderline in the class known as causes of mixed forum (*causae mixti fori*).[60] In these causes of mixed forum both Church and State are cumulatively competent and under the *same* aspect.

Matrimonial causes concerning the marriage bond, the spiritual effects, the inseparable temporal effects, and the canonical consequences[61] are properly and exclusively causes for the ecclesiastical forum because of the spiritual character of the sacramental bond and the spiritual effects, or the intimate connection with a spiritual matter as in the case of the inseparable temporal effects,[62] or by reason of their exclusive ecclesiastical nature as regards the canonical effects. Causes of this type the secular forum is absolutely incompetent to judge.

Questions arising in the purely political effects which the State attributes to marriage, such as the citizenship of the wife, her right to suffrage, her legal residence, are properly and exclusively causes for the civil magistrate. Among the separable

---

[56] C. 10, X, *de verb. signif.*, V, 40.

[57] Cogliolo, *Manuale delle Fonti del Diritto Romano*, p. 811; Noval, *De Iudiciis*, n. 56.

[58] Cavagnis, *Institutiones Iuris Publici Ecclesiastici*, I, n. 426.

[59] Wernz-Vidal, *Ius Canonicum*, VI, n. 33; Lega, *De Iudiciis Ecclesiasticis*, I, n. 324.

[60] Aichner, *Compendium Iuris Ecclesiastici*, n. 37.

[61] *E.g.* can. 93.

[62] Can. 1553 §1. Cf. "Accessorium sequitur principale."—Reg. 42, R. J., in VI°.

temporal effects can be listed the causes of mixed forum. In these the ecclesiastical and the civil forums are equally competent viewing the controversy under the same aspect. Here the court of trial is determined by priority of presentation (*praeventio*), being that tribunal to which the defendant is first cited.[63] Either forum acts of its own proper right for the matter concerns the temporal welfare. The ecclesiastical judge is competent—for the temporal good is contained in the spiritual well-being even as the greater includes the less—while temporal welfare of society is the direct and immediate concern of the secular officials.

Prevenience[64] between an ecclesiastical and civil court in matrimonial causes may be considered here. While a Catholic is free at first to present a matrimonial question of the *mixed forum* class to the decision of a secular judge he may suffer penalties if, having proposed the controversy before an ecclesiastical judge, he withdraws it and brings it to a secular court.[65] For this action he can be punished at the discretion of the bishop, even without previous admonition if scandal is imminent or the case bears special seriousness: but warning must precede the punishment if neither scandal nor special seriousness is present.[66] Further, the plaintiff is denied the right to reintroduce this cause or matters connected with it to an ecclesiastical court.[67] If canon 1554 provides punishment for transferring a cause of mixed forum from the ecclesiastical to the civil judge, does it not penalize the greater insult to ecclesiastical authority in proposing directly to the civil court a question which properly and exclusively belongs to the ecclesiastical forum? Canon 1554 is a penal enactment logically belonging to the fifth book of the Code. Like all penal laws it must be strictly interpreted. It applies only where a cause of the mixed forum type has been subtracted from the ecclesiastical court after the legitimate citation of the defendant and submitted to the secular power.[68]

---

[63] Can. 1553 §2, 1568, 1725-2°.

[64] Can. 1568; Wernz-Vidal, *Ius Canonicum,* VI, nn. 27, 28; "Qui prior est tempore potior est iure."—reg. 54, R. J., in VI°.

[65] Can. 1554.

[66] Can. 2222.

[67] Can. 1554. Martin V, Const., *Ad reprimandas,* Feb. 1, 1428, §3—*Fontes,* n. 46.

[68] Canon 19. Cf. canon 2219 §3.

It must be recalled that matrimonial causes of mixed forum include all and only matter of the temporal separable effects of the bond provided the issue is restricted to the temporal element and does not infringe upon the spiritual domain.[69] Examples may be furnished in cases of the restitution of dowry after separation (not separation itself), succession in nobility (not canonical legitimacy of child), action for damages resulting from breach of betrothal,[70] as well as crimes against marriage.[71]

Can a mere or nude spiritual fact be the object of a cause of mixed forum? In other words can a secular judge treat a cause to decide whether a person was married provided the question is one of fact which does not involve the validity of the marriage? It is purely a matter of fact which does not resolve itself into a question of law nor one on which the possession of some spiritual right depends. For example, if the question of an inheritance is based on the fact of a marriage having taken place, is a lay judge competent to decide the cause? Though Pius VI inveighed against laymen deciding mere spiritual facts[72] the more common opinion allows the questions of mere or nude spiritual facts as matters of mixed forum wherein a secular judge may be competent.[73] Being a question of fact the issue is also in the order of nature in that it is sensibly perceptible. The point concerns a temporal matter so that it is difficult to see why it cannot be a cause of mixed

---

[69] Roberti, *De Processibus,* I, p. 93.

[70] Pont. Comm. Inter. Cod., June 2-3, 1918, ad 10—*AAS,* X (1918), 345. *Ius Pontificium,* II (1922), 24.

[71] Cf. can. 1933 §3.

[72] "Ignotum Nobis non est, quosdam adesse, qui . . . potestatem relinquerint judicibus laicis cognoscendi saltem causas matrimoniales, quae sunt mere facti. Sed scimus etiam hanc captiunculum, et fallax hoc cavillandi genus omni fundamento destitui. Verba enim canonis (i. e. can. 12, C. Trent, sess. XXIV, *de matr.*) ita generalia sunt omnes ut causas comprehendant, et complectantur." Pius VI, litt. ad Ep. Motulense, Sept. 16, 1788—Feije, *De Impedimentis et Dispensationibus Matrimonialibus,* n. 12.

[73] Feije, *De Impedimentis et Dispensationibus Matrimonialibus,* n. 12, upholds the rigor of the law. The more tolerant opinion is held by: Cavagnis, *Institutiones Iuris Publici Ecclesiastici,* III, n. 460; Cappello, *Summa Iuris Publici,* n. 256; Gasparri, *De Matrimonio,* n. 1454; Wernz, *Ius Decretalium,* V, n. 273, note 58; Lega, *De Iudiciis Ecclesiasticis,* I, n. 324; Noval, *De Iudiciis,* n. 48; Roberti, *De Processibus,* I, p. 94; Coronata, *Ius Publicum Ecclesiasticum,* n. 88; Schmalzgrueber, *Ius Ecclesiasticum Universum,* IV, tit. 18, n. 8.

forum. If there is any doubt or dispute, the cause should be submitted to the ecclesiastical forum for the fact is a spiritual fact and inclines therefore to the religious court.[74]

§4. *Proper and exclusive jurisdiction*—Proper jurisdiction, or right, considers the *nature* and *source* of the judicial authority in itself while the quality of exclusiveness considers the *extent* of that authority, or its relation to the rights of others, in this case, the State. Judicial power belongs to the Church because the Church is a perfect society.[75] In the exercise of this power the Church is supremely free and independent. The authority is not conceded, derived, or delegated, either directly or indirectly, expressly or tacitly, by the secular power.[76] The term *iure proprio* of canon 1960 may not require as much explanation as the phrase *ex propria potestate* in canon 1961 where the merely civil effects of marriage are considered. It is to be recalled that the authority of the Church as the superior society is of a higher order than that of the State. Just as the greater contains the less and as the temporal should yield to the spiritual so the ecclesiastical judge is competent by his own power to decide incidental and accessory questions of a merely civil nature. The accessory follows the principal cause. It must be noted that this power of the ecclesiastical judge is not exercised when the temporal issue is the principal point, but only when the question is incidental and accessory.[77]

The exclusiveness of the Church's jurisdiction in the matrimonial causes of the baptized is an indication of the *absolute incompetence* of the secular forum in the matter. It denies that the proper power is shared with the State. Opponents of this exclusive competence are those who hold that the Church and State are equally competent, making all matrimonial questions causes of mixed forum (*mixti fori*) by seeking a real distinction between the Sacrament and contract. It must be noted that canon 1961 implies that both Church and State have proper authority over the merely civil effects, the latter society directly and in principal questions, the former indirectly (but none the

---

[74] Coronata, *Ius Publicum Ecclesiasticum,* n. 88.

[75] Cf. Bouix, *De Iudiciis,* I, p. 24 sq.

[76] Cf. canons 108, 109, 1553 §1; Coronata, *Ius Publicum Ecclesiasticum,* n. 50 sq; Wernz-Vidal, *Ius Canonicum,* V, n. 46.

[77] Sebastianelli, *De Iudiciis Ecclesiasticis,* p. 51.

less properly) in accessory and incidental cases. Here the *proper* authority in the matter is not *exclusive* either to the civil or ecclesiastical judge but shared by both.

§5. *Causes entered principally, incidentally, and accessorily*—The principal cause, or issue, in a trial is that which is directly and expressly mentioned in the petition as the immediate object of the judgment.[78] Other questions which perhaps are not expressed in the petition yet which pertain in one way or other to the main issue by having their origin or occasion in this principal question, are incidental causes.[79] The terms accessory and incidental causes are often used indiscriminately and there does not appear to be any grounds in the Code for drawing a distinction. The term "accessory cause" does not appear in the fourth book. But if a shade of difference is sought, it may lie in the notion that an incidental cause is one which, arising in the course of the discussion on the principal issue, impedes the final sentence and therefore should be decided prior to the principal question:[80] while an accessory cause is one connected indeed with the principal question but subordinately dependent and without a direct bearing on the solution of the principal cause. What is more likely in a matrimonial cause, an accessory question may be one in which the decision follows from or is based on the decision reached in the principal issue.[81]

It may be well to note here that while an ecclesiastical judge is properly competent in the incidental and accessory causes regarding the merely civil effects of the marriage bond, the secular magistrate, being absolutely incompetent in spiritual causes, cannot judge an accessory or incidental causes should it be of a spiritual nature, excepting as has been noted, a mere spiritual fact.[82]

---

[78] Noval, *De Iudiciis*, n. 575.

[79] Cf. canon 1837; Noval, *De Iudiciis*, n. 576; Lega, *De Iudiciis Ecclesiasticis*, I, n. 536.

[80] Cf. canons 1633, 1837, 1868.

[81] C. 3, X, *de donat. inter vir.*, IV, 20. Reg. 42, R. J., in VI°.

[82] C. 3, X, *de iud.*, II, I; C. X, *qui filii sint leg.*, IV, 17; Lega, *De Iudiciis Ecclesiasticis*, I, nn. 358, 536; Schmalzgrueber, *Ius Ecclesiasticum Universum*, IV, tit. 17, n. 44; Wernz-Vidal, *Ius Canonicum*, VI, n. 26, note 38.

Art. 2. Competence of the Ecclesiastical Forum in Matrimonial Causes

§1. *Marriage among baptized persons*—The Church does not claim that all matrimonial causes belong to the ecclesiastical judge, but those causes concerning the marriages between baptized persons are exclusively and properly causes for the ecclesiastical forum.

By baptism a man is constituted a person in the Church with all the rights and obligations[83] of a Christian unless as far as rights are concerned he is debarred from ecclesiastical communion or is under censure.[84] From the obligations assumed at baptism a man is never freed.[85] Once baptized a man remains under the jurisdiction of the Church until death. Further the contract of matrimony between baptized persons is a Sacrament.[86] The matrimonial causes of the baptized belong to the ecclesiastical forum not only because both parties are *subjects* of the Church but also because the question concerns a *Sacrament* and the ecclesiastical judge alone is competent in spiritual affairs.[87]

The term *baptized* includes all baptized persons—Catholics of the Western or Eastern Uniat Churches,[88] all heretics,[89] schismatics, apostates,[90] or excommunicated persons but not catechumens.[91] Over the matrimonial causes of these people the civil forum has no competence for their causes belong exclusively and properly to the ecclesiastical judge when the question concerns the intimate nature of the marriage contract as the bond itself, the spiritual effects, the inseparable temporal effects, or what is purely an ecclesiastical concern, the canonical consequences.[92] The civil forum cannot claim competence in the

---

[83] C. Trent, sess. VII, *de sacr. bapt.*, can. 7.

[84] Can. 87.

[85] Chelodi, *Ius de Personis*, n. 91. Wernz-Vidal, *Ius Canonicum*, V, n. 58.

[86] Can. 1012 §1.

[87] Can. 1553 §1-1°.

[88] S. C. S. Off., Instr. ad Ep. Orient, 1883—*Coll.*, n. 1588.

[89] S. C. S. Off., Mar. 28, 1860, §6—*Fontes*, n. 957.

[90] Cf. can. 1325 §2; Benedict XIV, Ep., *Singulari*, Feb. 9, 1747, §12—*Fontes*, n. 394; Pius IX, Litt. Ap., *Provida*, Jan. 18, 1906, §3—*Fontes*, n. 670; Roberti, *De Processibus*, I, p. 79.

[91] De Smet, *De Sponsalibus et Matrimonio*, n. 431.

[92] Pius IX, *Litt. ap. ad reg. Sardin.*, Sept. 9, 1852—*Fontes*, n. 514; *Syllabus errorum*, prop. 74—*Fontes*, n. 543; Leo XIII, Ep. encycl., *Arca-*

cause on the grounds that the contract is separable from the Sacrament.[93] It is scarcely necessary to remark that the Church is competent even though a ceremony of marriage may have been performed outside the Church before an heretical minister or a civil official.

If, in the progress of the trial, accessory or incidental causes concerning the separable effects of the marriage should arise, the ecclesiastical judge is properly competent to decide them. It is not necessary to submit them to the civil forum.[94] Yet it may be well whenever possible to leave the decision in such matters to the civil magistrate.[95]

§2. *Marriages between the baptized and the unbaptized*—The more probable opinion of theologians is that the matrimonial contract between a baptized person and an infidel does not possess the sacramental character.[96] The competence of the ecclesiastical judge in such marriage causes is not to be claimed on the basis of the Sacrament but rather on the reasons that one of the contracting parties is a *subject* of the Church and that the matrimonial contract is *individual.*

It is evident that the baptized party, Catholic or non-Catholic, is subject to the Church's power, yet is his marriage? Canon 1960 uses the phrase *inter baptizatos* in speaking of the judicial power in matrimonial causes while canon 1016 uses the genitive phrase *baptizatorum matrimonium* in treating of the Church's legislative power in matrimony. The Church can legislate even if only one party is baptized but can the ecclesiastical judge claim competence if a matrimonial cause arises?[97] Certainly one who is competent to legislate for a certain matter can judge that same case. Causes in mixed marriages belong properly and exclusively to the ecclesiastical forum. The bap-

---

num, Feb. 10, 1880— *Fontes,* n. 580; Pius VI, Const., *Auctorem Fidei,* Aug. 28, 1794, prop. 59—*Fontes,* n. 475.

[93] Cf. can. 1012.

[94] Can. 1961. C. 3, X, *de donat. inter vir.,* IV, 20; Santi, *Praelectiones Iuris Canonici,* IV, tit. 18, nn. 12, 13; Schmalzgrueber, *Ius Ecclesiasticum Universum,* IV, tit. 18, 4, 7.

[95] Chelodi, *Ius Matrimoniale,* n. 171; Gasparri, *De Matrimonio,* n. 1454.

[96] De Augustinis, *De Re Sacramentaria,* II, p. 637; Billot, *De Ecclesiae Sacramentis,* II, p. 372; Sasse, *Institutiones Theologicae de Sacramentis Ecclesiae,* II, p. 390; Noldin, *De Sacramentis,* n. 509; Aertnys-Damen, *Theologia Moralis,* II, n. 628; Hurter, *Compendium Theologiae Dogmaticae,* III, n. 736.

[97] Cf. Augustine, *A Commentary on Canon Law,* V, p. 25.

tized party is the subject of the Church and by reason of the *individuality of the marriage contract* the infidel is brought indirectly under the authority of the ecclesiastical forum. Like any other bilateral contract the marriage agreement is a contract in the strict sense of the term, consisting in the union of wills of the capable contracting parties in the same essential matter. In this, matrimony like any contract has the note of individuality in that it is either valid or invalid for both. But further the marriage contract had a stronger character of individuality in that, unlike other bilateral contracts, it can never *limp, i.e.* retain the force of a unilateral contract wherein the obligations on both parties are not equal. The marriage contract obliges both parties equally or not at all.[98] The individuality of the matrimonial contract was acknowledged in times past when the exemption of one party from the Tridentine prescription of the form of marriage was communicated to a person who was bound to observe the form.[99] Moreover the Church considers a marriage invalid where the diriment impediment exists on one side only[100] on the principle that if one party is bound by an impediment the other party is equally incapacitated in so far as this particular marriage is considered. In a matter of dispensation and its effects the individuality of the matrimonial contract has been expressly declared.[101] Accepting the notion of the individuality of the matrimonial contract, the civil magistrate cannot thereby claim competence by reason of the infidel party for then two distinct and independent authorities would be judging the same individual matrimonial cause.[102] And in a clash of authority the civil power yields to the ecclesiastical or higher power.[103] Consequently, causes concerning

---

[98] Schmalzgrueber, *Ius Ecclesiasticum Universum,* IV, tit. 1, n. 423.

[99] Cf. Acta et Decreta Balt. III, p. CVII; Cappello, *De Sacramentis,* III, n. 659-4°; Aichner, *Compendium Iuris Ecclesiastici,* p. 646; Benedict XIV, *De Synodo Dioecesana,* lib. VI, c. 6, n. 12; Wernz-Vidal, *Ius Canonicum,* V, n. 37; D'Annibale, *Summula Theologiae Moralis,* III, nn. 322, 333.

[100] Can. 1036 §3.

[101] ". . . ut inde hujus exemptio, propter contractus individuitatem, communicata remaneat." S. C. S. Off., Instr. ad Arch. Quebec, Sept. 16, 1824, ad 2—*Fontes,* n. 866. Cf. canon 1036 §3.

[102] De Smet, *De Sponsalibus et Matrimonio,* n. 438. Gasparri, *De Matrimonio,* n. 1456.

[103] Cavagnis, *Institutiones Iuris Publici Ecclesiastici,* I, n. 404; Benedict XIV, Const. *Singulari,* Feb. 9, 1749 §7—*Fontes,* n. 394; Leo XIII, Ep. ency., *Immortale Dei,* Nov. 1, 1885, §6—*Fontes,* n. 592.

marriages between a baptized person and an unbaptized person even as the causes between two baptized persons[104] belong to an ecclesiastical judge by proper and exclusive rights.[105]

What if the question of a doubtful baptism enters the case in that one of the parties either doubts the validity or the fact of his baptism? Should the difficulty arise in the cause of a marriage between two baptized persons, the matter claims the attention of the ecclesiastical forum as would any marriage cause between a baptized and an unbaptized person. But what if the doubt enters in a case of a supposedly baptized party who has married an infidel? Is the ecclesiastical forum competent? Even this cause belongs to the Church's field for if the validity of the baptism is doubted, the validity of the act is to be upheld in the external forum and the person considered as a subject of the Church.[106] If the fact of baptism is doubted presumptions are to be invoked. If the person was commonly looked upon as baptized the cause may be considered one for the ecclesiastical forum unless the fact of non-baptism is proved and this would be difficult.[107]

§3. *Marriages among unbaptized persons*—The Church claims no direct competence in the marriage causes arising among infidels, being especially competent neither as to *matter*—for the matrimonial contract is not a Sacrament here—nor as to the *persons* involved—as the unbaptized are not subjects of the Church. The care of such unions, authors generally agree,[108] belongs *per se* exclusively to the civil power. If the State can establish invalidating impediments for the marriage of infidels then the civil judiciary is competent to judge the matrimonial causes which arise among the unbaptized.[109] Whether this power is proper (*ex iure proprio*)[110] or derived (*ex iure devolutivo*)[111] is not clear. Assuredly the State is properly competent as to the persons involved but the nature of the civil authority in respect

[104] De Smet, *De Sponsalibus et Matrimonio,* n. 438.

[105] Chelodi, *Ius Matrimoniale,* n. 12.

[106] Vermeersch-Creusen, *Epitome* I, n. 79.

[107] Cf. can. 1070 §2.

[108] Gasparri, *De Matrimonio,* n. 288 in note; Cappello, *De Sacramentis,* III, n. 75; De Smet, *De Sponsalibus et Matrimonio,* n. 433; Wernz-Vidal, *Ius Canonicum,* V, n. 67.

[109] Wernz-Vidal, *Ius Canonicum,* V, n. 73.

[110] De Smet, *De Sponsalibus et Matrimonio,* n. 435.

[111] Cappello, *De Sacramentis,* III, n. 79.

to the matter, the marriage contract, is a mooted point,[112] and one in which the argument of the natural sacredness of marriage should not be overstressed.[113] Marriages among infidels are ruled by the natural and divine positive law of which the Church is the guardian and interpreter,[114] yet the State can have *per se* exclusive judiciary power in these matrimonial causes though the State, even as the Church, must respect the natural and divine positive laws involved.[115] While the Church can authoritatively interpret the divine and natural law in the matrimonial difficulties of infidels[116] the ecclesiastical judge's cognizance of a marriage contracted between infidels will come indirectly and by reason of its connection to some other marriage, for example, if divorce followed the marriage of the unbaptized parties and now one of them wishes to marry a Catholic[117] or the infidel party, having been baptized, wishes to contract another marriage.[118] Thus *per accidens* the ecclesiastical judge examines the marriage contracted between two infidels to determine the *status liber* or the freedom of the parties to contract marriage. Where a marriage had been contracted between two infidels and the later one or both parties become baptized, then by reason of the baptism of even the one party, any question of the marriage which might arise would be a matrimonial cause for the ecclesiastical forum.[119]

Art. 3. Competence of the Secular Forum in Matrimonial Causes

§1. *In the marriage of any baptized person*—Since the ecclesiastical judge is exclusively competent in the causes concerning the intimate nature of the marriage contract whenever one of the parties is baptized, it follows that the civil magistrate

---

112 Chelodi, *Ius Matrimoniale*, n. 13.

113 Wernz-Vidal, *Ius Canonicum*, V, n. 71. Cf. Leo XIII, Ep. ency., *Arcanum*, Feb. 10, 1880, §11—*Fontes*, n. 580.

114 Can. 1038 §1. Noldin, *De Principiis*, nn. 112-4, 117, 121.

115 Gasparri, *De Matrimonio*, n. 291.

116 Can. 1038 §1. De Smet, *De Sponsalibus et Matrimonio*, n. 437 bis.

117 De Smet, *De Sponsalibus et Matrimonio*, n. 702 in note. *Jus Pontificium*, VI (1926), 159.

118 Cappello, *De Sacramentis*, III, n. 866. Wernz-Vidal, *Ius Canonicum*, V, n. 687, note 16.

119 Cf. Aertnys-Damen, *Theologia Moralis*, II, n. 633 bis.

is absolutely incompetent in these causes. The secular forum is incompetent not only when the cause of this nature is the principal issue but even if in the discernment of a civil effect a question of the bond, a spiritual effect, or an inseparable temporal effect arises as an incidental or accessory issue.[120] Where a cause in which the ecclesiastical forum is exclusively competent arises incidentally, the secular judge should submit the question to the determination of ecclesiastical authorities, and having obtained a decision, proceed with the main issue.[121] The civil magistrate is most probably competent to decide a nude spiritual fact. Otherwise the only causes which can be defined by the secular forum are those concerned with the merely civil effects of matrimony. These the civil forum adjudges on its own proper authority and all such causes should be referred by the ecclesiastical judge to the secular court when they are the principal issue.[122] The secular forum is properly and exclusively competent in case involving the purely political effects of marriages. The civil forum cannot claim competence in a cause between a baptized person and an unbaptized person on the score that the infidel is the defendant (reus) in the case and that the principle "Actio sequitur forum rei" is to be applied.[123] The principle is not applicable in public law but only in private law, or between one ecclesiastical judge and another. No matter who is the defendant the cause belongs properly and exclusively to the ecclesiastical court.[124] Obviously in treating even causes of limited divorce where one of the parties is baptized the civil court is usurping ecclesiastical power.[125]

While laymen and civil judges cannot *per se* decide matrimonial causes, it is certain that the pope, but no lesser prelate, could delegate a layman to handle a matrimonial cause, endowing him at the same time with the necessary ecclesiastical jurisdiction.[126]

---

[120] Cf. can. 1553.

[121] C. 5, X, *qui filii sint legit.*, IV, 17.

[122] C. 7, X, *qui filii sint legit.*, IV, 17.

[123] Cf. can. 1559 §3. Cf. Sanchez, *De Matrimonio,* lib. VII, d. 4, n. 10.

[124] Gasparri, *De Matrimonio,* n. 1456; Wernz-Vidal, *Ius Canonicum,* V, n. 52.

[125] Noldin, *De Sacramentis,* n. 673.

[126] Bouix, *De Iudiciis, Ecclesiasticis,* I, p. 81. Ferraris, v. *Delegatio,* n. 40. Cavagnis, *Institutiones Iuris Publici Ecclesiastici,* I, n. 559.

§2. *In the marriages among infidels*—In any and all causes between infidels the matter is, according to common opinion, exclusively and properly a cause for the civil forum excepting *per accidens* when the ecclesiastical judge investigates the marriage in the cases mentioned.[127]

Art. 4. The Laws According to Which Marriages Are Judged

The proper and exclusive competence of the ecclesiastical forum is not surrendered when the clerical judge takes into consideration the exemptions allowed in canon law for baptized non-Catholics.[128] Fundamentally, the decision is based on the canon law which is *per se* the common norm for all the marriages of baptized persons.[129] Even non-Catholic teachings, beliefs, notions, and customs in marriage may have to be considered by the ecclesiastical judge. Erroneous though these opinions may be, they often have an important bearing on the validity of the marriage. An error or false judgment with respect to the properties of the marriage contract, for example the error that marriage is not perpetual or exclusive, may vitiate matrimonial consent even of a non-Catholic by being made a condition to the consent.[130]

A difficulty presents itself in the marriages between a baptized person and an unbaptized person. Is the validity of the marriage affected by the presence of a civil invalidating impediment? It is commonly agreed that the secular authority can establish diriment impediments for the marriages of infidels,[131]

---

[127] De Smet, *De Sponsalibus et Matrimonio,* n. 433; Chedodi, *Ius Matrimoniale,* n. 13; Cappello, *De Sacramentis,* III, n. 75; Cappello, *Summa Iuris Publici,* n. 416. Gasparri, *De Matrimonio,* n. 281; Wernz-Vidal, *Ius Canonicum,* V, nn. 67, 73; Cerato, *De Matrimonio,* p. 44; De Becker, *De Sponsalibus et Matrimonio,* p. 42; S. C. S. Off., Instr., June 20, 1883, §§43, 44—*Fontes,* n. 1076; Gasparri, "Du Pouvoir de L'Autorité Civil sur Le Mariage des Infidèls,"—*LCC,* XIII (1890), 201.

[128] Cf. can. 1070 §1, 1099.

[129] ". . . nisi postquam causa primi connubii ab haeretica parte iam antea initi cognita fuerit ecclesiastico iudicio ad canonum normam exacto, quo connubium idem fuerit irritum declaratum." Gregory XIV, Ep. encycl., *Summo iugiter,* May 27, 1832, §8—*Fontes,* n. 484.

[130] Wernz, *Ius Decretalium,* IV, pars I, n. 23. Cf. can. 1086 §2; Aertnys-Damen, *Theologia Moralis,* II, n. 816.

[131] Chelodi, *Ius Matrimoniale,* n. 11; Vlaming, *Praelectiones Iuris Matrimonii,* I, n. 51; Gasparri, *De Matrimonio,* n. 291.

but should an ecclesiastical judge take cognizance of such an impediment in judging the validity of a marriage contracted between a baptized and an unbaptized person? For all practical purposes he can ignore the civil impediment. The Church is properly and exclusively competent to adjudicate the marriage causes between a baptized and an unbaptized person. Exclusive judicial competence in a particular cause presupposes exclusive legislative power as well.[132] If recognition is given the civil impediment as invalidating such a marriage, then the civil power is granted a jurisdiction in the marriage of a baptized person which cannot be admitted according to the general principles of canon law.[133] Even if the civil impediment directly affects the infidel only, as the impediment of age, it does not appear that the impediment should be recognized in the ecclesiastical forum when the marriage has been contracted with a baptized person. Wherefore, if the civil law requires a greater age than the canon law (sixteen complete years for the man and fourteen complete years for the woman)[134] the validity of the marriage is not to be suspected. For where there is a conflict of laws on the same point the ecclesiastical as the law of the higher order is to prevail over the secular enactments.[135] Take, for example, the case where an infidel seventeen years of age has contracted marriage with a baptized party in violation of the civil law requiring the age of eighteen years for the validity of a marriage. In the eyes of the Church (granting the necessary dispensation of disparity of cult was obtained and the proper form of marriage observed) such a marriage is valid while in the eyes of the State the marriage is invalid. Two authorities, each supreme and independent in its own order, are exercising direct control in one and the same contract and the findings of one are contradictory to the judgments of the other. And though today as a matter of *fact* one and the same marriage valid in the eyes of the Church may be invalid in the estimation of the secular authorities, this condition of affairs cannot exist *de iure*.

---

[132] Wernz-Vidal, *Ius Canonicum,* V, n. 52.

[133] Cf. can. 1016; Chelodi, *Ius Matrimoniale,* n. 12.

[134] Canon 1067 §1.

[135] *Syllabus errorum,* prop. 42—*Fontes,* n. 543.

It is illogical.[136] Civil impediments as a rule only make the marriage contract rescindible. Yet granting the opinion that the civil impediment is truly invalidating even when an infidel contracts marriage with a baptized person,[137] what is the practical solution? Since the view upholding the invalidating force of the civil impediment is not certain for there is the opposite probability, namely, that the civil impediment has no force when marriage is contracted with a baptized person,[138] there is room for doubt and the principle enunciated in canon 1014 favoring the validity of the marriage furnishes the ecclesiastical judge reason for ignoring the civil impediment in this case.[139]

Whenever an ecclesiastical judge considers the marriage contracted between two infidels he applies not only the divine natural and divine positive law by which these marriages are regulated[140] but also the civil laws and their customary interpretation[141] in force at the time in that place where the marriage was contracted.[142] Care must be exercised to determine whether the civil legislator intended the impediment as nullifying[143] or merely prohibitive.[144]

There can be no appeal from the ecclesiastical to the civil

---

[136] De Smet, *De Sponsalibus et Matrimonio,* n. 438; Vermeersch-Creusen, *Epitome,* II, n. 297. Cf. Ryan-Millar, *The State and the Church,* p. 50.

[137] De Becker, *De Sponsalibus et Matrimonio,* p. 48; Vlaming, *Praelectiones Iuris Matrimonii,* I, n. 195. D'Annibale, *Summula Theologiae Moralis,* III, n. 294. Cf. however D'Annibale, *o. c.,* III, n. 335. Aertnys-Damen, *Theologia Moralis,* II, n. 697.

[138] Cappello, *De Sacramentis,* III, n. 67; Wernz, *Ius Decretalium,* IV, pars I, n. 60; Wernz-Vidal, *Ius Canonicum,* V, nn. 52, 69, note 72.

[139] The opinion of Gasparri, *De Matrimonio* (ed. 1892), n. 297, favoring the invalidating force of the civil impediment was reversed in the later edition of the work (ed. 1904), n. 306. The appeal made to Benedict XIV, Const., *Singulari,* Feb. 9, 1749, §§7, 8—*Fontes,* n. 394, is of little weight as it may be used in support of either opinion. Vermeersch, *Gregorianum,* VII (1926), 141, questions the authority of the Church to exempt or dispense the infidel party from the civil impediment yet in the *Epitome* (ed. 1927), II, n. 297, it is admitted that the divergence of opinions leaves a doubt and that for all practical purposes the invalidating force of the civil impediment may be ignored.

[140] Cf. can. 1069.

[141] Benedict XIV, Ep., *Postremo,* Feb. 28, 1747, §68—*Fontes,* n. 377.

[142] Wernz-Vidal, *Ius Canonicum,* V, n. 70. Cf. May, *Marriage Laws and Decisions in the United States,* for present civil laws.

[143] Cf. S. C. P. Fide, June 26, 1820—*Coll.,* n. 744.

[144] Cf. Cappello, *De Sacramentis,* III, n. 77.

forum in matrimonial causes whether the appeal is a simple appeal,[145] or what is known as *appeal from abuse*,[146] for the secular power can have no competence in the matter. An excommunication specially reserved to the Holy See is imposed on those who directly or indirectly hinder the exercise of ecclesiastical jurisdiction in either the external or internal forum by an effective recourse to any lay power.[147]

An ecclesiastical judge takes no notice of decisions in matrimonial causes which may be rendered by heretical or schismatical tribunals[148] for these courts have no juridical standing and their decisions are of no weight.[149] A cause previously submitted to a non-Catholic court must be entirely retried by judge and according to the prescriptions canon law. It is not forbidden, where it will expedite the trial, to peruse the acts of the heretical tribunal for a better understanding of the facts and circumstances of the cause but never can the Catholic judges adduce the sentence of the non-Catholic court as a motive for their decision. Because the decision of the competent court agrees with the decision rendered by the heretical tribunal, it does not follow that two conformable sentences have been had in the case and that an appeal to the court of second instance is unnecessary.[150]

In judging the marriage causes between infidels the secular judge is to be guided not only by the civil law but also the natural and divine positive laws.

Art. 5. Civil Divorce Courts and the Matrimonial Causes of the Baptized

In discussing secular divorce courts from the canonical, or juridical aspect, it is to be admitted that doctrine and practice

---

[145] Cavagnis, *Institutiones Iuris Publici Ecclesiastici,* II, pars 2ae, lib. III, n. 47*.

[146] Cappello, *Summa Iuris Publici,* n. 182. Cavagnis, *Institutiones Iuris Publici Ecclesiastici,* II, pars 2ae, lib. III, n. 51*. *Syllabus errorum,* prop. 41—*Fontes,* n. 543.

[147] Can. 2334-2°. Cf. Pont. Comm. Int. Cod., July 25, 1926—*AAS,* XVII (1926), 394.

[148] Pius VII, breve ad Arch. Moguntin, Oct. 8, 1803, §6—*Fontes,* n. 477.

[149] S. C. S. Off., resp. to Bishop of Agria, Aug. 28, 1794—*NRT,* XX (1888), 624; S. C. S. Off., *Instr.* 1883, §44—*Fontes,* n. 1076.

[150] S. C. S. Off., Instr. 1883, §44—*Fontes,* n. 1076.

differ that disagreeable civil consequences might be avoided.[151] Canonically the position of the secular court is clearly defined in the Code.[152] It is absolutely incompetent and usurps ecclesiastical jurisdiction in judging the matrimonial cause of any baptized person[153] excepting the proper authority it possesses to decide the merely civil and political effects of matrimony.[154] Yet today most civil legislation considers that civil divorce courts have power over the bond itself[155] and even in Spain and Austria where the causes of Catholics are remanded to the ecclesiastical forum the civil authorities do not hesitate to treat the matrimonial cases of baptized non-Catholics.[156] On the other hand the secular forum is recognized as competent in the matrimonial causes of the unbaptized.[157] Here the secular forum can declare nullity (due to civil invalidating impediments), permit separation, or decide nuptial promises among infidels but it cannot dissolve a valid marriage (*matrimonium legitimum*)[158] in contradiction to the divine law of indissolubility of the marriage bond.[159]

While the judgment of the matrimonial causes of baptized non-Catholics, whether they were contracted with other baptized non-Catholics or with infidels, belongs properly and exclusively to the ecclesiastical judge,[160] obviously the ecclesiastical authorities will rarely be asked to treat such a marriage directly.[161]

---

[151] De Smet, *De Sponsalibus et Matrimonio,* n. 402; Wernz-Vidal, *Ius Canonicum,* V, n. 706. Cf. "Mirizio v. Mirizio," *New York Sun,* April 25, 1928. *Mirizio v. Mirizio,* 242 N. Y. 74 (1926): 212 A. D. 524 (1925).

[152] Canons 1960, 1961.

[153] *I.e.,* matrimonial cause for dissolution of the bond, declaration of nullity, separation, or questions of sponsalia. Cf. Leo XIII, litt. *Il divisamento,* Feb. 8, 1893, §2—*Fontes,* n. 617.

[154] Canons 1016, 1961.

[155] Gasparri, *De Matrimonio,* n. 1535.

[156] Wernz-Vidal, *Ius Canonicum,* V, n. 706, notes 2, 4. Cf. *Apollinaris,* I (1928) 465.

[157] Wernz-Vidal, *Ius Canonicum,* V, n. 67.

[158] Canon 1015 §3.

[159] De Smet, *De Sponsalibus et Matrimonio,* n. 324; C. Trent, sess. XXIV, *de matr.,* canons 5, 7.

[160] Canon 1960.

[161] Smith, *Marriage Process,* p. 43. Cf. S. C. S. Off., Jan. 27, 1928—*AAS,* XX (1928), 75.

So discussion will be limited to a consideration of:

1. Catholic parties presenting their matrimonial causes to the secular forum;
2. Catholic judges and lawyers treating divorce cases.

§1. Hypothetically, *Catholic parties* may present a matrimonial cause to the secular court with (1) the concomitant dissolution, declaration of nullity, or permission of separation on the part of the ecclesiastical tribunal; (2) the license of ecclesiastical authorities when canonically the validity of the bond is undeniable; (3) or quite independently of any ecclesiastical sanction. These distinctions do not affect a defendant in a civil divorce action who can always oppose the suit either personally or through another. But for the plaintiff, or actor, the distinctions have a part. The last case is never justifiable. Where a Catholic seeks a civil divorce independently of any permission from ecclesiastical authorities and with no intention of having the matter adjusted by an ecclesiastical decision, he effects nothing. If a remarriage is attempted while the first bond endures, he becomes *ipso facto* infamous and liable to other ecclesiastical penalties.[162] In this country if a remarriage is attempted after a civil divorce there is also an excommunication, *latae sententiae*, reserved to the Ordinary.[163] This penalty remains in force today.[164]

Where the cause was, or is about to be, properly treated in the ecclesiastical courts the usual and advisable practice today is that the matter be also presented in the secular courts yet always with the knowledge and advice of the ecclesiastical officials lest penalties be incurred.[165] The Catholic plaintiff in such an action will intend merely the civil safeguarding of his rights

---

[162] Can. 2356.

[163] ". . . poenam excommunicationis statuimus, Ordinario reservatam, ipso facto incurrendam ab eis, qui postquam divortium civile obtinuerint, matrimonium ausi fuerint attentare."—n. 124, *Acta et Decreta Balt. III*, p. 64.

[164] Cf. canon 6. Neuberger, *Canon 6, or The Relation of the Codex Juris Canonici to Preceding Legislation*, p. 53.

[165] ". . . iis omnibus, qui matrimonio conjuncti sunt, praecepimus, ne inconsulta auctoritate ecclesiastica, tribunalia civilia adeant ad obtinendam separationem a thoro et mensa. Quod si quis attentaverit, sciat se gravem reatum incurrere et pro Episcopi judicio puniendum esse."—n. 126, *Acta et Decreta Balt. III*, p. 64.

and the civil effects of marriage. Today this is the only remedy for avoiding unpleasant and serious legal consequences both for himself and for ecclesiastical authorities,[166] especially if the parties wish to remarry or if the case in question is a mixed marriage since a non-Catholic might fail to appreciate the Catholic viewpoint of the matter. In the civil court the action for divorce or separation can be based on the titles allowed in civil legislation. It is imprudent to expect the secular tribunal to recognize canonical reasons unless the civil code embodies the same points.[167] The parties may and should institute civil action in conjunction with the ecclesiastical process where a ratified non-consummated marriage has been, or is to be, canonically severed by the solemn religious profession of one party or by papal dispensation. Moreover a convert whose legitimate marriage has been severed by the application of the Pauline privilege or through papal authority[168] should, if possible, secure a civil pronouncement. Where a marriage is canonically invalid (*i. e. in facie ecclesiae*) by reason of a diriment canonical impediment, defect of consent, or more commonly, defect in form because the ceremony took place before a civil magistrate, non-Catholic minister, or even before an unauthorized priest as witness,[169] the recognition of the invalidity should be secured in the eyes of the secular authorities by any possible legal means.

Limited divorce, or separation, too should be fortified by the sentence of a secular tribunal through which any molestation from the dismissed party may be quite effectively interdicted. The canonical reasons should be present.[170] As the reasons advanced in civil legislations for complete divorce are generally similar to those for which the Church allows separation,[171] no difficulty should be experienced. The bishop's permission to

---

166 Wernz-Vidal, *Ius Canonicum,* V, n. 711, note 13; Smith, *Marriage Process,* p. 32; S. C. S. Off., May 22, Dec. 19, 1860, ad 4—*Collect.,* n. 2272.

167 Cf. Herbert v. Cloutre, Quebec Superior Court, Mar. 23, 1911, where the invalidity of the bond was urged because the ceremony had taken place before a non-Catholic minister.—Stockton, *Marriage, Civil and Ecclesiastical,* p. 89; cf. S. C. S. Off., Sept. 9, 1824—*NRT,* XVIII, p. 412; S. C. S. Off., June 25, 1885—*Fontes,* n. 1093.

168 Cf. *e. g.,* S. C. S. Off., Nov. 5, 1924—*AER,* LXXII (1925), 188.

169 Canons 1094-1096.

170 Canons 1129-1131.

171 Chelodi, *Ius Matrimoniale,* n. 162.

enter such a civil suit for effecting a separation should be obtained,[172] though the obligation is not so grave as in cases where complete divorce is sought since the Code allows separation to be effected even on private authority.[173] Theoretically, a difficulty may be found where no canonical reasons for separation are present when a civil separation is sought.[174] The case may be most rare but should it occur Catholics, apparently, would not be justified in going to the secular court. No difficulty should be experienced between the power of the ecclesiastical and civil forums in the matter of espousals (*sponsalia*),[175] or breach of promise suits, as they are civilly known. Causes concerning espousal, however, are by nature spiritual and so proper to the ecclesiastical forum.[176]

What of cases where the marriage is canonically valid so that no declaration of nullity is obtainable in the ecclesiastical forum? Can the solution of the marital difficulties be sought through a civil divorce? Catholic authors disagree as to whether or not civil divorce is intrinsically evil.[177] As there has been no general decision of the Holy See declaring civil divorce intrinsically evil[178] and as the attitude of the State in regarding marriage as a merely civil contract and the State's total indifference as to what the Church may decide in a matrimonial cause may alter circumstances considerably,[179] the matter may be summarized in the corollary of one author: "The petition for civil divorce on the part of a Catholic who is indissolubly united in a valid marriage, does not appear to be an intrinsically evil action but merely unseemly (*male sonans*): wherefore, excepting special circumstances and positive ecclesiastical prohibition, it

---

172 *Acta et Decreta Balt. III*, n. 126.

173 Canons 1130, 1131.

174 Wernz-Vidal, *Ius Canonicum*, V, n. 712.

175 Gasparri, *De Matrimonio*, n. 1445; Wernz-Vidal, *Ius Canonicum*, V, n. 706.

176 Pius VI, const., *Auctorem fidei*, Aug. 28, 1794, §58—*Fontes*, n. 475.

177 Cerato, *De Matrimonio*, n. 118; Wernz-Vidal, *Ius Canonicum*, V, n. 712, take the stricter view: Lehmkuhl, *Theologia Moralis*, II, n. 701, note 1; Noldin, *De Sacramentis*, n. 673; De Becker, *De Sponsalibus et Matrimonio*, p. 429; Cappello, *De Sacramentis*, III, nn. 834, 837, teach the milder opinion.

178 Cf. De Smet, *De Sponsalibus et Matrimonio*, n. 400; Wernz-Vidal, *Ius Canonicum*, V, n. 712.

179 Smith, *Marriage Process*, p. 37; Noldin, *De Sacramentis*, n. 674; *AER*, LXXI (1924), 599.

may be justifiable at times, though rarely so."[180] At any event the civil action should not be instituted before the ecclesiastical authorities have been consulted. Canonically, there will generally be present reasons for a canonical separation.[181] A pastor should not decide the matter but should bring it to the attention of the bishop who will grant permission for the civil suit and advise the necessary precautions.[182]

§2. *Catholic judges and lawyers*—Canonically no civil judge has jurisdiction over the matrimonial causes of any baptized person for these cases belong to the ecclesiastical forum and *per se* a layman is incapable of judging spiritual concerns.[183] While, as has been noted, the pope could delegate a layman,[184] it is to be seriously questioned whether the Church supplies jurisdiction to any civil judge when it tolerates the granting of civil divorces.[185] To tolerate the action of the civil authority is quite distinct from supplying ecclesiastical jurisdiction to the secular judge. Should any judge, lawyer, or any other person, pertinaciously *say* that matrimonial causes of the baptized do not belong to ecclesiastical judges, he is to be considered an heretic[186] and is liable to the penalties for heresy.[187] Yet *in fact* a judge, or any other person, may act against the implications of Canon 1960 by having part in a civil divorce action without being a formal heretic, though such a person may sin by the sacrilegious usurpation of ecclesiastical judgment.[188]

It appears that Catholic judges and lawyers may be justified in assisting at those divorce actions which Catholic parties are justified in presenting to the secular tribunal.[189] What these

---

180 De Smet, *De Sponsalibus et Matrimonio,* n. 401.

181 Can. 1130 sq.

182 Cf. n. 126, *Acta et Decreta Balt. III,* p. 64; De Smet, *De Sponsalibus et Matrimonio,* n. 403; *Acta et Decreta Concilii Prov. Mechliniensis IV (1920)*, sectio moralis, n. 81.

183 S. C. S. Off., July 6, 1817—*Fontes,* n. 855; Cavagnis, *Institutiones Iuris Publici Ecclesiastici,* I, n. 559.

184 Bouix, *De Iudiciis, Ecclesiasticis,* I, p. 81.

185 Cf. Gasparri, *De Matrimonio,* n. 1457; Bassibey, *Le Mariage,* p. 54; Noval, *De Iudiciis,* n. 836; Cappello, *De Sacramentis,* n. 839, note 16; Bouuaert-Simenon, *Manuale Juris Canonici,* n. 1173.

186 C. of Trent, sess. XXIV, *de matr.,* canon 12.

187 Canon 2314. Cf. Gasparri, *De Matrimonio,* n. 1458.

188 Wernz-Vidal, *Ius Canonicum,* V, n. 711.

189 Lehmkuhl, *Theologia Moralis,* II, n. 701, note 1; De Smet, *De Sponsalibus et Matrimonio,* nn. 393, 401; Pighi, *De Sacramento Matri-*

cases are has already been noted. But in any and all causes certain conditions must be observed by the civil judge in places where the ecclesiastical authorities expressly or tacitly tolerate civil divorce. The judge who does not recognize the Church's authority in matrimonial causes of the baptized acts illicitly and perversely. Where the judge admits the jurisdiction of the ecclesiastical forum it is the opinion of some moralists that he acts licitly, provided he:

(a) intends to affect the civil effects only;
(b) has very grave reasons for acting in the case;
(c) avoids scandal by explicitly warning the parties as well as others that his sentence does not touch the bond itself but merely the civil effects;
(d) is not restricted by any special prohibition of ecclesiastical authorities.[190]

The Catholic judge should first settle his conscience as to his own formal competence lest he sin formally by usurpation of ecclesiastical jurisdiction and then he should consider the circumstances of the locality, noting whether explicit or tacit toleration of civil divorce is allowed by the Church. Circumstances in this country seem to warrant the assumption that the civil court does not expect its sentences to contravene the religious principles of the parties.[191] The Catholic Church's regulation of marriage is generally known and respectfully tolerated by the secular tribunals. Speaking of religious marriages, Mr. Chief Justice White said: "It is of the essence of these religious unions, and of their right to establish tribunals for the decision of questions arising among themselves, that those decisions should be binding in all cases of ecclesiastical cognizance subject only to such appeals as the organism itself

---

monii, n. 143-4; Telch, *Epitome Theologiae Moralis,* pp. 389, 445. Cf. *AER,* LXXI (1924), 600.

[190] S. C. S. Off., June 25, 1885—*Fontes,* n. 1636; Sacred Penit., Sept. 23, 1887—Gasparri, *De Matrimonio,* n. 1551; Noldin, *De Sacramentis,* n. 673; Cappello, *De Sacramentis,* III, n. 839; De Smet, *De Sponsalibus et Matrimonio,* n. 393; Aertnys-Damen, *Theologia Moralis,* II, n. 925.

[191] Sabetti-Barrett, *Theologia Moralis,* n. 559, p. 40; Telch, *Epitome Theologiae Moralis,* p. 390.

provides for."[192] Again Mr. Justice Miller remarked: "The right . . . to create tribunals for the decision of controverted questions of faith within the association, and for the ecclesiastical government of all the individual members, congregations and officers within the general association, is unquestioned."[193] The Supreme Court of New Jersey (Everett v. First Baptist Church) is quoted as writing ". . . with respect to the spiritual and temporal acts of the Church, not affecting the civil right of individuals . . . the ecclesiastical courts and governing bodies of the religious society have exclusive jurisdiction and their decisions are final."[194]

Conditions vary in the different nations accordingly as civil legislation is tolerant, hostile, or indifferent to the exercise of ecclesiastical jurisdiction in matrimonial causes. Wherefore a general decision of the Holy See on the relation of Catholics and civil divorce courts cannot be expected. Catholic judges universally should have the will to consult the local Ordinary when doubts arise. If the Ordinary cannot settle the matter, the question with an explanation of the peculiar local circumstances should be sent to the Holy See.[195]

The part played by the Catholic lawyer is more akin to that of the parties whom he represents. Catholic lawyers may always oppose a suit for divorce in the secular court provided the bishop recognizes the integrity of the advocate and the lawyer does not act against the principles of the natural and ecclesiastical law.[196] Where Catholic parties are justified in presenting their cause to the secular forum the lawyer seems thereby implicitly justified and licensed in assisting the case.[197] And where other than Catholic parties (i. e. non-Catholics in divorce suits among themselves) act licitly, the Catholic lawyer

---

[192] Reynolds v. U. S., 8 Otto 145, 25 L. Ed. 244, 250—as quoted by Martin, "The American Judiciary and Religious Liberty,"—*Catholic Historical Review*, VIII (1928), p. 24.

[193] Watson v. Jones, 13 Wall. 679, 20 Law Ed. 666—as quoted by Martin, *o. c.*, p. 31.

[194] *New York Times*, Oct. 10, 1928.

[195] Noval, *De Iudiciis*, n. 836; S. C. S. Off., Dec. 19, 1860—*Coll.*, n. 2272.

[196] S. C. S. Off., Dec. 19, 1860 ad 2—*Coll.*, n. 2272; S. C. S. Off., April 3, 1878, ad 5, 6—*Coll.*, n. 1491; Cappello, *De Sacramentis*, III, n. 840; Gasparri, *De Matrimonio*, n. 1538.

[197] De Smet, *De Sponsalibus et Matrimonio*, n. 401.

in assisting them acts licitly also.[198] In accepting any divorce case where the clients are acting without reason or with perverse intentions the Catholic lawyer needs a very grave reason before he can cooperate in the intended evil.[199] This is more especially true where the advocate is free to undertake the case or not than where the case is assigned to the lawyer by the court.[200] The advocate should consult the Ordinary in such an assignment.[201]

---

[198] Noldin, *De Sacramentis,* n. 676; Cappello, *De Sacramentis,* III, n. 840-2º.

[199] Cappello, *De Sacramentis,* III, n. 840-3º.

[200] De Smet, *De Sponsalibus et Matrimonio,* n. 404. Aertnys-Damen, *Theologia Moralis,* II, n. 925.

[201] Gasparri, *De Matrimonio,* n. 1556.

PART II

Matrimonial Competence Within the Church

CHAPTER III

Historical Sketch

Art. 1. The Early Period (to Innocent III)

What ecclesiastical authorities took cognizance of the matrimonial causes among the early Christians? Undoubtedly, the bishop was the proper judge in these matters for he was the recognized judge in each community.[1] The first ecclesiastical proceedings must have been informal processes in which the substance of justice and court procedure was observed.[2] Matrimonial doubts were submitted to the Pope who informed inquiring bishops how to act in certain cases. Julius I settled the point that a slave could legitimately marry the master,[3] Leo I gave advice on the presumption of the death of the spouse,[4] while Vigilius determined what penance should be meted out for an incestious marriage.[5] Bishops often took the initiative when invalid nuptials were found. This made the bishop both the custodian of the law and the judge.[6] The Pope, of course,

---

[1] Didascalia, II, 22, 23—Funk, *Didascalia et Constitutiones Apostolorum,* I, pp. 80, 114; Benedict XIV, *De Synodo Diocesana,* L. IV, c. 2, n. 1; St. Augustine, Confessions, VI, 3—*Corpus Script.* Eccl. Lat., XXIII, p. 117.

[2] Cornelius à Lapide, *Commentaria* (I Cor. V), p. 228; Prat, *The Theology of Saint Paul,* I, p. 103; Hurter, *Compendium Theologiae Dogmaticae, III,* p. 551.

[3] Decreta Julii I, §10—Labbe, II, 1269.

[4] Ep. ad Nicetam.—*Coll.,* n. 606.

[5] Ep. ad Caesar. Arelet.,—*MPL,* LXIX, 21.

[6] Cf. C. of Agatha (506), c. 25—Mansi, VIII, 329. Cf. Hincmar, *De Divortio Lotharii, Regis—MPL,* CXXV, 652; C. of Toledo IV (633), c. 63—Mansi, X, 634; C. of Leptin (743)—Mansi, XII, 371.

was ever the supreme judge in matrimonial causes. Popes personally threatened royal culprits, replied to episcopal queries,[7] and sent legates to preside at councils where matrimonial cases were to be discussed.[8]

The growth and complexity of matrimonial impediments in the fifth and sixth centuries demanded special care in the treatment of matrimonial causes. Where earlier councils had passed disciplinary measures[9] directing the several bishops to carry them out,[10] the provincial councils of the later days not only legislated but acted as the usual tribunal for matrimonial causes in the province.[11] The case of Lothar II and Teutberga, typical of the more prominent matrimonial causes of that time, shows the provincial synod as the initial tribunal with the Holy See as the court of appeal.[12]

However, it cannot be definitely stated that the local bishops did not act in matrimonial causes during this same period for there are indications that individual bishops treated matrimonial causes in their diocesan synod. In 949 Fulbert, Bishop of Cambray, is said to have proceeded in a case of incest;[13] Sigismund of Halberstad (1012) declared the separation of Count Henry and Hateburga;[14] while Yves, the well known bishop of Chartres, had the marriages of minors annulled as seen from his letter directed to the bishop of York regarding the treatment of matrimonial cases.[15] Definite rules for ecclesiastical competence in matrimonial cases cannot be found in this era wherein bishops proceeded *ex officio* against invalid marriages.[16] Provincial

[7] C. 4, 6, X, *de divortiis,* IV, 19.

[8] C. 13, X, *de donat. inter vir.,* IV, 20; c. 18, X, *de sponsal. et matr.,* IV, 1; Synod of Quedlimberg (1085)—Mansi, XX, 608; Synod of Poitiers (1100)—Mansi, XX, 1117.

[9] Cf. Esmein, *Le Mariage en Droit Canonique,* I, p. 204.

[10] Synod of Leptin (743), can. 3—Mansi, XII, 371. Cf. Hartzheim, *Concilia Germaniae,* I, p. 50.

[11] Cf. Hincmar's account of Synod of Tousy II (860)—Mansi, XV, 571; c. 10, C. XXXV, q. 6; c. 1, C. XXXIII, q. 2. Cf. Esmein, *Le Mariage en Droit Canonique,* I, p. 18.

[12] Cf. Jungmann, *Dissertationes in Historiam Ecclesiasticam,* III, p. 233; C. of Poitiers (1100)—Mansi, XX, 1117; Epist. CCXI of Yves—*MPL,* CLXII, 215; C. of Rheims (1119)—Mansi, XXI, 239.

[13] Perrone, *De Matrimonio Christiano,* II, p. 391.

[14] Hartzheim, *Concilia Germaniae,* II, p. 586.

[15] Epist. 214—Perrone, *De Matrimonio Christiano,* II, p. 392.

[16] Perrone, *De Matrimonio Christiano,* II, p. 393.

synods are known to have treated causes even in what is now known as the first instance, and the popes, personally or through delegates, examined cases appealed to Rome. The arrangement of grades was not well defined, yet the steps were as a rule from the bishop and his diocesan synod to the provincial synod and then to the Holy See. With the press of litigation in the ecclesiastical courts of the Middle Ages the tribunals of the delegated archdeacons and deans came to be the common court of matrimonial causes with the episcopal tribunal as the court of appeal.[17]

Art. 2. The Age of the Inferior Prelates (Innocent III-Council of Trent)

From the care of the provincial council matrimonial causes devolved upon the local bishop who found himself so overburdened with litigations (he enjoyed not only ecclesiastical but civil authority) that the judgment of cases was delegated to the archdeacons, deans, archpriests, and prelates of inferior rank. The bishop delegated these men and later so amplified their powers that the inferior prelates came to consider their jurisdiction as ordinary,[18] not hesitating to judge cases in the very presence of the bishop[19] though they were originally appointed to handle only those cases where the bishop could not be present.[20] The Fourth Lateran Council warned the inferior judges, especially the abbots, to leave matrimonial causes to the care of the bishop unless they had special reason for interposing their authority. The power of these lower tribunals was such that the bishop appeared to have but little power in his own diocese.[21]

These inferior tribunals, apparently, were such not only in rank but in their knowledge of matrimonial causes and judicial procedure as well. Innocent III complained that the required solemnities were not universally observed[22] and councils re-

---

[17] Thomassinus, *Nova et Vetera Ecclesiastica Disciplina*, P. I, lib. 2, c. 9, n. 8.

[18] Synod of Bremen (1266)—Mansi, XXIII, 1159.

[19] Cf. C. of Samur (1253), can. 7—Mansi, XXIII, 811.

[20] C. 13, X, *de restitut. spol.*, II, 13.

[21] C. Lateran IV (1215), can. 60—Mansi, XXII, 1047.

[22] C. 1 X, *de lite non cont.*, II, 6.

marked that archdeacons and others often lacked the necessary skill required for matrimonial causes.[23] The years from Innocent III to the Council of Trent mark the struggle to strip the inferior prelates, especially the archdeacon, of authority over major causes among which matrimonial questions held prominent place. To counteract the archdeacon offices such as the present vicar general and official were introduced into the diocesan curia.[24]

In the British Isles the gradual undermining of the archdeacons' matrimonial competence is seen when they were forbidden to decide causes where any doubt remained without first consulting the bishop.[25] Rural deans were absolutely prohibited from hearing causes on the presumption that they lacked sufficient knowledge and were out of contact with capable advisors.[26] The council of London (1237) insisted on the presence of sound knowledge of matrimonial legislation as well as competent jurisdiction in the cleric who judged a matrimonial case. The council did admit that the inferior prelates could act (apparently they were considered ordinary judges) yet ordered that they define no sentence until the local bishop had been consulted.[27]

On the Continent various councils and synods likewise insisted that these inferior prelates possess proper knowledge and required that a special mandate be obtained to sit in judgment of a cause.[28] Benedict VIII insisted that appeals were not to be taken from the official to the bishop,[29] emphasizing the notion that the bishop and his official formed one court and that consequently the metropolitan, or the official of the metropolitan, was the proper court of appeal.[30] The official was gradually displacing the archdeacon and came to be the ordinary judge for

---

[23] C. of Bude (1279), can. 38, 39—Mansi, XXIV, 287; C. of York (1367), cap. 8—Mansi, XXVI, 468.

[24] Cf. Migne, *Encyclopedie Theologique,* X, 669.

[25] C. of Durham (1220)—Wilkins, *Concilia Magnae Britanniae et Hiberniae,* I, p. 582.

[26] C. of Oxford (1222)—Wilkins, *o. c.,* I, p. 588; Synodal Constitutions of an unknown bishop (1237)—Wilkins, *o. c.,* I, p. 660.

[27] Can. 23—Wilkins, *o. c.,* I, p. 654.

[28] C. of Lavall (Vallem Guidonis) (1242), can. 4—Mansi, XXI, 551; Synod of Poitiers (1280)—Mansi, XXIV, 382.

[29] C. 2, *de consuetudine,* I, 4 in VI°.

[30] C. of Cologne (1423), can. 3—Mansi, XXVIII, 1051; c. 3, *de appell.,* II, 15 in VI°; c. 1, *de officio ord.,* I, 16 in VI°.

episcopal causes.[31] This official was to stay in the city [32] caring for the major cases which included matrimonial matters. The bishops had reduced the power of the inferior prelates and were bringing matrimonial cases more closely under their own observation.[33] The waning power of the inferior judges was further circumscribed by the declaration that their sentences, when passed without special episcopal mandate, were invalid [34] except where the authority had been prescribed by legitimate custom.[35] The decisions of the inferior tribunals were often scandalously erroneous. In some places the penalty of excommunication was threatened for the inferior prelate who presumed to decide a matrimonial cause.[36] The Council of Trent came out strongly against the excesses of the inferior prelates and thenceforth their power was universally broken. But a few faint echoes of the old struggle were still to be heard.

Art. 3. The Reorganization of Judicial Procedure (Council of Trent—Benedict XIV, 1563-1741)

The struggle which the bishops had been carrying on with the inferior prelates was recognized by the general council of Trent. Deans, archdeacons, and other inferior prelates were now deprived of their competence in matrimonial causes by general law. Hereafter the tribunal of first instance was to be that of the local bishop alone. Higher dignitaries were forbidden to interfere with the bishop's exercise of authority. Causes which the Holy See reserved to itself by law or special reservation were noted as being withdrawn from episcopal competence.[37] The general restriction laid upon the competence of the

---

[31] Thomassinus, *Nova et Vetera Ecclesiastica Disciplina,* P. I, lib. 2, c. 18, n. 10.

[32] Cf. Statutes of Robert of Canterbury, cap. 4—Mansi, XXIV, 1149.

[33] Synod of Bessin (1300), can. 95, 100—Mansi, XXV, 78; Constitutions of Bishop Giberti, tit. 7, cap. 5—Roskovany, *Matrimonium in Ecclesia Catholica,* I, p. 79.

[34] C. of Merciac (1326), can. 4—Mansi, XXV, 777; cf. c. 2, *de offic. vicar.,* I, 13 in VI°.

[35] C. of Bourges (1286), can. 3—Mansi, XXIV, 627; C. of Lavaur (1368), can. 25—Mansi, XXV, 499.

[36] C. of York (1367), cap. 8—Mansi, XXVI, 468; C. of Cambray (1550), tit. 6, n. 3—Roskovany, *Matrimonium in Ecclesia Catholica,* I, p. 80.

[37] C. of Trent, sess. XXIV, *de ref.,* cap. 20.

inferior judges did not prevent them from being delegated to judge matrimonial causes. They could not however act on their own authority.[38] The bishop,[39] his official,[40] or the vicar general[41] were the usual judges in matrimonial causes with the metropolitan tribunal as the court of appeal.[42] The inferior prelates were loath to relinquish an authority which they had come to consider as ordinary. In some places they were required to have special mandates to act.[43] One means open to those inferior prelates who would retain their competence in matrimonial causes was to lay claim on the title of an immemorable custom. It was held that the Council of Trent, sess. XXIV, *de ref.*, c. 20, did not revoke the competence of inferior prelates who had obtained their judicial powers from immemorable custom. According to the Sacred Congregation of the Council, January 22, 1598, if the immemorable existence of the custom was proven by three conformable sentences then the inferior prelates were not to be denied the exercise of judgment in matrimonial causes. While these claims were pending the matrimonial causes were to be decided by the bishop.[44] The bishop, however, was considered the usual judge of matrimonial causes.[45]

In France the civil power is seen upholding the bishop's competence in matrimonial causes against the claims of the inferior prelates.[46] The struggle was not ended for bishops were found insisting under threat of censure on their exclusive compe-

---

[38] Benedict XIV, *De Synodo Diocesana,* lib. IX, c. 9, n. 3; Benedict XIV, Const., *Dei miseratione,* Nov. 3, 1741, §4—*Fontes,* n. 318.

[39] C. of Augsburg (1610), P. II, c. 10, n. 31—Hartzheim, *Concilia Germaniae,* IX, 55.

[40] C. of Narbonne (1609), cap. 42—Mansi, XXXIV-B, 1525; C. of Mexico (1585), L. I. tit. 8, n. 12—Mansi, XXXIV-B, 1045.

[41] C. of Constance (1609), P. I, tit. 16, n. 43—Roskovany, *Matrimonium in Ecclesia Catholica,* I, p. 90; Thomassinus, *Nova et Vetera Ecclesiastica Disciplina,* P. I, L. II, c. 20, n. II.

[42] Cf. C. of Trent, sess. XIII, *de ref.*, cap. 2.

[43] Cf. Synod of Trent (1593), cap. 22—Roskovany, *Matrimonium in Ecclesia Catholica,* I, p. 88.

[44] Mansella, *De Impedimentis Matrimonium Dirimentibus ac de Process u Iudiciali,* p. 171; Pignatelli, *Consultationes Canonicae,* t. 4, con. 35, n. 22; Gallemart, *Sacrosanctum Concilium Tridentinum,* p. 571.

[45] DeOliva, *Tractatus de Foro Ecclesiae,* p. III, q. XI, nn. 11, 12.

[46] Thomassinus, *Nova et Vetera Ecclesiastica Disciplina,* P. I, lib. 2, c. 20, n. II.

tence to judge matrimonial causes.[47] Even the endeavors of the general council had not perfected matrimonial competence and it remained for Benedict XIV to arrange a definite system for the treatment of matrimonial causes.

The rash and hasty decisions with which some tribunals declared a marriage invalid and allowed the parties to pass to a new union was a problem which confronted Benedict XIV.[48] In the beginning of a sweeping reform in matrimonial procedure this pontiff called attention[49] to the appointment of synodal judges[50] and their qualifications as demanded by the Council of Trent.[51] These were to be learned and prudent men designated in each diocese, whom the Holy See could select as judges in a particular case. But these provisions had evidently been disregarded.[52]

The document that stabilized matrimonial procedure and became the basis of the modern judicial system for matrimonial causes, was the constitution "Dei miseratione" issued by Benedict XIV on November 3, 1741.[53] Difficulties had arisen from the poor qualifications of judges who had acted as delegates of the Holy See in matrimonial causes either in the first instance (in cases which apparently were beyond the competence of the local Ordinary or his official by reason of the case having been immediately introduced to the Holy See) or in the second instance when there was no tribunal lower than the Holy See for accepting an appeal, or where the court of second trial was not competent.[54] After one decision by these careless judges the separated parties contracted new and frequently invalid unions. With reason did the Pope again complain that properly qualified men were not being designated as synodal judges. The Council of Trent had deprived the inferior judges of the power they had exercised in judging matrimonial causes but it did not prevent them from being delegated by the Holy See. Indeed, inferior

[47] Synod of Bisuntin (1707), stat. 20—Roskovany, *Matrimonium in Ecclesia Catholica,* I, p. 101; C. of Sedun (1626), cap. V, n. 11—Hartzheim, *Concilia Germaniae,* IX, 389.

[48] Ep. ency., *Matrimonii,* Apr. 11, 1741—*Fontes,* n. 307.

[49] Cf. Ep. ency., *Quamvis paternae,* Aug. 26, 1741—*Fontes,* n. 315.

[50] C. 11, *de rescript.,* I, 3 in VI°.

[51] Sess. XXV, *de ref.,* cap. 10.

[52] Benedict XIV, *De Synodo Diocesana,* L. IV, c. 5, n. 6.

[53] *Fontes,* n. 318.

[54] *Dei miseratione,* §3.

prelates had sometimes acted as delegated judges in tribunals of second importance. But for the future the constitution "Dei miseratione" ordered that any delegation to act as the judge of second instance should be committed only to some bishop, preferably one of the vicinity, or in defect of a bishop, to a well qualified judge who should have been selected according to the method determined in the encyclical "Quamvis paternae." [55]

The defender of the marriage bond, a new figure in matrimonial trials, was introduced. His presence was now required in all causes which concerned the bond of marriage.[56] Two conformable sentences were required before the parties could contract a second union, and even then the sentence in a marriage case was never considered as a definitely final decision (*rem iudicatam*).[57] The proper court of second instance was the tribunal of the metropolitan, papal nuncio, neighboring bishop, or delegated judge.[58] The Holy See might be the tribunal of the first, second or third instance. Cases sent to Rome were entrusted either to the Congregation of Cardinals, Interpreters of the Canons of the Council of Trent (now the Congregation of the Council), or to the Rota unless the pontiff remanded the case to a particular congregation. Here at Rome the presence of the defensor [59] and two conformable sentences were likewise required.[60] Cases first tried by the Congregation of Cardinals were retried in the second instance by the same body. The Tribunal of second instance for cases tried by a particular Congregation was some other Congregation. Causes initially tried before the Rota were resubmitted to another group, or turn, of auditors in the Rota. When the entire assembly of the Rota had adjudged the first instance then the entire body retried the case again.

Art. 4. From Benedict XIV to the Code (1741-1918)

The legislations of Benedict XIV gave matrimonial procedure distinctive characteristics. The local Ordinary was firmly estab-

---

[55] Aug. 26, 1741—*Fontes*, n. 315. Cf. *Dei miseratione*, §4.
[56] *Dei miseratione*, §5 sq.
[57] *Dei miseratione*, §14.
[58] *Dei miseratione*, §10.
[59] *Dei miseratione*, §13.
[60] *Dei miseratione*, §14.

lished as the judge of the first instance. The general grades of appeal were observed. Succeeding years marked the rise of the official and the limitation of the vicar general's activities to the administrative affairs of the local curia. The determination of the proper court in relation to the subject of matrimonial competence came to be further developed.

The Sacred Congregation of the Council observed that the prescriptions of the Benedictine constitution must be observed under penalty of the invalidity of all the judicial acts; that the bishop was the ordinary judge and should himself, or through a delegated judge, not only pronounce sentence but even preside at the trial; that the absence of the defensor in cases in which his attendance was required would invalidate the acts of the court. The procedure at a matrimonial trial was sketched with special attention to the proofs for the non-consummation of the marriage. Appeals were to be made according to the grades determined in the constitution "Dei miseratione" and the bishop was to send an authentic copy of the acts to the judge of second instance.[61]

A treatise on matrimonial causes entitled "Instructio pro Iudiciis Ecclesiasticis Imperii Austriaci quoad Causas Matrimoniales" more commonly referred to as "The Austrian Instruction" was drawn up by Cardinal Rauscher for use in his country.[62] While the document had no official character it reflects the condition of those times. It bears the date of May 4, 1855[63] and received the personal commendations of five learned Roman theologians and canonists. The Third Council of Baltimore suggested its use by ecclesiastical judges in the United States.[64] The matrimonial instruction issued by the Propaganda to the United States in 1883 repeats verbatim one paragraph of this Austrian Instruction.[65]

After some preliminary notions of marriage and the matrimonial impediments[66] the Austrian Instruction noted that matrimonial causes belong solely to ecclesiastical judges. The proper judge was the bishop in whose diocese the husband had

[61] S. C. C., Instr., Aug. 22, 1840—*Coll.*, n. 911.
[62] *Coll. Lacen.*, V, 1286 sq.
[63] Bassibey, *Le Mariage*, p. 2.
[64] *Acta et Decreta Balt. III*, n. 304.
[65] Cf. Prop. Fide, Instr. 1883, §2; Austrian Instruction, §96.
[66] §§1-94.

a domicile. Exception was made however when separation or the malicious desertion of the wife by the husband had intervened. In the former event either party could accuse the other before the bishop of the diocese where the party (actor) had a domicile. In the latter case the deserted wife could institute proceedings before the bishop within whose diocese her domicile had been located. Change of domicile after judicial citation did not affect the judge's competence.[67] A collegiate tribunal of at least four or at most six members selected by the bishop should hear the case.[68] The defensor was an important member of the court.[69] The decision of the tribunal was reached by an absolute majority of votes. In case of a tie the presiding official decided the matter with his vote except it was a question of the validity of the marriage. Then the validity was to be upheld in event of a tie vote.[70] Before the tribunal gave sentence the decision reached and the motives upon which the findings had been based were to be submitted to the bishop who either approved or ordered a further examination.[71] Appeal was from the diocesan court to the Metropolitan and then to the Holy See. Causes tried in the first instance in Metropolitan courts or before tribunals of exempt bishops went in the second instance to the Holy See.[72] While the Instruction gave detailed directions on appeals and the necessity of two conformable sentences [73] it unduly demanded two conformable sentences even for the validity of the marriage,[74] and in some places the treatise seemed to imply that there was no room for an appeal after two conformable sentences.[75] The matter of appeal and two conformable sentences is better expressed in the Propaganda Fide Instruction to the United States.[76] The Austrian Instruction noted that a sentence by an incompetent judge was invalid.[77] It continued with a detailed account of

[67] §96.
[68] §§97, 98.
[69] §§124, 125.
[70] §99.
[71] §178.
[72] §§101, 180.
[73] §§179-182.
[74] §179.
[75] §§180, 181.
[76] Prop. Fide, Instr., 1883, §30—*Coll.*, n. 1587.
[77] §187.

processes in cases of separation [78] and alleged death of a spouse.[79]

An instruction of the Holy Office gave special information on processes instituted in cases where a papal dispensation from a ratified non-consummated marriage was to be sought.[80] Another instruction of the same congregation was given in 1868 relative to the process to prove the death of a spouse.[81] Answers to a questionnaire addressed to several bishops by the Sacred Congregation of the Council [82] afford some evidences of how matrimonial causes were handled in the diocesan curia. The bishop of Rottenburg responded that matrimonial causes were tried by the bishop, or in his absence, by the vicar general. Preparatory steps in annulment cases were taken by the pastor or rural dean but the judicial action was held in the episcopal curia before the bishop's syndic aided by two canons and in the presence of the defender of the bond. When the trial had terminated the acts were presented to the bishop who pronounced the sentence in the presence of the defensor.[83] At Spires matrimonial causes were heard by a collegiate tribunal directed by the vicar general. The defensor was ever in attendance. The tribunal of appeal was the metropolitan court while the Roman curia was the tribunal of third instance.[84] The bishop of Breslau related that the vicar general exercised voluntary jurisdiction only and that the official sitting with the consultors tried matrimonial causes.[85]

Two similar instructions were given on matrimonial processes in the year 1883, the one by the Congregation de Propaganda Fide to the United States [86] and the other from the Holy

---

[78] §§205-245.

[79] §§246-251.

[80] S. C. S. Off., Instr., 1858—*Fontes,* n. 946.

[81] S. C. S. Off., Instr., 1868—*Fontes,* n. 1002.

[82] "Quonam modo Episcopi iudiciariam qua pollent potestatem in cognoscendis causis ecclesiasticis, potissimum matrimonialibus, exerceant, et quaenam procedendi atque appellationes interponendi methodo utantur." S. C. C., June 6, 1867, n. 15—Roskovany, *Matrimonium in Ecclesia Catholica,* I, p. 835.

[83] Roskovany, *Matrimonium in Ecclesia Catholica,* III, p. 110.

[84] Roskovany, *Matrimonium in Ecclesia Catholica,* III, p. 112.

[85] Roskovany, *Matrimonium in Ecclesia Catholica,* III, p. 113.

[86] *Coll.,* n. 1587.

Office to the Oriental Bishops.[87] The instruction to the American bishops shows that the proper episcopal tribunal is that of the bishop in whose diocese the husband has a domicile. Two exceptions are allowed, namely, in event of separation or malicious desertion. Indeed this part of the instruction is taken over verbatim from the Austrian Instruction.[88] The Instruction speaks of the bishop, vicar general, or approved delegate as the moderator of the acts. The judge, the Ordinary or his delegate, was to have the opinion of two or three skilled consultors before pronouncing sentence. If the first sentence defined the validity of the marriage and the parties did not appeal, the defensor was not obliged to take the matter to a higher court. It is in this case of appeal and the need of a second conformable sentence that the Instruction of the Congregation is more concise than the Austrian Instruction. If the first sentence declared the invalidity of the marriage then the defensor had to appeal the case to the tribunal of second instance. Only after two conformable sentences could the parties marry again and not even then if the defensor had appealed this second sentence. Appeal was addressed to the metropolitan tribunal. Where the metropolitan court itself had first tried the case the tribunal of second instance was that of a nearby metropolitan. The Holy See was ordinarily the court of third instance. The parties however could introduce the cause for the first instance trial to the Roman tribunal itself. The sentence in a matrimonial cause never became decisively final though the parties might remarry when two conformable sentences had been pronounced for the invalidity and the defensor did not consider himself bound in conscience to appeal this second sentence. The instruction concluded with rules to be observed in special causes. In the similar instruction issued by the Holy Office to the Oriental Bishop [89] to care for the special conditions obtaining in the East a few notions were added. In the Oriental Church the order of appeal was from bishop to patriarch. If the patriarch had heard the cause

[87] *Coll.*, n. 1588; *Fontes*, n. 1076; Bassibey, *Le Mariage*, p. 50* gives the date as June 20, 1883.

[88] The case of malicious desertion has been further clarified in the response of the Commission for the Interpretation of the Code given on July 14, 1922—*AAS*, XIV (1922), 529.

[89] *Fontes*, n. 1076.

in the first instance the court of appeal was the Holy See. Orientals, however, were free to introduce a marriage cause directly to the Holy See. In the specific instruction on particular impediments the Holy Office instruction of 1858 is repeated for cases of impotence. If the impediments of solemn vow or sacred orders entered into the matrimonial cause then the Oriental bishops, after holding an informative process to gather the necessary documents and information, were to send the matter to the Holy See for decision.

A particular instruction of the Holy Office was issued in 1890[90] which relaxed the rigorous demands of the Benedictine constitution "Dei miseratione" in view of conditions in a certain mission area.

The Third Council of Baltimore allowed the bishop to delegate the vicar general or another cleric to pronounce the sentence in a matrimonial cause provided it had been approved by the bishop.[91] The old rule of the forum of contract[92] came to be applied in matrimonial causes.[93] The determination of the proper tribunal when a marriage of mixed religion was to be judged was settled by the decision that it was the bishop in whose territory the Catholic party had a domicile. If the heretic became a Catholic, the proper judge was the bishop of the husband.[94] A query as to competence based on the forum of contract and the forum obtained by reason of connected cases was answered by a reference to the Instruction of the Propaganda of 1883 and the Holy Office reply of June 30, 1892, but with an additional note. If a Catholic is to contract a marriage with a heretic who had been previously married to a non-Catholic and had secured a civil divorce, the bishop of the Catholic party was the one to inquire into the first marriage as he was the one to establish the freedom of the parties to marry.[95]

The twentieth century brought further perfection to matrimonial procedure. The reorganization of the Roman curia was effected through the efforts of Pius X. His constitution "Sapi-

---

[90] S. C. S. Off., Instr. (Myssur.), Aug. 6, 1890—*Fontes*, n. 1127.
[91] *Acta et Decreta Balt. III*, n. 304, p. 174.
[92] C. 20, X, *de foro competenti, II*, 2.
[93] S. C. C., resp. ad Milev.—*Anal. Juris Pontif.*, VII (1899), 403.
[94] S. C. S. Off., June 30, 1892—*Fontes*, n. 1157.
[95] S. C. S. Off., June 23, 1903—*Fontes*, n. 1266.

enti consilio"[96] with its appended "Ordo Servandus in S. Congregationibus, Tribunalibus, Officiis Romanae Curiae,"[97] the "Lex Propria Sacrae Romanae Rotae et Signaturae Apostolicae,"[98] the "Regulae Servandae in Iudiciis apud S. R. Rotae Tribunal,"[99] and the corresponding "Regulae Servandae in Iudiciis apud Supremum Signaturae Apostolicae Tribunal,"[100] introduced a general division of jurisdiction into the judicial power of the Tribunals and the administrative competence of the Congregations. Benedict XV in 1915 increased the competence of the Signatura in certain phases of matrimonial procedure.[101]

The Code of Canon Law effective May 19, 1918, adopted the distinction between judicial and administrative competence as introduced in the Roman curia by Pius X but did not clarify the matter. Indeed the strict lines of competence are said to have then somewhat relaxed by the Code.[102] Prorogation of jurisdiction was abolished.[103] The bishop's tribunal was competent in matrimonial causes even as the forum of contract.[104] Previously the legality of this title was not certain.[105] Title to proper competence in matrimonial causes continued to be based mainly on the domicile of the parties. The Code indicated the determination of the proper court accordingly as one party was the defendant, or in the cases of mixed marriage, the Catholic party.[106] Further, provision was made for the Official, a judge with ordinary power, distinct from the vicar general and bishop, yet forming one tribunal with the bishop.[107]

---

[96] June 29, 1908—*Fontes*, n. 682.

[97] *AAS*, I (1909), 36.

[98] *AAS*, I (1909), 20.

[99] Aug. 4, 1910—*AAS*, II (1910), 783.

[100] Mar. 6, 1912—*AAS*, IV (1912), 187.

[101] Benedict XV, chirog., *Attentis expositis*, June 28, 1915—*Fontes*, n. 705.

[102] Biccari, "Ricorsi alla Santa Sede,"—*Perfice Munus*, II (1927), 908.

[103] Cf. c. 18, X, *de foro competenti*, II, 2; c. 66, X, *de appellat.*, II, 28; yet, cf. canon 1559.

[104] Canon 1964.

[105] S. C. S. Off., June 23, 1903—*Fontes*, n. 1266; *LCC*, XXVI (1903), 659.

[106] Can. 1964.

[107] Can. 1573. Cf. c. 2, *de consuetudine*, I, 4 in VI°; Noval, *De Iudiciis*, n. 112.

CHAPTER IV

Matrimonial Competence in the Roman Curia

Art. 1. The Pope and the Matrimonial Causes of Rulers

The Pope's exclusive and absolute competence to judge the matrimonial causes of rulers, either personally or through specially delegated Congregations, Tribunals, or Commissions, is a provision induced by custom [1] and now explicitly reserved in the Code.

***Canon 1962.*—Causas matrimoniales ad eos spectantes de quibus in can. 1557, §1, n. 1, illa Sacra Congregatio vel illud Tribunal aut specialis ea Commissio exclusive cognoscet, cui eas toties quoties Summus Pontifex delegaverit; . . .**

***Canon 1557.*—§1. Ipsius Romani Pontificis dumtaxat ius est iudicandi:**

1°. Eos qui supremum tenent populorum principatum horumque filios ac filias eosve quibus ius est proxime succedendi in principatum.

Previously, no direct mention of this reservation was to be found aside from the general reservation of all major causes to the judgment of the Holy See.[2]

The basis for this exclusive competence is found, no doubt, in the Middle Ages when the temporal rulers, sons of the Church, turned to the Pope as the prince among princes to seek approval for their various undertakings. The marriage causes of royalty were of great concern for they could have unsuspected and incalculable results. A prince's right to the throne frequently depended on the validity of the wedlock

[1] Gasparri, *De Matrimonio,* n. 1459. Bassibey, *Le Mariage,* p. 39.

[2] Letter of Celestine III—Bassibey, *Le Mariage,* p. 39; C. of Trent, sess. XIV, *de ref.,* cap. 5; Leo XIII, litt. encycl., *Trans oceanum,* Apr. 18, 1897, XIV-3—*Fontes,* n. 633. Cf. Vives, *Compendium Iuris Canonici,* p. 133.

whence he sprung.[3] The reservation removed the suspicion and the real danger, too often present, of an obsequious tribunal of local bishops. Further, unless the desires of some sovereigns were curbed by a recognized authority, royal divorces might have become a pattern as well as a scandal to the people. Stephen III,[4] Gregory V,[5] Paschal II,[6] Clement IV,[7] Celestine III,[8] and Innocent III,[9] had their difficulties with royal marriage cases. The cases of Lothar II [10] and Philip Augustus [11] typify conditions which made advisable the reservation of royal marriage causes to the Pope. These causes had been treated by bishops in provincial synods but the intervention of the Pope was demanded sooner or later for he alone could gainsay the bold determination of the monarchs. For the most causes the popes appointed legates [12] or commissions.[13] An anonymous defense of the action of Clement VII in bringing the case of Henry VIII to Rome states that the case was one which pertained to the Holy See alone and mentioned that no place was more fitting, open to less suspicion, or allowed more freedom of discussion than Rome.[14]

In the early nineteenth century the matrimonial difficulties of the Bonaparte family occasioned observations that the matrimonial causes of rulers were matters for the personal judgment of the Sovereign Pontiff. Pope Pius VII refused to comply with Napoleon's request that the marriage of his brother Jerome

---

[3] Cf. c. 3, X, *de ordine cognit.*, II, 10; Bouix, *De Iudiciis*, I, p. 77.

[4] Ep. ad Carolum—*MPL*, XCVIII, 256.

[5] Cf. C. of Rome (998)—Mansi, XIX, 223.

[6] Cf. C. of Paris (1105)—Mansi, XX, 1193; Perrone, *De Matrimonio Christiano*, II, pp. 86, 393.

[7] Ep. III ad Reg. Aragon—Roskovany, *Matrimonium in Ecclesia Catholica*, I, p. 65.

[8] Letter Celestine III, Mar. 13, 1196, to bishops of France in case of Philip and Ingelburge—Bassibey, *Le Mariage*, p. 39.

[9] Cf. Jungmann, *Dissertationes in Historiam Ecclesiasticam*, V, p. 248; *Annales Baronii*, ed. Theiner, XIX, p. 671.

[10] Jungmann, *Dissertationes in Historiam Ecclesiasticam*, III, p. 233; Hincmar, *De Divortio Lotharii*, Regis—*MPL*, CXXV, 653; Esmein, *Le Mariage en Droit Canonique*, I, p. 208.

[11] Jungmann, *Dissertationes in Historiam Ecclesiasticam*, V, p. 248.

[12] C. 4, C. XXXI, q. 2; C. 4, C. XXXIII, q. 2; Benedict XIV, *De Synodo Diocesana*, L. VIII, c. 12, n. 4; Jungmann, *Dissertationes in Historiam Ecclesiasticam*, III, p. 240.

[13] Bassibey, *Le Mariage*, p. 40.

[14] Roskovany, *Matrimonium in Ecclesia Catholica*, I, p. 78.

and Elizabeth Patterson of Baltimore be adjudged invalid.[15] Later Napoleon desired his own marriage with Josephine to be severed. He did not wish to submit the matter to the Pope but created three sets of French tribunals which would decide the case. Many ecclesiastics who were assigned parts in the divorce proceedings realized that the cause was one in which all others except the Pope were incompetent.[16] The situation was later remarked by the Fathers of the Second Council of Baltimore in these words: ". . . the anger of the first Napoleon was incurred by the refusal of Pius VII, of holy memory, to declare invalid a marriage contracted between that ruler's brother and a Protestant lady of the city in which we are assembled. When this same monarch sought to break his first faith, he was obliged to have recourse to an extinct tribunal of the diocese of Paris resusitated for that special purpose which presumed to decide a question which the wisdom of the Holy See has reserved for its own exclusive jurisdiction."[17] The matrimonial causes of the Bonapartes are cited by authors as examples of causes wherein the local officials were absolutely incompetent.[18] In the later nineteenth century the matrimonial cause of the Prince of Monaco and the Princess Hamilton was decided by the Holy See through a special Commission.[19]

This reservation makes any ecclesiastical judge or tribunal other than the Roman Pontiff *himself*[20] absolutely incompetent to treat the matrimonial causes of rulers,[21] who cannot renounce this privilege of a special forum.[22] Prior to the Code these causes were considered major causes by reason of the dignity

---

[15] Allies, *The Life of Pope Pius the Seventh,* p. 93; Jomini, *Life of Napoleon,* I, p. 406; Artaud, *Histoire du Pape Pius VII,* II, p. 55.

[16] Allies, *The Life of Pope Pius the Seventh,* p. 195; Artaud, *Histoire du Pape Pius VII,* II, p. 262 sq.

[17] Pastoral Letter of the Fathers of II Plenary Council of Baltimore, 1866, chap. V—*Acta et Decreta Balt. II,* p. XXXVIII.

[18] Feije, *De Impedimentis et Dispensationibus Matrimonialibus,* p. 473, note 4; DeBecker, *De Sponsalibus et Matrimonio,* p. 446; Gasparri, *De Matrimonio,* n. 1459; Wernz-Vidal, *Ius Canonicum,* V, p. 26, note 34.

[19] De Smet, *De Sponsalibus et Matrimonio,* p. 312, note. Cf. *ASS,* XII, 403.

[20] Cf. cans. 1557 §1, n. 1; 1597.

[21] "In causis de quibus in can. 1556, 1557, aliorum iudicum incompetentia est absoluta"—Can. 1558; cf. can. 1892.

[22] Can. 72 §3.

of the parties concerned[23] but now, reserved by ecclesiastical law,[24] there is no longer any room for doubt. Each case is specially reserved to the Pope, *personally*, and not to the Roman Curia,[25] and the pontiff will assign the cause (delegating at the same time the necessary competence) to any of the existing Congregations, the Rota, Signatura Apostolica, or to a specially appointed Commission. Further should a royal marriage cause arise as an incidental or accessory question in another marriage cause the entire matter would be reserved to the Pope because inferior judges are absolutely incompetent.

The persons[26] whose matrimonial causes are reserved, include the man or woman holding the supreme authority of the people, their legitimate sons and daughters, and stepchildren,[27] and those next in right of succession. Blat denies that application of the reservation outside the countries of monarchial government.[28] Cappello considers this a controverted point.[29] While some incline to the opinion that presidents are included,[30] others do not hesitate to include the supreme magistrate of a republic as long as he actually holds the power.[31] And their view is acceptable. The ruler must not be one in title alone but he should actually possess the power.[32] In a republic this would include the president, or the equivalent magistrate, and his immediate family during the tenure of office, as well as the vice-president (though not his family) who would succeed in event the executive office was vacated. Beyond this there is no need to extend the reservation, for example, in the United States to the Cabinet officials. Moreover, the president-elect would be included prior to his inauguration because his is the

---

[23] Cf. Gasparri, *De Matrimonio*, n. 1459.

[24] Noval, *De Iudiciis*, n. 64.

[25] Cf. cans. 7; 1569; 1600.

[26] Physical persons only are considered. If the supreme rule of a country is invested in a moral person, the individuals constituting the moral personage are not under this reservation.

[27] Blat, *Commentarium*, IV, n. 12.

[28] Blat, *Commentarium*, IV, n. 12.

[29] *De Sacramentis*, III, n. 870.

[30] Farrugia, *De Matrimonio et Causis Matrimonialibus*, p. 506; Vlaming, *Praelectiones Iuris Matrimonii*, n. 787, note 3.

[31] Roberti, *De Processibus*, I, p. 110; Wernz-Vidal, *Ius Canonicum*, VI, n. 49; De Smet, *De Sponsalibus et Matrimonio*, n. 705.

[32] Gasparri, *De Matrimonio*, n. 1459.

right, not the hope, of succession in office.[33] In the present American system of presidential selection this would mean the period from the casting of the votes by the presidential electors until the inauguration (March 4). Indeed, in the United States in view of the unique political constitution of the Union which leaves each State sovereign: and considering that there is no national marriage legislation as in Europe but that each State legislates for itself, it does not appear as forcing an interpretation of canon 1557 §1, n. 1, to include the governors of states and their children and the lieutenant-governor. Senators, cabinet officials, and in monarchies, regents, are not included.

Would the matrimonial cause of a ruler coming within the scope of canon 1990 be reserved? Without going into the nature of the authority employed in that canon, may it be remarked here that the case would without doubt be reserved. If the power spoken of in canon 1990 is judicial, the reservation by law of canon 1962 holds. If the power is administrative, the case is reserved, by reason of the persons concerned, to the Holy See if not to the Pope, personally, as a matter of major moment.[34] The decree of the Congregation of the Sacraments, March 7, 1910, by which the granting of dispensations (*administrative* by nature) in the matrimonial affairs of kings and their royal line (*regibus ac regiae stirpis principibus*) is listed as a major cause specially reserved to the Holy See,[35] seems to bear out the opinion. The reservation of the coercive power to the Roman Pontiff personally in the cases of rulers[36] and the care with which the Holy Office in the recent response[37] disclaimed any competence in the cases reserved by canon 1557 §1—1°, seem to leave no doubt in the matter that all marriage cases of rulers are reserved to the Pope personally.

Art. 2. The Sacred Congregation of the Sacraments and Dispensations "Super Matrimonio Rato et Non Consummato"

The chapter on the competent forum contains references in canons 1962 and 1963 to the special competence of the Congre-

[33] Wernz-Vidal, *Ius Canonicum,* VI, n. 49.

[34] Can. 220.

[35] *AAS,* II (1910), 147.

[36] Can. 2227 §1.

[37] S. C. S. Off., Jan. 27, 1928, ad 2—*AAS,* XX (1928), 75.

gation of the Sacraments in cases where a dispensation *super matrimonio rato et non consummato* is sought. Though placed in this section among judicial causes these cases are not fundamentally judicial. While the most minute details of judicial process are to be observed in establishing the fact of non-consummation and the reasons for dissolving the marriage yet the power which actually severs the bond is *administrative* being exercised by way of papal dispensation.[38] The legislations affecting competence in these cases are found not only in the Code but also in the Regulations issued by the Congregation of the Sacraments in 1923.

(a) *Can. 1962.*—". . . causas dispensationis super matrimonio rato et non consummato, Sacra Congregatio de disciplina Sacramentorum; . . ."

(b) *Can. 1963.*—§1. Quare nullus iudex inferior potest processum in causis dispensationis super rato instruere, nisi Sedes Apostolica facultatem eidem fecerit.

§2. Si tamen iudex competens auctoritate propria iudicium peregerit de matrimonio nullo ex capite impotentiae et ex eo, non impotentiae, sed nondum consummati matrimonii emerserit probatio, omnia acta ad Sacram Congregationem transmittantur, quae iis uti poterit sententiam super rato et non consummato ferendam.

(c) *Can. 249.*—§3. Ipsa cognoscit quoque et exclusive de facto inconsummationis matrimonii et de existentia causarum ad dispensationem concedendam, nec non de iis omnibus, quae cum his sunt connexa. Potest tamen cognitionem horum omnium, si id expedire iudicaverit, ad Sacram Romanam Rotam remittere . . ."

(d) Regulae servandae in processibus super matrimonio rato et non consummato.[39]

---

[38] "Inde duo consequuntur magni ponderis: primo quod huiusmodi causae, utpote quae non promoventur ab actione iudiciali contentiosa aut criminali, sed ex benigna concessione Sanctae Sedis annuentis oratoris precibus, non sunt vere iudiciales, sed magis gratiosae seu administrativae; quae tamen cum eo spectent ut Summus Pontifex legitime uti valeat Sua suprema potestate dispensandi super matrimonio rato et non consummato cum plena rerum cognitione, in his veritas inquirenda est non minus religiose ac sedulo, quam in negotiis proprie iudicialibus." Decretum S. C. de Sacr., May 7, 1923—*AAS,* XV (1923), 389.

[39] *AAS,* XV (1923), 389 sq.

Caput I—*de foro competenti.*

3. §2. Si vero probationes de non secuta matrimonii consummatione hactenus instructae, habeantur non sufficientes iuxta normas heic positas, eaedem compleantur et acta dein plene instructa ad H. S. C. remittantur.

4. Pariter si in iudicio in prima aut in altera instantia peragendo de matrimonii nullitate, ex alio capite (ex. gr. ex defectu consensus, ex vi et metu, etc.) matrimonii nullitas evinci non possit, sed *incidenter* dubium valde probabile emerserit de non secuta matrimonii consummatione, tunc integrum est alterutri, vel utrique parti, libellum porrigere Romano Pontifici inscriptum, pro dispensatione a matrimonio rato et non consummato; at quin preces ad hanc Sacram Congregationem remittantur pro obtinenda consueta commissione facultatum, fit potestas iudici, vi huius praescriptionis seu ex delegatione a iure, causam instruendi iuxta *Regulas* heic determinatas.

§1. *Notion of a marriage ratified but not consummated*—A valid marriage between two Christians, in which the conjugal act *per se* apt for generation has not taken place, is known as a ratified but non-consummated marriage.[40] Strictly speaking, a *matrimonium ratum et non consummatum* is had in case of a valid marriage between two baptized persons which has not been consummated and, most probably, in a valid marriage between two infidels after both have received baptism and have not thereafter consummated the marriage.[41] Valid marriages between infidels, or between an infidel and a baptized person, entered with or without a dispensation from the impediment of disparity of cult, are not considered as "matrimonia rata."

Merely ratified marriages can be severed *ipso iure* by

---

[40] Can. 1015 §1.

[41] De Smet, *De Sponsalibus et Matrimonio*, n. 157; Vermeersh-Creusen, *Epitome,* II, n. 426. A recent case occurred in which two infidels had obtained a civil divorce from their (consummated) marriage. The man was later baptized in an heretical sect: the woman became a convert. The diocesan curia petitioned the Holy See for a dispensation in a *matrimonium legitimum*. The Holy See solved the case by a dispensation super matrimonio rato et non-consummato.

solemn religious profession or, for a just reason, by a papal dispensation granted at the petition of one of the parties.[42] There can be no doubt that canons 1962 and 1963 enunciate the competence of the Sacred Congregation of the Sacraments in cases of particular papal dispensations but what of a case where one party to a merely ratified marriage wishes to enter religion and take solemn vows? The solemn religious profession is capable of severing *ipso facto* the marriage tie but who is competent to establish the fact of non-consummation in such a case? May this be done in the local curia or must faculties first be sought from the Sacred Congregation of the Sacraments?[43] The two methods, mentioned in canon 1119, of dissolving a non-consummated marriage imply dispensation. The one, the power of solemn religious profession, is by a general dispensation of ecclesiastical law.[44] This is effective in all cases where the conditions are had, *viz.*, non-consummation of the marriage and actual solemn religious profession. The other, particular papal dispensation, is granted personally by the Supreme Pontiff at the request of one of the parties, for reasons deemed sufficient. Is the process to establish non-consummation of a marriage which is to be severed by religious profession included under reservation of canons 1962 and 1963 §1?

The decree of the Sacred Congregation of the Sacraments does not indicate any solution for while it quotes canon 1119, the course to be followed in the event of solemn religious profession is not treated. The decree speaks only of particular papal dispensations while the appended Regulae are devoted *ex professo* to cases for particular papal grants of dispensation.[45] Canon 249 §3 indicates that the Sacred Congregation of the Sacraments takes exclusive competence of the fact of non-consummation *and* the existence of the reasons for granting the dispensation, as well as all connected matters. Does this prohibit the local curia from the judgment of non-consummation where the bond is to be severed by solemn religious profession? The general dispensation is granted *ipso iure* for the Code ad-

[42] Can. 1119.

[43] Cf. Vlaming, *Praelectiones Iuris Matrimonii*, n. 707 e.

[44] Chelodi, *Ius Matrimoniale*, n. 153; Cappello, *De Sacramentis*, III, n. 759; Wernz-Vidal, *Ius Canonicum*, V, n. 626.

[45] S. C. de Sacr., Decr. et Instr., May 7, 1923—*AAS*, XV (1923), 389. Cf. *e.g.*, reg. n. 102.

mits the sufficiency of the reason, the fact of non-consummation alone is to be established. It appears that the local curia, one judge being sufficient to hear the case as it does not concern the bond of matrimony directly,[46] can without seeking license of the Sacred Congregation of the Sacraments, institute a process to establish the fact of non-consummation. If this is established the defensor (yet in the case it can be questioned whether his presence is necessary[47]) need not make the customary appeal for the decision of the court does not declare the nullity of the marriage[48] but only the fact of non-consummation. The matter should be carried to the Congregation of the Sacraments if the correctness of the decision of the local curia as to the fact is questioned.

A case which happened in Naples in 1761 may be of interest. The validity of a marriage had originally been attacked on the grounds of impotence of the man, who later expressed the desire to enter a religious order. The local curia passing over the question of impotence, defined that the marriage stood but was non-consummated and the man could enter an approved religious institute for the purpose of taking solemn vows. The decision was upheld on an appeal to the Sacred Congregation of the Council which did not suggest seeking a particular papal dispensation *super matrimonio rato.*[49]

§2. *Historical survey*—The authority to dispense *super matrimonio rato et non consummato* is reserved to the Supreme Pontiff. Though the Sacred Congregation of the Sacraments examines the case and advises whether the dispensation can and should be granted, the actual grant is made when the Pope in audience with the secretary of the Congregation directly and personally grants the dispensation which severs the valid bond of matrimony then and there.[50] Ratified and non-consummated marriage, the strongest of any non-consummated marriage ties, is by the natural and divine positive law intrinsically indissoluble. The parties themselves cannot recede from the con-

---

[46] Cf. can. 1576 §1—1°. The question is considered apart from the prescription of canon 542—1°.

[47] ". . . sive de probandis inconsummatione *et* causis ad dispensandum super rato, . . ."—Can. 1967.

[48] Cf. can. 1986.

[49] S. C. C., *Neapol.*, April 3, 1761—Thesaurus resol., XXX, 54.

[50] Cf. S. C. de Sacr., Instr., May 7, 1923, reg. 6, 102, 103.

tract. Extrinsically, however, the bond can be dissolved by the Pope in the grant of a dispensation (improperly speaking) for a just cause even as he dispenses in the case of vows. The Pontiff cannot and does not dispense in the strict sense of that word from the divine law of indissolubility of marriage. Dispensation here is used in the broad sense of the term, and describes rather than defines the action of the Pope wherein by virtue of his vicarious power to bind and loose, he grants the right to a person to withdraw or retract the act of the will that begot the obligation (in this case the marital consent). The matter of the obligation being changed the obligation no longer urges.[51]

At one time the power of the Pope to grant such a dispensation was questioned.[52] Doctors of the thirteenth century defended this papal prerogative and several popes as a matter of fact used it. By the sixteenth century the authority had often been invoked.[53] A commission of cardinals appointed by Clement VIII studied the matter and returned an answer favoring the Pope's authority to dispense.[54] Early cases were treated by the Pope personally and he has ever retained the final decision in this grave matter. The Congregation of the Council as an outgrowth of the cardinal consultors came to be the group to which the examination of these cases was usually referred.[55]

When Benedict XIV effected the reorganization of procedure in matrimonial causes, he declared that the petitions for dispensation *super matrimonio rato et non consummato* were to be presented directly to the Pope who would either reject the petition or assign the examination of the case to some division of the Roman Curia. Ordinarily cases were to be submitted as formerly to the consultive vote of the Sacred

---

[51] Cf. Noldin, *De Principiis,* I, nn. 117, 183; *Catholic Encyclopedia,* V, p. 41; Vlaming, *Praelectiones Iuris Matrimonii,* II, n. 709; De Smet, *De Sponsalibus et Matrimonio,* n. 329; Cappello, *De Sacramentis,* III, n. 756; Wernz-Vidal, *Ius Canonicum,* V, n. 624.

[52] Cf. c. 2, X, *de conver. coniugatorum,* III, 32.

[53] *E.g.,* Martin V, Eugene IV, Julius III, Paul III, Pius IV—cf. Sanchez, *De Sacramento Matrimonii,* lib. II, disp. XIV, n. 2; Perrone, *De Matrimonio Christiano,* III, p. 531.

[54] Cf. Thesaur. Resol. S. C. C., I, p. 190; Richter, *Canones et Decreta Concilii Tridentini,* n. 96, p. 259.

[55] For a list dating from 1711—cf. Feije, *De Impedimentis et Dispensationibus Matrimonialibus,* p. 829.

Congregation of the Council but might be remanded at the Pontiff's discretion to some other specially designated Congregation. Then the Pope would approve the findings of the consultors, or if further examination was desired, resubmit the matter to another Tribunal or Congregation.[56] An instruction in 1840 repeated the Benedictine Legislation.[57]

Ordinaries were competent in matrimonial causes where the impediment was that of impotence.[58] But as these cases required the greatest of care for the existence of this impediment has always been difficult to establish, often the best solution was to apply for a papal dispensation *super matrimonio rato.*[59] In 1858 the Holy Office issued an instruction entitled: Pro conficiendo processu super viri impotentia, et non secuta matrimonii consummatione, accedente Pontificis dispensatione ab accurata observantia praescriptionum Bullae Benedicti XIV, Dei miseratione. The title explains the nature of the instruction which does not make express mention of any papal commission being given to the inferior tribunal to institute this process *super rato.* In concluding, the instruction gives the admonition that all the acts were to be sent to the Sacred Congregation of the Council for a decision.[60]

The Instruction of the Propaganda to the United States refers to the Instruction of the Holy Office of 1858.[61] At the same time a clear instruction was issued to the Oriental bishops that if the impediment of impotence was proven they were to judge the marriage as invalid but if the fact of impotence was not firmly established or if the proofs showed rather that the marriage had never been consummated, then the entire matter was to be sent to the Holy See.[62] At the end of the nineteenth century the legislation in these cases reached the stage of the

---

[56] Const., *Dei miseratione,* Nov. 3, 1741, n. 15—*Fontes,* n. 318. Cf. Const., *Justitiae et pacis,* Oct. 10, 1746—*Bullarium Benedicti XIV,* II, 157, where it is noted that the Rota and S. C. Council handled most matrimonial causes at Rome.

[57] S. C. S. Off., *Instr.,* Aug. 22, 1840—*Coll.,* n. 911.

[58] Esmein, *Le Mariage en Droit Canonique,* I, 263.

[59] Esmein, *Le Mariage en Droit Canonique,* II, 286; cf. *e.g., Thesaur. Resol. S. C. C.,* I, 32, 189; S. C. C., Jan. 25, 1873—*ASS,* VII, 491.

[60] *Fontes,* n. 946.

[61] S. C. Prop. Fide, Instr. 1883, n. 46—*Coll.,* n. 1587. Cf. S. C. S. Off., Instr. (Myssur.), Aug. 6, 1890—*Fontes,* n. 1127.

[62] S. C. S. Off., Instr. (ad Ep. Rituum Orient.), 1883—*Fontes,* n. 1076.

present discipline. As the Benedictine legislation had indicated bishops were reminded that special delegation of the Holy See was required to handle a case wherein a dispensation *super matrimonio rato et non-consummato* was sought.[63] When a tribunal found that a cause, entered on the grounds of the impediment of impotency, revealed rather the fact of non-consummation the case was to be completed and then all the acts sent to the Holy See together with the petition for a dispensation *super rato.* The Holy See implicitly commissioned the Ordinaries to complete the process in such an event.[64] When the case came to the Holy See the Congregation of the Council, which according to the *Regulae of 1847* was a judicial and also an administrative body,[65] the Holy Office, or the Propaganda (for mission countries) received the petition.[66] By the constitution *Sapienti consilio* competence in the cases of dispensations *super matrimonio rato et non-consummato* was taken from the scope of any other Roman Congregation and assigned to the Congregation of the Sacraments,[67] which could of its own authority remit the case to the Sacred Roman Rota for a further examination.[68] This brings the survey of competence in cases of dispensation *super rato* well within the period when the codification of canon law was under way.[69]

§3. *Competence of the local curia*—In case of a non-consummated marriage only the parties themselves, or one of them, can petition the Holy See for a dispensation.[70] They are known not as "actors" (*actores*) but as "petitioners" (*oratores*)[71] which denotes the administrative or non-judicial character of the jurisdiction employed in these cases.[72] Though the parties

---

[63] S. C. C., Jan. 25, 1890—*ASS,* XXII, 665. S. C. S. Off., Jun. 16, 1894—*ASS,* XXVII, 153.

[64] S. C. S. Off., resp. June 16, 1894—*ASS,* XXVII, 153.

[65] Lega, *De Iudiciis Ecclesiasticis,* II, n. 169.

[66] Gasparri, *De Matrimonio,* n. 1459.

[67] Pius X, Constit., *Sapienti consilio,* June 29, 1908—*Fontes,* n. 682; *Ordo Servandus, etc. Normae Peculiares,* cap. VII, art. III, 11a; Monin, *De Curia Romana,* p. 248; Ojetti, *De Romana Curia,* p. 73.

[68] S. C. Consist., Jan. 28, 1909—*AAS,* I (1909), 213.

[69] Pius X, Motu proprio, *Arduum sane,* Mar. 19, 1904—*ASS,* XXXVI, 549.

[70] Can. 1973.

[71] S. C. de Sacr., Instr., May 7, 1923, reg. 5 §2.

[72] Cf. S. C. de Sacr., decr. May 7, 1923, §4—*AAS,* XV (1923), 389.

are free to petition the Holy See directly, the advisable and usual method is to dispatch the petition through their proper Ordinary.[73]

According to the Instructión of 1923, the Ordinary who may accept this task is not only the Ordinary competent in judicial matters according to canon 1964, but even the Ordinary of the place where the petitioner is actually staying.[74] The local Ordinary who accepts the petition should make an extrajudicial investigation of the general facts of the case and ascertain the characters of the parties involved. These findings should be added to the petition when it is transmitted to the Congregation. In making this investigation the Ordinary is not acting contrary to canon 1963 §1.[75] Should the application be received favorably by the Congregation, the local Ordinary who sent the request for the parties is generally designated as the Ordinary in whose curia the process is to be instituted. To this Ordinary the Sacred Congregation will delegate the faculties to institute the process according to the regulations of the Instruction of 1923 with such particular instructions as the Holy See shall have determined for this particular case.[76]

Only one judge called the "judge instructor" is required for the process.[77] It is his duty to direct the proceedings according to the regulations given in the Instruction of 1923 and any particular instructions which may have been given by the Holy See for this individual case. At the completion of the process the judge instructor does not publish the process[78] nor give a sentence on the fact of non-consummation or the reasons for the granting of the dispensation. The acts are to be given the defensor that he may prepare his opinions on the case. Then all the acts are to be signed with the written opinion (*votum*) of the *bishop*[79] (but not the judge instructor unless

[73] S. C. de Sacr., Instr., May 7, 1923, reg. 7.

[74] S. C. de Sacr., Instr., May 7, 1923, reg. 8 §§1, 2. Cf. can. 93 §2, 1964.

[75] S. C. de Sacr., Instr., May 7, 1923, reg. 9.

[76] S. C. de Sacr., Instr., May 7, 1923, reg. 12. Cf. S. C. C., *Chien.*, Mar. 12, 1729, where the bishop was delegated to grant the dispensation—Richter, *Canones et Decreta Concilii Tridentini*, n. 141, p. 283.

[77] Can. 1966.

[78] Formerly the acts could be published. Cf. Gasparri, *De Matrimonio*, n. 1504.

[79] Can. 1985. During the vacancy of the see this is to be done by the administrator selected by the diocesan consultors (can. 427, 429 §3),

the bishop himself was moderator of the process) and the defensor and sent to the Sacred Congregation of the Sacraments.[80] There is no need for a second hearing in the court of second instance as in a judicial process. At Rome the Congregation can of its own proper authority submit the matter to the Sacred Rota should it deem it advisable to have the case examined by that tribunal.[81] If one of the petitioners seeking a dispensation *super rato* is a non-Catholic how is the local Ordinary to act in view of recent decisions of the Holy Office?[82] If one of the petitioners is a non-Catholic the proper Ordinary, without previously securing the permission of the Holy Office, can accept the petition for transmission to the Holy See for the non-Catholic is not an *actor*.[83] The real difficulty appears in the matter of where the Ordinary should address the petition. Should it be sent to the Holy Office or to the Sacred Congregation of the Sacraments? By the Code the Congregation of the Sacraments is exclusively competent in the cases of dispensations *super rato*,[84] and by the Instruction of 1923 even if the dispensation is sought by a non-Catholic party, the Ordinary is instructed to direct the petition to the Congregation of the Sacraments with an explanation of the circumstances.[85] Does the recent decision of the Holy Office stating that the Holy Office has exclusive competence in any matrimonial cause between a Catholic and a non-Catholic, whether baptized or not, brought in any way to the Holy See, qualify the competence of the Sacred Congregation of the Sacraments when one of the parties, whether the petitioner or the "pars conventa," is a non-Catholic? Cases for a dispensation *super rato* are not truly judicial but rather administrative.[86] The recent decision

---

the vicar capitular, apostolic administrator, or other person who may legitimately supply the place of the bishop. Cf. S. C. S., Instr., May 7, 1923, reg. 98.

[80] Can. 1985.

[81] Can. 249 §3. S. C. Consist., Jan. 28, 1909—*AAS*, I (1909), 211. In six years six such cases were presented to the Rota. Cf. *AAS*, XII (1922), 560.

[82] S. C. S. Off., Jan. 27, 1928—*AAS*, XX (1928), 75.

[83] S. C. S. Off., Jan. 27, 1928, ad I—*AAS*, XX (1928), 75. Cf. S. C. de Sacr., Instr., May 7, 1923, reg. 9 §2.

[84] Can. 249 §3.

[85] S. C. de Sacr., Instr., May 7, 1923, reg. 9 §2. Cf. *ibid.*, reg. 98 §2.

[86] S. C. de Sacr., Decr., May 7, 1923, §4—*AAS*, XV (1923), 389.

of the Holy Office seems directed against the notion that cases in the judicial order are to be sent to the Roman Rota directly even if the question concerns a mixed marriage. Canon 247 §3 has no direct denial of the absolute competence of the Congregation of the Sacraments in the matter of dispensations *super rato* [87] which the Instruction of May 7, 1923, related as including even cases where a non-Catholic was an interested party.[88] While cases of dispensations *super rato* may not be matrimonial *causes* in the sense of being judicial in nature yet the clause in the decision "brought in any manner to the Holy See" (*quocumque modo ad Sanctam Sedem delatis*) seemingly embraces not only matrimonial cases deferred in a judicial manner but even those of an administrative character. For the Holy Office is both a Tribunal and a Congregation and the scope of its competence is extensive. Consequently, it appears that petitions for a dispensation *super rato* which are sent to the Holy See should, in cases where one party is a non-Catholic, be addressed to the Holy Office. The diocesan tribunal is properly competent to treat a matrimonial cause in which the nullity of the marriage is based on the impediment of impotency. When a local tribunal, competent on any of the titles allowed in canon 1964, undertakes such a case and in the course of the trial proof emerges not of the impotency but rather of the non-consummation of the marriage, then the acts are to be completed and transmitted to the Sacred Congregation of the Sacraments that they may be used for giving a decision on the possibility of a papal dispensation.[89] If antecedent impotence is proven with great probability it is reason enough for seeking the dispensation.[90] When the case assumes the aspect of a non-consummation procedure the diocesan collegiate tribunal may remain in the hearing the case but are all three judges[91] delegated or is only one of them to become the judge instructor of the procedure to establish the non-consummation? The question will be taken up after a similar delegation is considered.

The Instruction of the Sacred Congregation of the Sacra-

[87] Can. 249 §3.

[88] S. C. de Sacr., Instr., May 7, 1923, reg. 9 §2; 98 §2.

[89] Can. 1963 §2. S. C. S., Instr., May 7, 1923, reg. 3. Cf. S. C. C., June 16, 1894—*ASS*, XXVII, 153.

[90] Cf. *ASS*, XXVIII, 543.

[91] Can. 1576 §1—1°.

ments of May 7, 1923, provides for events similar to the case mentioned in canon 1963 §2. A delegation of faculties by law (*a iure*) to hold a process *super rato* is given to the diocesan curia under certain circumstances. Often in the diocesan court the nullity of a marriage is based on such reasons as defect of consent, fear, violence, error of person, or defect in the proper form, which, by reason of their internal, mental, or intangible nature, are often difficult to prove. If the cause has already been introduced before the local tribunal on the score of defect of consent, etc., and while the point at issue cannot be firmly established, there arises *incidentally* a very probable doubt that the marriage was ever consummated, then one or both parties are in a position to seek a dispensation *super rato.* Under such circumstances the diocesan tribunal which has been hearing the case up to this (whether sitting as the tribunal of the first or second instance) need not halt the proceedings to seek the faculty to initiate the process *super rato.* Here, as in the case contemplated in canon 1963 §2 and explained in the Instruction of 1923,[92] the faculty to hold a process *super rato* is delegated by law (*a iure*) to the *judge* to institute a procedure according to the Instructions of May 7, 1923.[93] When the process is completed the acts are signed and sent to the Congregation in the usual manner.

Now a return may be made to the problem which presented itself in the consideration of canon 1963 §2, and which reoccurs in the case just considered. When the matrimonial cause was originally entered before the local tribunal the court was composed of at least three judges.[94] Delegation in canon 1963 §2 and in the Instruction (reg. 4) is given to the judge.[95] Is the term judge to be rendered as tribunal or its the faculty to be considered as devolving on one man? It is hard to say. When the process *super rato* is undertaken it is by virtue of delegated faculties. The procedure changes from a process

---

[92] Reg. 3 §§1, 2.

[93] ". . . at quin preces ad Hanc Sacram Congregationem remittantur pro obtinenda consueta commissione facultatum, fit potestas iudici, vi huius praescriptionis seu ex delegatione a iure, causam instruendi iuxta *Regulas* heic determinatas."—S. C. de Sacr., Instr., May 7, 1923, reg. 4.

[94] Can. 1576 §1—1°.

[95] "Si tamen judex . . ."—can. 1963 §2; ". . . potestas fit iudici . . ." —S. C. de Sacr., Instr., May 7, 1923, reg. 4.

fundamentally judicial to a process which is rather administrative.[96] In the administrative procedure but one judge instructor is needed.[97] A solution of the difficulty may be found in the general principle that if many obtain delegated jurisdiction for the same matter and there is doubt as to whether the delegation was made "in solidum" or collegiately, it is to be presumed that it was "in solidum" in voluntary matters, collegiately in judicial matters. But the Sacred Congregation of the Sacraments in the decree of May 7, 1923, declared that these processes *super rato* are rather administrative or *in forma gratiosa* than judicial. From this it may be inferred that any one of the local collegiate tribunal enjoys the faculty to direct the process *super rato* as the judge instructor.

If the indications of the non-consummation emerge in the course of the trial before the court of second instance then it is to the judge of that curia that the delegation is extended by the law. The case cannot be returned to the tribunal of first instance for that court would not have received the necessary delegation.

Art. 3. The Competence of the Holy Office

§1. *The competence of the Holy Office in matrimonial causes in which the actor is a non-Catholic*—No inferior tribunal can validly undertake the trial of a matrimonial cause in which a non-Catholic, whether baptized or not, has the role of plaintiff (actor) without first obtaining the permission of the Holy Office. The special reasons for admitting the non-Catholic actor are to be explained to the Holy See.[98] This does not mean that the hearing of case itself is reserved to the Holy Office, but that the permission for the non-Catholic to bring the matrimonial cause as actor to the ecclesiastical tribunal must first be obtained from the Holy Office. This includes all matrimonial

---

[96] S. C. de Sacr., Decr., May 7, 1923, §4—*AAS,* XV (1923), 389.

[97] Can. 1966.

[98] "I. Utrum in causis matrimonialibus *acatholicus,* sive baptizatus sive non baptizatus, *actoris* partes agere possit.

Ad. I: *Negative,* seu standum Codici I. C., praesertim can. 87. Siquidem autem speciales occurrant rationes ad admittendos acatholicos ut *actores* in huiusmodi causis, recurrendum ad Supremam Sacram Congregationem Sanctii Officii in singulis casibus." S. C. S. Off., Jan. 27, 1928—*AAS,* XX (1928), 75.

questions of a judicial nature[99] but not those of an administrative character, *e. g.*, the declaration of nullity due to absence of form.[100]

Before the Code, though heretics and infidels were generally denied the right to be the actor in an ecclesiastical trial, an exception was allowed in matrimonial causes.[101] The qualifications for an actor demanded by the Code[102] did not clearly define the position of non-Catholics as actors in matrimonial causes. While some post Code writers do not expressly treat the juridical capacity of a non-Catholic to appear as the plaintiff in a matrimonial cause,[103] Wernz-Vidal stated that *baptized* non-Catholics may be admitted as actors in matrimonial causes.[104] The matter is now defined for the response of the Holy Office shows clearly that there is an obstacle to the exercise of the rights conferred by baptism.[105] Where the Catholic party is plaintiff (*actor*) against the non-Catholic party as defendant (*reus, pars conventa*) the local tribunal may accept the matrimonial cause for permission of the Holy Office is only required when the non-Catholic is to be admitted as *actor.*

§2. *The competence of the Holy Office in any mixed marriage cause brought to the Holy See*—At the same time that the question just discussed was settled another point in matrimonial competence was clarified. Obviously, the Holy Office was exclusively competent in marriage matters involving non-Catholics which were presented to the Holy See for administrative cognition. However, the Holy Office is not only a Congregation but also a Tribunal and as such possesses judicial

---

[99] Cf. *causis.*

[100] Cf. Pont. Comm. Int. Cod., resp. Oct. 16, 1919, ad 17—*AAS,* XI (1919), 479.

[101] C. 13, X, *de haeret.,* V, 7. Sanchez, *De Matrimonio,* L. VII, d. 3, n. 9. Cf. Austrian Instruction, §115. "Acatholici, haeretici atque infideles ordinarie ad agendo in foro ecclesiastico repelluntur; vel qua excommunicati vel qua a iurisdictione ecclesiastica remoti, quales sunt infideles. Sed hi omnes aliquando agere vel respondere valent apud eccl. iudices, veluti in causis matrimoniorum mixtorum."—Lega, *De Iudiciis Ecclesiasticus,* I, n. 63.

[102] Cf. can. 1646, 1654 §2, 87, 1971 §1—1°.

[103] Cf. Noval, *De Iudiciis,* nn. 262, 263. Roberti, *De Processibus,* I, p. 323.

[104] Wernz-Vidal, *Ius Canonicum,* VI, n. 210.

[105] Cf. *Ius Pontificium,* VIII (1928), 9.

power.[106] The Roman Rota was commonly considered the competent tribunal to hear a matrimonial cause which had been appealed to the Holy See. Now the competence of the Rota in causes where one party is a non-Catholic is explained by the recent response of the Holy Office. Inquiry was made: Whether in any matrimonial cause between a Catholic party and a non-Catholic party, baptized or not baptized, which is brought in any manner to the Holy See, the Supreme Sacred Congregation of the Holy Office has exclusive competence? The reply of the Holy Office was in the affirmative and special reference was made to canon 247 §3. It disclaimed competence, however, in any cause reserved under canon 1557 §1-1°.[107] This response gives a clearer understanding of canon 1962 which determines matrimonial competence among the members of the Roman Curia. Even judicial matrimonial causes as well as administrative matters in which a non-Catholic is concerned must be brought to the attention of the Holy Office. An appeal to the Holy See is not to be sent directly to the Sacred Roman Rota if a non-Catholic is a party to the cause. The Holy Office has exclusive competence in the matter. As has been seen even petitions *super rato* in which one party is a non-Catholic must apparently be sent to the Holy Office. While these are not strictly matrimonial causes yet the words of the decision "brought in any manner to the Holy See" seem to include these cases.

§3. *The competence of the Holy Office in the Pauline Privilege.*

Canon 1962.—. . . **causas vero quae referuntur ad privilegium Paulinum, Sacra Congregatio S. Officii.**

Canon 247 §3.—**Ipsa sola cognoscit ea quae, sive directe sive indirecte, in iure aut in facto, circa privilegium, uti aiunt, Paulinum, et matrimonii impedimenta disparitatis**

[106] Cf. Canons 247, 1555 §1.

[107] II. Utrum in quibuslibet causis matrimonialibus inter partem catholicam et partem acatholicam, sive baptizatam sive non baptizatam, quocumque modo ad Sanctum Sedem delatis, Suprema Sacra Congregatio Sancti Officii exclusivam habeat competentiam. Ad. II. Affirmative, habita praesertim ratione can. 247 §3, et salvo praescripto can. 1557 §1—1°. S. C. S. Off., Jan. 27, 1928—*AAS,* XX (1928), 75. This regulation is not exactly new.—cf. Peries, *Procédure Canonique,* n. 44.

cultus et mixtae religionis versantur; . . . Quare quaelibet huiusmodi quaestio ad hanc Congregationem est deferenda, quae tamen potest, si ita censeat et casus ferat, quaestionem remittere ad aliam Congregationem vel ad Tribunal Sacrae Romanae Rotae.

When a matrimonial case involving the Pauline privilege is presented to the ecclesiastical authorities, there is the task of verifying the existence of the conditions requisite for the effective application of the privilege. This may be done in a summary (extrajudicial) or judicial manner for the valid marriage contracted by the two infidels is not dissolved or declared null by the sentence of an ecclesiastical judge but is severed *ipso iure* by the second marriage of the convert.[108] Since the interpellations are necessary, unless the Holy See declares otherwise, the exclusive competence of the Holy Office to the exclusion of lower authorities in cases where such a dispensation is sought, or where any doubt in law or fact as to the valid application of the privilege remains, is easily perceived.[109]

In the early Church bishops referred doubtful cases to the Pope[110] for it was generally recognized that cases of this character required prudent care.[111] Because of the close connection which these cases had with faith itself the Holy Office came to be entrusted with the questions which were brought to the Holy See.[112] In the reorganization of the Roman Curia under Pius X the Holy Office retained this competence, being empowered to allow the omission of the interpellations and to judge cases presented to it.[113] Its scope was universal, extending directly even to territories under the Propaganda[114] and to Orientals.[115] Further should the Holy Office see fit it could of its own authority remit a case of the Pauline privilege to the Rota or any other Congregation for further examination.[116]

Canon 1962 delineates matrimonial competence in the Roman

---

108 Canon 1126.
109 Cf. canons 1120-1127.
110 E. g., c. 7, *de divortiis*, IV, 19.
111 Gregory XIII, Const., *Populis*, doc. VIII in Codex.
112 E. g., S. C. S. Off., June 23, 1671—*Fontes*, n. 745.
113 Const., *Sapienti consilio*, I—1, n. 5—*Fontes*, n. 682.
114 Cf. *Ordo Servandus*—pars altera, cap. I—1°a.
115 S. C. Consist., Nov. 12, 1908, ad. 6—*AAS*, I (1909), 149.
116 S. C. Consist., Jan. 21, 1910—*AAS*, II (1910), 56.

Curia and the reservation of the Pauline privilege to the Holy Office, so far as inferior judges are concerned, is not as strict as the other two reservations mentioned. Inferior tribunals are incompetent in the cases of rulers and in cases of dispensation from a ratified but non-consummated marriage not by reason of canon 1962 but by reason of other canons of the Code.[117] The competence of the local Ordinary in the matter of Pauline privilege is not so absolutely restricted.[118] The local Ordinary can verify in a summary investigation or in a judicial fashion through the diocesan curia[119] the existence of the conditions necessary for the application of the Pauline privilege, *viz.*, a. a valid marriage contracted between two infidels (can. 1120); b. the reception of baptism by one party (can. 1121 §1); c. the refusal of conversion or, at least, of peaceful cohabitation on the part of the unbaptized party when asked by the baptized party prior to the second marriage which will sever the former bond (can. 1121 §1, 1122, 1126).

If the omission of the interpellations is desired, the Holy Office alone is competent. So the competence of the local Ordinary in these cases does not contradict the reservation of canon 1962. Indeed the Pauline privilege can be validly employed on private authority.[120] If a marriage case under consideration in a local curia involves a former marriage severed by virtue of the Pauline privilege, the local authorities retain competence and there is no need of placing the matter before the Holy Office except in the circumstances mentioned above.

§4. *The competence of the Holy Office in other matrimonial causes*—Distinct from cases of ratified non-consummated marriages and cases of the ordinary Pauline privilege, there are other matrimonial cases which are difficult to classify and which require careful treatment. There is, for example, the special provision made in canon 1125 and treated at length in the three Constitutions appended to the Code. Whatever the exact nature of these cases may be,—whether they are special applications of the Pauline privilege, as it seems in the Constitutions "Altitudo"

---

117 Canons 1558, 1963.

118 Cf. Richter, *Canones et Decreta Concilii Tridentini*, p. 286, n. 151; *AER*, LXXII (1925), 623.

119 Cf. canon 1122 §1. Peries, *Procédure Canonique*, p. 224.

120 Cf. can. 1122 §2. Chelodi, *Ius Matrimoniale*, n. 158.

and "Romani Pontificis," or the solution of a legitimate marriage (*matrimonium legitimum*) through a papal dispensation, as it seems in the Constitution "Populis,"—[121] general provision is made by the Code for the treatment. As Chelodi remarks, only in one constitution (Gregory XIII, *Populis*) is the intervention of local ecclesiastical authorities necessary, though the local authorities will, no doubt, be called upon to verify the conditions in all cases. Such cases as these need not be submitted to the Holy See. If advice is sought, it would be asked of the Holy Office. In other matrimonial cases where the marriage is not a ratified and consummated marriage, there is the possibility of a dissolution of the bond *ab extrinseco* by a papal dispensation. The extent of this papal power is not as yet clearly determined but an example is seen in the celebrated Helena (Montana) case of a few years ago when the marriage between a baptized person and a non-baptized person was severed by a papal dispensation.[122] If such a case is brought to the local curia, the local authorities should gather the data possible and send the case to the Holy Office for a decision.

Art. 4. The Sacred Roman Rota

Apart from the special competencies noted in canon 1962, or already explained, the usual Roman tribunal for matrimonial causes is the Rota.[123] The Rota is the usual permanent tribunal, collegiate in nature, enjoying ordinary [124] vicarious [125] judicial authority.[126] Its competence is restrained by no territorial limitations,[127] but certain matrimonial causes are, by reason of the matter or the persons involved, beyond its scope. The Rota is

---

[121] Cf. Gasparri, *De Matrimonio*, n. 1349; Chelodi, *Ius Matrimoniale*, n. 160; Wernz-Vidal, *Ius Canonicum*, V, n. 635 sq.

[122] S. C. S. Off., Nov. 5, 1924—*AER*, LXX (1924), 59; LXXII (1925), 186. Cf. S. C. S. Off., July 10, 1924—*L'Ami du Clerge*, XLVII (1925), 409.

[123] Canons 259, 1598-1601. Pius X, *Sapienti consilio*, June 29, 1908—*Fontes*, n. 682; *Regulae Servandae in Iudiciis apud S. R. Rotae Tribunal*, Aug. 4, 1910—*AAS*, II (1910), 783; *Lex Propria Sacrae Romanae Rotae*, June 29, 1908—*AAS*, I (1909), 20. Cf. for history, Lega, *De Iudiciis Ecclesiasticis*, II, n. 42; Ojetti, *De Romana Curia*, p. 175.

[124] Canon 1598.

[125] Canon 1597.

[126] Cf. canon 1598 §1.

[127] Roberti, *De Processibus*, I, p. 213.

the ordinary tribunal for matrimonial causes legitimately appealed to the Holy See for a hearing in the second,[128] third, or further instances.[129] It is *per turnum* a tribunal of appeal from its own sentences.[130] The Rota is not the court of first instance unless a matrimonial cause is remanded to it by the Pope[131] or by some Roman Congregation, as the Holy Office,[132] Oriental Congregation,[133] or the Sacred Congregation of the Sacraments.[134]

The Rota follows the general prescriptions of the Code in its procedure[135] and such further details as given in its proper law and regulations.[136] The tribunal has by nature only judicial competence though administrative power may be employed in dispatching some incidental question.[137] A recourse to the Rota in a matrimonial case that has been treated administratively (e.g., declaration of the nullity of a marriage due to *lack* of form) would be of no avail. Administrative matters are for the Congregations.[138] By the recent response of the Holy Office, already mentioned, it is the Holy Office which has exclusive competence in any matrimonial cause involving a non-Catholic which is presented to the Holy See. Consequently, any matrimonial cause of this type, if appealed from the tribunal of second instance, would be sent not to the Rota but to the Holy Office. The Rota appears to be absolutely incompetent to judge these causes until the Holy Office has first seen the matter.

Art. 5. The Supreme Tribunal of the Apostolic Signatura[139]

As the title indicates, this tribunal ranks foremost among the permanent courts of the Church. It is often likened to our own

---

[128] Canon 1599 §1, 1°; *Lex Propria,* can. 14 §2.

[129] Canon 1599 §, 2°; *Lex Propria,* can. 14 §3.

[130] *Lex Propria,* can. 33 §2; *Regulae Servandae,* §§224 sq.

[131] Canon 1559 §2; *Lex Propria,* can. 14 §1.

[132] Canon 247 §3.

[133] Canon 257 §3.

[134] Canon 249 §3. Cf. S. C. Consist., Jan. 28, 1909—*AAS,* I (1909), 211.

[135] Canon 1555 §2.

[136] *Lex Propria,* June 29, 1908—*AAS,* I (1909), 20 sq; *Regulae Servandae,* etc.,—*AAS,* II (1910), 783 sq.

[137] Cf. *AAS,* XV (1923), 296.

[138] Canon 1601; *Lex Propria,* can. 16; Noval, *De Iudiciis,* n. 174.

[139] Canons 259, 1602-1605. Pius X, Const., *Sapienti consilio,* June 29, 1908—*Fontes,* n. 682; *Regulae Servandae in Iudiciis apud S. T. Ap. Sig-*

United States Supreme Court. Like the Rota, the Signatura enjoys ordinary [140] vicarious [141] judicial [142] power, but further it possesses delegated administrative authority in certain matters.[143] The Signatura is not so much a court of trial as one which reviews the merits of a case to decide if the inferior court acted validly or licitly. This tribunal has great power in matrimonial causes though it does not directly decide them. As sentences in matrimonial causes never become settled (*res iudicata*)[144] there was always the possibility of the cause being reopened. What legal steps could be taken if the Rota, after two conformable sentences had been given and the time for appeal had passed, refused to reopen a matrimonial cause? By the Constitution *"Sapienti consilio"* of 1908 [145] the Signatura was empowered to hear cases that a restitution of the entire matter (*restitutio in integrum*) might be granted in causes where the sentence had passed into a permanent state (*rem iudicatam*).[146] When the Signatura was asked to discern a matrimonial cause so that a *"restitutio in integrum"* might be given, the legal incongruity of a matrimonial cause, in which the sentence could never become fixed (*res iudicata*), being capable of a restitution was apparent. An interpretation of the Signatura's authority was needed and Cardinal Lega addressed a letter to Benedict XV explaining the situation. The papal response, the chirograph *"Attentis expositis,"* [147] is the foundation for the present fifth number in canon 1603 §1. It is now clearly established that the Signatura is competent by virtue of ordinary power to consider *recourses* against a sentence of the Rota when the Rota refuses to admit the matrimonial cause to a new hearing. This power is really administrative and it ap-

---

naturae, Mar. 6, 1912—*AAS*, IV (1912), 187 sq; *Lex Propria, etc.*, June 29, 1908—*AAS*, I (1909), 29 sq; *Appendix ad Regulas Servandas, etc.*, Benedict XV, Chir., *Attentis expositis*, June 28, 1915—*Fontes*, n. 705. For history, Roberti, *De Processibus*, I, p. 215.

[140] Canon 1603.

[141] Canon 1597.

[142] Canon 259.

[143] Canon 1603 §2. *AAS*, VII (1915), 184.

[144] Benedict XIV, Const., *Dei miseratione*, Nov. 3, 1741, §11—*Fontes*, n. 318. Cf. canon 1989.

[145] *Fontes*, n. 682.

[146] Cf. *Lex propria*, can. 37 and canon 1603 §1, 1°—4°.

[147] June 28, 1915—*Fontes*, n. 705.

pears incorrect to say that the power of the Signatura in canon 1603 §1 is strictly judicial.[148] The Signatura reviewing the case generally considers the plea to renew the cause because of some new evidence uncovered.[149] In giving decision in cases the Signatura need not append the reasons though it is free to do so.[150] The Signatura's competence to consider a recourse against an interlocutory sentence or incidental decree of the Rota given in the course of a matrimonial cause, was called into question by a Rotal defensor in 1922. The decision of the Signatura was that it was competent in this matter.[151] Further, in any controversies arising over matrimonial competence between inferior tribunals, where there is no other superior court to decide the question, or lacking these, no Apostolic Legate, then the Signatura is competent to adjust the difficulty.[152] Controversies in matrimonial competence among the branches of the Roman Curia are decided by a special commission of cardinals specially designated each particular time.[153]

---

[148] Cf. Vermeersch-Creusen, *Epitome,* III, n. 55.
[149] Cf. canons 1786, 1903.
[150] Canon 1605 §2.
[151] Nov. 25, 1922—*AAS,* XV (1923), 180.
[152] Canon 1603 §1, 6°.
[153] Canon 245.

CHAPTER V

Formal Judicial Procedure in the Diocesan Curia

***Canon 1964.*—In aliis causis matrimonialibus iudex competens est iudex loci in quo matrimonium celebratum est aut in quo pars conventa vel, si una sit acatholica, pars catholica domicilium vel quasi-domicilium habet.**

Art. 1. Causes Proper to the Diocesan Court

Matrimonial causes in which the local curia is competent are noted in the opening words of canon 1964. Cases reserved to the higher authorities are beyond the scope of the episcopal curia. To recall what has been said the diocesan court is absolutely incompetent [1] in the marriage causes of rulers [2] or in any matrimonial cause legitimately brought to the Holy See in the first instance.[3] The local judge cannot *per se* validly institute the inquiry preliminary to the petitioning for a papal dispensation from a ratified but non-consummated marriage.[4] Cases beyond the scope of the Pauline privilege requiring the exercise of papal authority may be investigated by the diocesan officials but obviously the matter must be referred to the Holy See for final settlement.[5] Involved cases of the Pauline privilege may have to be submitted to the Holy Office for decision. Permission to omit the interpellations must be sought from the Holy Office.[6] In other cases the verification of the conditions requisite for the application of the Pauline privilege may be made by the local Ordinary.[7] The diocesan court cannot validly accept a matrimonial cause in which the actor is a non-Catholic without first

---

[1] Canon 1892—1°.

[2] Canon 1558.

[3] Cf. canons 1559 §2, 1569, 1597.

[4] Canon 1963 §1.

[5] E. g., *AER*, LXXII (1925), 188.

[6] Canon 1121 §2.

[7] Canon 1122. Cf. *AER*, LXX (1924), 623.

securing in each case the permission of the Holy Office.[8] The local curia, too, is to consider certain Catholics as juridically incapable of becoming *actors* in matrimonial causes. These persons are Catholics who have been wittingly responsible for the impediment whence the nullity of the marriage arose.[9] These include not only persons who have caused the impediment of crime to arise [10] or who contracted marriage consciously concealing a diriment impediment, but even persons responsible for impediments in the broad sense, *e.g.* substantial error, condition against essence of matrimony, *etc.* This teaching of authors [11] is now confirmed by a response of the Pontifical Commission for the Interpretation of the Code.[12] Though the diocesan court is itself properly competent to try certain causes it may not accept the petition of a person juridically incapable of becoming an actor. Only the Holy See can dispense from this general disqualification. An innocent person can always accuse the marriage. Further, the Promoter of Justice is competent to institute an action of nullity in all cases where the invalidating impediments are public *natura sua.*[13]

Matrimonial causes in which the diocesan court is competent are those wherein the nullity is based on defect of consent, defect in the proper form,[14] or the presence of a diriment impediment. Causes of separation [15] or any other matrimonial concern may be treated by the local court. The competence of the diocesan tribunal has been questioned where the impediment was that of disparity of cult but there is no doubt but that the local curia

---

[8] Cf. S. C. S. Off., Jan. 17, 1928—*AAS,* XX (1928), 75; canons 1892—2°, 1609 §2.

[9] Canon 1971 §1—1°: cf. 1609 §2.

[10] Blat, *De Processibus,* n. 526.

[11] Cf. Vermeersch-Creusen, *Epitome,* III, n. 286; Chelodi, *Ius Matrimoniale,* n. 176; Cappello, *De Sacramentis,* III, n. 879; Noval, *De Iudiciis,* n. 850.

[12] Utrum vox *impedimenti* canons 1971 §1, n. 1, inteligenda sit tantum de impedimentis proprie dictis (cann. 1067-1080), an etiam de impedimentis improprie dictis matrimonium dirimentibus (cann. 1081-1103). Resp. Negative ad primam partem, affirmative ad secundam. Pont. Comm. Intr. Cod., March 12, 1929—*AAS,* XXI (1929), 171.

[13] Canon 1971 §1—2°.

[14] Absence of form is a distinct title for invalidity and, as it can be treated administratively, does not properly come under canon 1964. Cf. Pont. Comm. Inter. Cod., Oct. 16, 1919, ad 17—*AAS,* XI (1919), 479; *Ius Pontificium,* III (1923), 73.

[15] Canons 1130, 1131 §1.

is competent in these cases.[16] The local Ordinary is competent in disparity of cult matters coming under canon 1990. Further, the reservation of disparity of cult causes is not even hinted in canon 1962. Noval discloses the private information that all causes of disparity of cult not meeting the exactions of the briefer process detailed in canon 1990 are reserved to the Holy Office.[17] Nevertheless, there appears no bases in the general prescriptions of the law for denying the competence of the local curia in judging matters of disparity of cult in the ordinary judicial procedure.[18]

Art. 2. Determination of the Proper Diocesan Curia

The proper diocesan court to which a matrimonial cause should be presented for the trial of the first instance is that of the diocese in which the marriage had been contracted or that in which the defendant has a domicile or quasi-domicile, unless the defendant be a non-Catholic, in which event the domicile or the quasi-domicile of the Catholic party determines the proper tribunal.[19] The general rule that the forum of the defendant (*reus*) is preferred and that in case of the multiplicity of proper courts the plaintiff (*actor*) has the choice of forum,[20] is applicable in matrimonial causes in which both parties are Catholics. Both the judge of the diocese of contract and the judge of the diocese of domicile are equally competent, and in the former case no distinction is made whether both parties are Catholics or not. The circumstances of the case may make one forum preferable to the other.

Canon 1964 treats of marriages that have been contracted prescinding from any indication that a second marriage is contemplated. The canon considers the cause as a question arising between husband and wife who are the "parties" mentioned by the canon. Where a Catholic may wish to contract a marriage with a person who has been previously married, the

---

[16] Bouuaert-Simenon, *Manuale Iuris Canonici*, n. 1174. Cf. *Apollinaris*, I (1928), 219.

[17] Noval, *De Iudiciis*, n. 840.

[18] Cf. Wernz-Vidal, *Ius Canonicum*, V, n. 690; Bassibey, *Le Mariage*, p. 40; *Decisiones S. R. Rotae*, III, p. 258; *AER*, LXXII (1925), 623

[19] Canon 1964.

[20] Canon 1559 §3.

validity of that previous union must be determined. Then the Ordinary of the Catholic, who wishes to marry, has the task of establishing the freedom to marry. This Ordinary, being competent to make the investigation prior to marriage,[21] would be competent in the connected question or the judicial inquiry into the validity of any previous marriage.[22] Prior to the Code the Holy Office declared that when a previous marriage between two heretics had been followed by a civil divorce and later a Catholic wished to marry one of the divorced parties, the Ordinary of the Catholic contemplating the marriage was competent to determine the validity of the first marriage.[23] The Catholic person in such a case could not be termed the "pars catholica" of canon 1964 for he is not yet a party to any marriage. This notion is supported by canon 1971 §1—1° which shows that only the married persons themselves are capable of entering a formal private accusation against the validity of the marriage. Nowhere under canon 1971 §1—1° is the Catholic, who contemplates a marriage with a person previously married, capable of accusing the former union directly and of becoming the actor in a cause against the first marriage. In such instances the Ordinary of the Catholic person becomes competent to judge the validity of the prior union because of its connection with a matter in which he is properly competent, *i.e.,* in establishing the freedom of the Catholic to contract this determined marriage (*status liber*). The investigation may be made judicially and the question of the previous marriage becomes proper to the Ordinary by title of connected cause.[24] This notion simplifies matters for while the Ordinary of the place where the first marriage had been contracted is competent to judge the validity of a marriage even between non-Catholics,[25] there would be the difficulty of admitting a non-Catholic as an actor. For this special permission of the Holy Office would be required.[26] The difficulty would remain whenever the first marriage had been contracted between non-Catholics, whether baptized or not, as long as the parties remained non-Catholics. If the prior union

---

21 Canons 1019 sq.
22 Canon 1567. Cf. *AfkK,* CV (1925), 113.
23 S. C. S. Off., June 23, 1903—*Fontes,* n. 1266.
24 Canon 1576.
25 Cf. *Ius Pontificium,* VI (1926), 159.
26 S. C. S. Off., Jan. 17, 1928—*AAS,* XX (1928), 75.

had been contracted with a Catholic or if one party to a non-Catholic marriage had in the meantime become a Catholic, the Ordinary of the place where the marriage was contracted may undertake the cause; the Ordinary of the Catholic party to the first marriage may accept the case; or, further, the Ordinary of a Catholic person wishing to contract marriage with one of these persons to the first marriage in deciding the *status liber*, may settle the question of the validity of the first marriage by title of connected cause. Yet it may be well to have the Catholic party to the first marriage accuse the validity of the first union and seek a decision from the tribunal determined on the principles of canon 1964, *i.e.* either the forum of contract or the forum of domicile or quasi-domicile.[27]

With the view that canon 1964 directly considers matrimonial causes concerning existing marriages a further understanding of the canon will be attempted in treating:

1. The forum of contract;
2. The forum of domicile or quasi-domicile;
3. Other special titles;
4. Cases of spoliation;
5. Prevenience.

§1. *The forum of contract*—The competence of the local judge of the place where the marriage had been contracted to decide questions affecting that marriage was once uncertain.[28] This is a particular application of the title of judicial competence by reason of the forum of contract.[29] Prior to the Code, a few held it was applicable even in matrimonial causes.[30] Yet there was always the difficulty of the general principle that a judge, competent on this title, could legitimately issue a citation only where the defendant was in his territory.[31] Consequently, the presence of the defendant in the territory of the judge was demanded even in matrimonial causes.[32] Now the Code in canon

[27] Cf. *Apollinaris,* I (1928), 303.

[28] S. C. S. Off., June 23, 1903—*Fontes,* n. 1266. Cf. *LCC,* XXVI (1903), 659.

[29] Canon 1565.

[30] Cf. Lega, *De Iudiciis Ecclesiasticis,* I, n. 339; Wernz, *Ius Decretalium,* IV, p. II, n. 736, note 42.

[31] Lega, *De Iudiciis Ecclesiasticis,* I, n. 339; Sebastianelli, *De Iudiciis Ecclesiasticis,* p. 58.

[32] Bassibey, *Le Mariage,* p. 58.

1964 admits without qualification the competence of the local judge of the place where the marriage had been contracted to cite the parties even if they are not within his territory.

The new legislation of competence in judicial affairs generally by title of the place of contract [33] must be understood according to the general prescriptions of law. It is generally true at the present time that the defendant in any action must be present in the territory of the judge competent by reason of this title of place of contract to be legitimately cited.[34] There are two admitted exceptions to this rule. The one is contained in canon 1565 §2 which provides for the designation of an elected forum and the other is found in canon 1964 wherein the judge of the place where the marriage was contracted is competent in a matrimonial cause though the defendant, or even both parties, are beyond the territorial jurisdiction of the court.[35]

For judging marriages which had been contracted between infidels the forum of contract is preferable. In that place the civil laws and solemnities governing marriage will be better known.[36] The forum is the forum of true contract for the selection of a legal forum by the parties themselves, as allowed in canon 1565 §2, does not apply in matrimonial contracts.[37] The forum of contract is only applicable where the marriage has taken place [38] but not where the marriage is to be contracted in the diocese.[39]

§2. *The forum of domicile or quasi-domicile*—By reason of the domicile or quasi-domicile of the married parties, the competent local judge in a matrimonial cause is the judge of the diocesan domicile [40] or quasi-domicile.[41] For people with no fixed abode (*vagi*) the court of the diocese in which they are staying is the proper tribunal.[42] While either the tribunal of

---

[33] Canon 1565.

[34] Pontif. Comm. Inter. Cod., July 14, 1922—*AAS*, XIV (1922), 529. Cf. Vermeersch-Creusen, *Epitome*, III, n. 20.

[35] Cf. canon 201.

[36] Cf. May, *Marriage Laws and Decisions in the United States*, for various state legislations.

[37] Cf. Noval, *De Iudiciis*, n. 81.

[38] Cf. *Ius Pontificium*, VI (1926), 159; *Apollinaris*, I (1928), 304.

[39] Cf. Gasparri, *De Matrimonio*, n. 1463.

[40] Canon 92 §§1, 3.

[41] Canon 92 §2.

[42] Canons 94 §2, 1563.

the domicile or that of the quasi-domicile may be selected, the tribunal of the place of domicile is to be preferred.[43]

Where both parties are Catholic the general principle *"Actio sequitur forum rei"* obtains,[44] and the cause is entered either in the court of the domicile or quasi-domicile of the defendant. If the husband is the defendant the proper tribunal is that of his domicile or quasi-domicile: when there is a multiplicity of forums the choice belongs to the wife. Should the wife be the defendant in the action a different aspect arises in view of the necessary domicile of married women.

One effect of a valid marriage is that the wife, unless barred by special law, shares the husband's state so far as the canonical effects of marriage are considered.[45] Among these effects is the legal, or necessary, domicile of the wife[46] which must be considered in determining the proper tribunal when the Catholic wife is the defendant in a matrimonial action.[47] Though the validity of the marriage may be under question, the canonical effect of a valid marriage giving the wife the domicile of the husband remains, since the validity of marriage enjoys the favor of law.[48] Yet, it is possible for a married woman to have her own quasi-domicile and, at times, even her own domicile. This matter of domicile is presented in an outline.

Forums of husband defendant:

1. Domicile.
2. Quasi-domicile.

Forums of wife defendant:

A. Living with husband:
   1. Domicile of husband (canon 93 §1).
   2. Quasi-domicile of husband (canon 93 §1).[49]

---

[43] Maroto, *Institutiones Iuris Canonici*, I, n. 415; Bassibey, *Le Mariage*, p. 58.

[44] Canon 1559 §3.

[45] Canon 1112.

[46] Canon 93.

[47] Canon 1561.

[48] Canon 1014.

[49] Cf. Chelodi, *Ius de Personis*, p. 166; Maroto, *Institutiones Iuris Canonici*, I, nn. 412, 413; Wernz-Vidal, *Ius Canonicum*, II, n. 12. Vermeersch-Creusen, *Epitome*, I, n. 185, denies that the wife has, as a necessary quasi-domicile, the quasi-domicile of the husband.

B. Separated from husband:
   a. Legitimately (canons 1130, 1131 §1).
      1. Domicile of own (canon 93 §2).
      2. Quasi-domicile of own (canon 93 §2).
   b. Illegitimately (includes malicious desertion).[50]
      1. Domicile of husband (canon 93 §1).
      2. Quasi-domicile of own (canon 93 §2).

Therefore, if a Catholic wife is the defendant in an action the proper court of trial is determined by the domicile or quasi-domicile of the wife. If she is living with the husband the forum is that of the husband's domicile or quasi-domicile. If the wife is legitimately separated (a court sentence is not always necessary for a legitimate separation),[51] the place of trial is the wife's proper domicile or quasi-domicile. If the separation is illegal, which includes cases where the woman has been maliciously deserted, the court of trial (where the wife is the defendant) is either the domicile of the man (the wife's necessary domicile) or the quasi-domicile proper to the woman.[52]

If the marriage in question is a mixed marriage the proper forum is determined according to the domicile of the Catholic party, whether defendant or plaintiff.[53] When the husband is the Catholic, no difficulty is found in determining the properly competent tribunal. When the wife is the Catholic, the selection of the proper court may cause some doubt. If the marriage is one of mixed religion the proper court is determined in the same manner as it would be in cases between two Catholics when the wife is the defendant (*reus*).[54] But what of cases where the husband is an infidel? Would the infidel husband be considered as having a canonical residence[55] and the Catholic wife, as a consequence, a necessary domicile in the place where the husband has his domicile?[56] This question is possible should a Catholic wife be maliciously deserted by the unbaptized partner

[50] Pontif. Comm. Inter. Cod., July 14, 1922—*AAS*, XIV, (1922), 529.
[51] Canons 1130, 1131 §1.
[52] Cf. Pontif. Comm. Inter. Cod., July 14, 1922—*AAS*, XIV (1922), 529, which considers the case where the deserting husband is the defendant.
[53] Canon 1964.
[54] Cf. S. C. S. Off., July 27, 1892—*Fontes*, n. 1158.
[55] Canon 92. Cf. Canons 12, 87.
[56] Canon 93.

or illegally separated from him. Apparently the infidel husband is to be considered as having a canonical domicile and the wife therefore a necessary domicile in the place where the husband resides. The natural law supposes that the wife follow the domicile of her husband.[57] Further, the determination of residence as outlined in the Code[58] is applied even to the non-baptized as canon 738 mentions the proper pastor[59] of an unbaptized *"peregrinus."*

§3. *Other titles of competence*—While canon 1964 considers only the forum of domicile or quasi-domicile there are other ways of acquiring a forum for judicial matters generally and these may in special instances be applicable in matrimonial causes. One who has a domicile or quasi-domicile somewhere and is a visitor in Rome (*peregrinus*), even for a short time, is privileged to accept citation before the tribunal of the diocese of Rome (not the Rota).[60] Such a defendant has, however, the right of seeking that the cause be decided by his proper Ordinary. This request must be made before the official citation to appear in the local court of the Cardinal-Vicar of the Eternal City is accepted.[61] One who has been in Rome a year has the right of declining citation in the forum of the proper Ordinary and of demanding that he be cited before the diocesan tribunal of the City.[62] As the diocesan court of Rome would be competent on the title of quasi-domicile the main concession here is the right granted the person to decline the forum of his proper Ordinary.[63] In crimes against marriage the Ordinary of the place where the crime was committed is competent in any judicial procedure.[64]

§4. *Spoliation as applicable in matrimonial causes*—There is the possibility of having a question of spoliation arise between married people when there is the action to recover the exercise of matrimonial rights. This suit may be directed against a

---

[57] De Smet, *De Sponsalibus et Matrimonio*, n. 206.

[58] Canons 90-95.

[59] Canon 94 §1.

[60] Canon 1599 §2; Roberti, *De Processibus*, I, p. 120.

[61] Canons 1562 §1, 1568, 1725. Cf. Roberti, *De Processibus*, I, p. 120; Noval, *De Iudiciis*, n. 77; Burke, *Competence in Ecclesiastical Tribunals*, p. 38. Cf. c. 20, X, *de foro compet.*, II, 2.

[62] Canon 1562 §2.

[63] Cf. Wernz-Vidal, *Ius Canonicum*, VI, n. 55, note 18.

[64] Canon 1566.

third party who is hindering the exercise of these rights or against the spouse.[65] Such matrimonial causes would be known as actions to recover possession (*actio de spolio*) [66] and on this title would obtain a necessary forum.[67] The competent judge in a case of spoliation is the one in whose territory the object of dispute is located (*rei sitae*) or where the rights are exercised.[68] It may be the court of the diocese where the actor is staying or it may be the forum of the place where the defendant resides. The forum of the defendant seems preferable.[69] For example, a husband unjustly deserts his wife or vice versa.[70] An action to compel the deserting partner to resume community of life is possible.[71] The properly competent judge would be ascertained by applying canon 1560—1°.

What if the deserting party enters exception to the demand that cohabitation be restored by claiming that the marriage is invalid by reason of some defect? [72] While the general principles of law require that the object disputed must first be restored to the one who claims to have been despoiled, before any counter action (*exceptio spolii*) is considered,[73] the principle does not apply in matrimonial causes because of the spiritual concern, or the danger of sin perhaps, if the restoration of cohabitation is demanded before the counter claim is settled.[74] This matter of the restoration of the disputed right to the despoiled party is left to the decision of the judge and while

---

[65] Canon 1698 §1.

[66] Bouix, *De Iudiciis Ecclesiasticis*, II, p. 421. Wernz-Vidal, *Ius Canonicum*, VI, n. 351. Roberti, *De Processibus*, I, p. 406. Noval, *De Iudiciis*, n. 365.

[67] Canon 1560—1°. A necessary forum is in contradistinction to an optional forum (canons 1561-1566). It is one which is preferred by law. The fact that certain cases are considered as having a necessary forum to which they should be presented does not imply that any other judge is *absolutely* incompetent to treat the case (cf. canon 1559 §2).

[68] Canons 1560—1°, 1564.

[69] Cf. Roberti, *De Processibus*, I, p. 114.

[70] Cf. Roberti, *De Processibus*, I, p. 409; Wernz-Vidal, *Ius Canonicum*, VI, n. 355 for other examples.

[71] C. 8, 10, 12, X, *de restit. spol.*, II, 13; Lega, *De Iudiciis Ecclesiasticis*, I, n. 221; Wernz-Vidal, *Ius Canonicum*, VI, n. 355; Roberti, *De Processibus*, I, p. 409.

[72] Cf. Wernz-Vidal, *Ius Canonicum*, VI, n. 355.

[73] Canon 1699 §1.

[74] Canon 1699 §3. Cf. Roberti, *De Processibus*, I, p. 410.

authors distinguish different cases[75] practically it is better not to try to apply the general principle and so not to insist upon the restoration of community of life until the counter action is decided and the existence of the alleged invalidity of the marriage bond proved or disproved.[76]

§5. *Prevenience*—When two or more diocesan courts are equally competent to try a matrimonial cause, the right to decide the matter becomes proper to that tribunal to which the defendant was first legitimately cited. This is known as prevenience (*preventio*).[77] Thus by canon 1964 both the diocesan court of the place where the marriage had been contracted and the tribunal of the domicile of the defendant are equally competent to undertake a cause. The proper court would be decided by prevenience. Once the court has issued legitimate citation, or the parties have freely appeared before the tribunal, the cause ceases to be integral (*res integra*) and becomes proper to this particular court.[78]

Proper competence by reason of prevenience is only possible between *equally* competent tribunals. Judges are not equally competent when one forum is the necessary forum[79] and the other forum is an optional forum.[80] The diocesan tribunals in matrimonial causes are, excepting the forum in causes of spoliation, all optional forums and, being equally competent, there is the possibility of prevenience. The forum of necessity in the matter of spoliation as applied in matrimonial causes would be rarely found in the present day.

Art. 3. By Whom and How This Competence Is Exercised

Matrimonial causes are to be tried regularly in the first instance before the diocesan tribunal. Under the term diocesan judge are included the Ordinaries possessing judicial authority:[81] resident bishops and archbishops once they have taken

---

[75] Cf. Bouix, *De Iudiciis Ecclesiasticis*, II, p. 421; Wernz-Vidal, *Ius Canonicum*, VI, n. 355.

[76] Lega, *De Iudiciis Ecclesiasticis*, I, n. 231.

[77] Canon 1568.

[78] Canon 1725, Cf. Roberti, *De Processibus*, I, p. 447.

[79] Canon 1560.

[80] Canons 1561-1567. Cf. Noval, *De Iudiciis*, n. 91.

[81] Canon 198.

canonical possession of their sees, even prior to consecration,[82] but not the vicar general of a diocese,[83] abbots and prelates *nullius*,[84] administrators, vicars and prefects apostolic,[85] and the interregnum successors. While the bishop is the judge in the diocese, the Code advises that this office be performed generally through another.[86] Each bishop is held to select an Official, *per se* distinct from the Vicar General. This Official has ordinary judicial power and constitutes one tribunal with the bishop: consequently, there is no appeal from the Official to the bishop. The Official cannot judge causes which the bishop reserves to himself.[87] To the Official may be given helpers called vice-officials,[88] who have powers equal to the Official, enjoying even ordinary judicial authority.[89] Wherefore the Official and vice-officials may substitute one for the other when there is reason.[90] During the vacancy of the see the Official and the vice-officials retain their powers.[91] As the Official and vice-officials have ordinary power and as there is no express prohibition to the contrary, they may delegate this authority.[92] Besides selecting these judges who obtain *ipso facto* ordinary judicial power, the bishop may delegate other priests of approved life and canonical science, even externs, to the number of twelve at most, who may act as judges, even in matrimonial causes. These men are known as synodal or prosynodal judges accordingly as their designation was made in the diocesan synod or outside of the synod.[93]

A matrimonial cause concerned with a question of the bond

---

[82] Canon 334 §3.

[83] Canon 1573 §1.

[84] Cf. S. C. Counc., Aug. 22, 1840—*Coll.*, n. 911. Feije, *De Impedimentis et Dispensationibus Matrimonialibus*, n. 587. DeBecker, *De Sponsalibus et Matrimonio*, p. 446.

[85] Noval, *De Iudiciis*, n. 98.

[86] Canon 1578.

[87] Canon 1573. Noval, *De Iudiciis*, n. 114.

[88] Canon 1573 §3.

[89] Cf. canons 1577 §2, 1578. Roberti, *De Processibus*, I, p. 165.

[90] Roberti, *De Processibus*, I, pp. 165, 263.

[91] Canon 1573 §6.

[92] Canon 199 §1. Roberti, *De Processibus*, I, p. 165, denies that the power can be delegated but the citations in support of his view (canon 199 §§2, 4) deal with the subdelegation of delegated power. The Official and the vice-officials have ordinary judicial power.

[93] Canons 1572 §1, 1574.

of marriage itself is reserved to a collegiate tribunal of three judges.[94] The Official or vice-official usually presides at such trials assisted by two synodal or prosynodal judges.[95] If a matrimonial cause concerning the bond arises as an incidental cause in the course of some other trial, three judges are required to settle the question of the marriage bond.[96]

The Code requires the collegiate tribunal to proceed collegiately.[97] Where the bishop, Official, or vice-official, all of whom possess ordinary power, preside over the tribunal, the court is to be considered as exercising ordinary power even though the two synodal judges have delegated power.[98] If the court is composed entirely of judges enjoying delegated power, *e.g.*, three synodal judges, then the tribunal is acting with delegated power.[99] Whether a tribunal possesses ordinary or delegated authority it should proceed collegiately [100] and indeed the intervention of all three judges in the pronouncement of the sentence in a matrimonial cause is absolutely required for the validity of the sentence.[101] All the judges of the collegiate tribunal must sign the sentence.[102] But is the presence of all three judges of a tribunal treating a matrimonial cause required at all the acts other than the sentence? [103] This is rather hard to say since the tribunal may accomplish many judicial acts [104] through the auditors [105] and the presiding judge.[106] The question really arises in relation to those acts which require discernment and which should be performed by the judge or, in this case, the tribunal.[107] It is difficult to say just what acts

[94] Canon 1576 §1—1°.

[95] Canons 1576 §3, 1577 §2, 1574.

[96] Roberti, *De Processibus,* I, p. 177.

[97] Canon 1577 §1.

[98] Roberti, *De Processibus,* I, p. 173; Wernz-Vidal, *Ius Canonicum,* VI, n. 90; ". . . tribunali ordinario, cui praesit officialis vel vice officialis."—Canon 1578.

[99] Cf. canon 1574. Lega, *De Iudiciis Ecclesiasticis,* I, n. 95.

[100] Canon 1577 §1.

[101] Canons 1892—1°, 1874 §5.

[102] Pontif. Comm. Inter. Cod., July 14, 1922—*AAS,* XIV (1922), 529.

[103] Cf. canons 1576 §1—1°, 1577 §1.

[104] Canon 1642.

[105] Canons 1580-1583.

[106] *E. g.,* canons 1614 §3, 1643 §2.

[107] *E. g.,* canons 1844, 1799, 1861 §2, 1871 §3. Cf. Roberti, *De Processibus,* I, p. 174.

of this type, apart from the sentence, must under pain of nullity be treated by the entire tribunal. The general principle can be offered that if the tribunal has ordinary power the acts (other than the sentence) cannot be considered as invalid if all three judges are not present whereas if the tribunal possesses delegated authority apparently all the judges should be present at sessions in which the decision of the court is needed lest the acts be challenged as invalid.[108] As the auditors are generally given a wide range by the court, the necessity for all members of a delegated tribunal to be present, excepting at the final sentence, would be rare.

Art. 4. The Tribunal of Appeal

Whenever the court of first instance returns a verdict favoring the invalidity of the marriage bond the defensor must *ex officio* appeal this sentence to the tribunal of second grade.[109] Appeals are to be made from grade to grade. When the diocesan court has treated the cause in one instance it becomes incompetent to judge the same cause in another grade.[110] This incompetence is absolute, being prescribed for the public good, and holds even where all the judges of the diocesan tribunal may have been changed. Change in personnel in any court, the Rota excepted,[111] does not change the grade, or instance.[112]

Decretal law recognized the principle *"A delegato appellatur ad delegantem."*[113] Yet this was due, Roberti claims,[114] to a misunderstanding of the Roman law sources whence the principle was drawn. Authors sought a distinction in the Roman law terms "give a judge" (*iudicem dare*) and "mandated judgment" (*mandans*): in the former the delegator was considered as retaining his authority in the matter while in the latter the delegator was looked upon as having completely abdicated his

---

108 Cf. canon 205 §3. Cf. c. 16, X, *de offic. iud. deleg.*, I, 29. Noval, *De Iudiciis*, n. 126; Roberti, *De Processibus*, I, p. 230.

109 Canon 1986. Cf. Benedict XIV, const., *Dei miseratione*, Nov. 3, 1741, §8—*Fontes*, n. 318.

110 Canon 1571.

111 Canon 1599 §1—2°.

112 Cf. Noval, *De Iudiciis*, n. 105; Lega, *De Iudiciis Ecclesiasticis*, I, n. 318. Cf. canon 1615 §1.

113 C. 27, X, *de off. iud. deleg.*, I, 29. Cf. Noval, *De Iudiciis*, n. 641.

114 Roberti, *De Processibus*, I, p. 233.

authority in favor of the delegate.[115] Wherefore there was another principle applicable to mandated power: *"A delegato appellandum ad superiorem delegantis."* This was mentioned and rejected by Lega as without foundation.[116] Does the principle "a delegato appellatur ad delegantem" apply today? Certainly there is no place for its application when the sentence has been given by the ordinary tribunal, *i.e.* any diocesan court presided over by the bishop, official, or vice-official. Such a tribunal acts with ordinary, not delegated, power. Even prior to the Code it was a legal principle that there was no appeal from the vicar-general or official to the bishop.[117] What if the diocesan court which rendered the sentence was a delegated tribunal?[118] Would appeal be directed to the Ordinary who delegated the tribunal? According to some post Code authors an appeal from a delegated tribunal is taken to the delegator.[119] This may have been true prior to the Code for delegation in judicial affairs generally,[120] but even in those times the principle could scarcely be applied to the appeals from tribunals delegated by the bishop to act in matrimonial causes. Such action was entirely out of harmony with the general tenor of the legislation of the Council of Trent which did away with the inferior tribunals, making the bishop alone the ordinary judge of matrimonial causes:[121] and with the Benedictine regulation requiring two conformable sentences in distinct grades of judgment.[122] The common interpretation, at least in matrimonial causes, was that the delegate of the bishop acted with a delegation *in totum* if he (the delegate) gave the definitive sentence so that appeal was to be directed to the metropolitan curia.[123] Today the principles

---

[115] C. 18, 27, X, *de off. iud. deleg.*, I, 29. Cf. Devoti, *Institutiones Canonicae*, III, tit. XV, n. 1, note 1; Santi, *Praelectiones Iuris Canonici*, I, tit. XXIX, n. 31; Bassibey, *Le Mariage*, n. 539.

[116] Lega, *De Iudiciis Ecclesiasticis*, I, n. 622, note 2.

[117] C. 2, *de consuet*. I, 4 in VI°. Cf. Bassibey, *Le Mariage*, n. 539; Peries, *Procédure Canonique*, n. 2.

[118] Canons 1606, 1607 §2.

[119] Noval, *De Iudiciis*, nn. 157, 643; Vermeersch-Creusen, *Epitome*, III, n. 57.

[120] Cf. Lega, *De Iudiciis Ecclesiasticis*, I, n. 622.

[121] C. of Trent, sess. XXIV, *de ref.*, cap. 20.

[122] Benedict XIV, Const., *Dei miseratione*, Nov. 3, 1741, §8—*Fontes*, n. 318.

[123] Peries, *Procédure Canonique*, n. 132, note 13; Bassibey, *Le Mariage*,

of delegation and the system of appeals in judicial matters are well defined. The opinion of Roberti that appeal from the delegated tribunal is taken to the tribunal of higher grade is more acceptable.[124] The Code with its carefully defined steps of appeals or grades from which any exception is rare seems to have given the death blow to the general pre-Code principle that appeal from a delegate went to the delegator. The delegated tribunal is indeed held to observe the general principles governing the use of delegated authority [125] but these principles make no mention of appeal when delegation is had in judicial matters. The mode of action then should be rather according to the rules for appeal defined in the Code than by the pre-Code principle. For in the Code appeal is from grade to grade not from inferior to superior. In the general procedure,[126] in criminal [127] and matrimonial procedure,[128] the appeal is always to the tribunal superior *ratione gradus*.

The metropolitan court has no direct jurisdiction over the diocesan court of the suffragan bishop. It is merely superior by reason of grade, or instance.[129] Indeed, if the metropolitan should select the tribunal of one of his suffragans as the tribunal of appeal for causes treated in the first instance in the archdiocesan court,[130] the diocesan tribunal becomes the superior tribunal of the archdiocesan court by reason of grade.[131] Where a delegated diocesan tribunal has given the first sentence in a matrimonial cause the defensor should direct the appeal not to the one who delegated the tribunal but to the court of second instance. The bishop who delegated the tribunal is to be considered as having seen the cause through the delegates.[132] Wherefore, he cannot see the cause in the higher grade.[133] Further, once the sentence has been given, a tribunal delegated for

---

n. 539; Mansella, *De Impedimentis Matrimonium Dirimentibus ac de Processu Iudiciali*, p. 217.

[124] Roberti, *De Processibus*, I, p. 233.

[125] Canon 1606.

[126] Canons 1594, 1599 §1—1°, 1891.

[127] Canon 1959.

[128] Canons 1986, 1987.

[129] Cf. canons 274—7°, 1594 §1.

[130] Canon 1594 §2.

[131] Cf. Wernz-Vidal, *Ius Canonicum*, VI, n. 605, note 46.

[132] Canon 1572 §1.

[133] Canon 1571.

this individual cause loses its authority:[134] if the delegated tribunal is considered as quite distinct from the bishop and the ordinary diocesan tribunal, before whom then would a complaint of nullity (*querela nullitatis*),[135] opposition of a third party,[136] or other questions arising subsequent to the sentence, be presented?

From a matrimonial sentence given in the diocesan curia the appeal is to be carried to the metropolitan court which will decide the cause on the merits of the case to determine whether the first sentence is to be upheld or not.[137] If the episcopal curia has no proper metropolitan tribunal because the local Ordinary is immediately subject to the Holy See, the court of second instance is that metropolitan tribunal which the prelate shall designate, once for all, with the approval of the Holy See.[138]

The court of appeal for causes tried in the first instance in the metropolitan curia is that tribunal of the local Ordinary which the metropolitan has once permanently designated, with the approval of the Holy See, as the court of appeal.[139] Metropolitans formerly selected some neighboring metropolitan curia.[140] Now they are free to select any Ordinary, archbishop or bishop—even one of their own suffragans.[141] No obligation for the metropolitan to select one of the suffragan bishops as the judge for appeals can be based on the implication in canon 1594 §3.[142]

The tribunal of second instance should be constituted in the same manner as the court of first instance. In the discussion of the cause the same regulations, accommodated to the matter in hand, should be observed as were followed in the first curia.[143] Matrimonial causes in the first instance must be decided by a collegiate tribunal of at least three judges lest the sentence be

---

[134] Canons 1606, 207. Cf. Noval, *De Iudiciis*, n. 184; Lega, *De Iudiciis Ecclesiasticis*, I, n. 97.

[135] Canons 1893, 1895.

[136] Canon 1899 §1. Cf. Roberti, *De Processibus*, I, p. 235.

[137] Canons 274—7°, 1594 §1.

[138] Canons 1594 §3, 285.

[139] Canon 1594 §2. Cf. Roberti, *De Processibus*, I, p. 146.

[140] S. C. Prop. Fide, Instr., 1883, §26—*Coll.*, n. 1587.

[141] Canon 1594 §2.

[142] Vermeersch-Creusen, *Epitome*, III, n. 45, mention such an obligation.

[143] Canon 1595.

null: [144] the tribunal of appeal should be composed of judges in no less number than was had in the first trial. This is not required, however, under pain of invalidity of the sentence. Canon 1576 §1—1° legislates for the ordinary tribunal of first instance. Canon 1596, which treats of the ordinary tribunal of second grade, does not require any definite number of judges under penalty of invalidity.[145]

Appeals from the tribunals of the second instance are carried to the Holy See unless by special arrangement, as in Spain, a tribunal of third instance is provided.[146] At the Holy See the usual court is the Rota [147] but if the matrimonial cause involves a non-Catholic party the matter must first be sent to the Holy Office.[148] The Rota may, in particular causes, be the court of second instance for those matrimonial causes which, judged in the tribunal of the local Ordinary, have been legitimately appealed to the Holy See. In missionary countries the hierarchy is often lacking so that the appeal is directed to the Rota.[149] Appeals from a sentence given by the Rota are received by another turn of the same tribunal.[150]

In a matrimonial cause two conformable sentences must have been given before the parties are free to enter another marriage. If the decision of the metropolitan court confirms the sentence of the diocesan tribunal and the defensor of the metropolitan curia does not in conscience consider that an appeal should be taken to the third instance, then the parties are free to marry ten days after the second sentence has been given.[151] These ten days permit the defensor of the metropolitan curia to file notice of appeal before the tribunal which gave this second sentence.[152] Once the defensor files notice of appeal the parties are not able to contract new marriages for the appeal suspends the second

---

[144] Canon 1576 §1—1°.

[145] Roberti, *De Processibus,* I, p. 178; Vermeersch-Creusen, *Epitome,* III, n. 46.

[146] Cf. Wernz-Vidal, *Ius Canonicum,* VI, n. 605. Cf. *AfkK,* LV (1886), 353, for former Austrian concession.

[147] Canons 1598 §1, 1599 §1.

[148] S. C. S. Off., Jan. 27, 1928, ad 2—*AAS,* XX (1928), 75.

[149] Canon 1599 §1—1°.

[150] Canon 1599 §1—2°.

[151] Canon 1987.

[152] Canon 1881.

sentence so the parties cannot act upon it.[153] When the court of appeal informs the local curia that the first sentence of invalidity of the bond has been upheld it becomes the duty of the Ordinary of the place where the first trial was held to have this declaration of nullity inscribed in the baptismal and matrimonial registers where the marriage had been recorded.[154] This detail, being administrative, may be attended to by the vicar general.[155] As causes concerning the state of a person never become settled (*res iudicata*), no matter how many sentences may have been given,[156] the sentence in a matrimonial causê is never absolutely final. There is ever the possibility of the case being reopened especially if new arguments are found.[157]

Art. 5. Avoiding Judgments

***Canon 1965.*—Si matrimonium accusatur ex defectu consensus, curet ante omnia iudex ut monitionibus opportunis partem, cuius consensus deesse affirmatur ad consensum renovandum inducat; si ex defectu formae substantialis vel ex impedimento dirimenti quod dispensari potest et solet, partes inducere studeat ad consensum in forma legitima renovandum vel ad dispensationem petendam.**

In this canon is formulated the constant policy of the Church to avoid litigation,[158] to guard the stability of the marriage state, and to validate an invalid union, thereby effecting the Sacrament of Matrimony with its God-given graçes. Bishops have ever been counseled to act first as fathers and only as a last resort accept the role of judge.[159] Modern civil courts have a similar mode of action in trying to effect a reconciliation before a decree of divorce is finally granted.

Though this directive canon serves a purpose akin to those canons suggesting ways to avoid litigations through transactions

---

[153] Canon 1889.

[154] Canon 1988.

[155] Noval, *De Iudiciis,* n. 870.

[156] Canon 1902.

[157] Canons 1989, 1903.

[158] Titus III: 2. Cf. *Didascalia,* II, n. 45 §5—Funk, *Didascalia et Constitutiones Apostolorum,* I, p. 154.

[159] deMendoza, *De Confirmando Concilio Illibertano,* I, cap. 20—Labbe, II, 155; C. of Arles (314), c. 10—Labbe, II, 472; S. C. S. Off., Instr., 1883 (ad Orient. Episc.)—*Coll.,* n. 1588. Cf. Canon 2214 §2.

and compromise by arbitration [160] it stands alone in view of the fact that matrimonial causes, so far as the dissolution of the bond is concerned, admit neither transaction [161] nor compromise in arbitration.[162] The private settlement of the parties out of court certainly has no place in a matrimonial cause concerning the severance of the bond,[163] for the divine natural law forbids such pacts.[164] And whether the marriage is ratified and consummated, merely ratified, or simply a legitimate matrimony (matrimonium legitimum)[165] it remains by natural law indissoluble.[166] If parties agree to have their ratified marriage severed by solemn religious profession or papal dispensation,[167] their agreement is lawful for the severance of the bond is not effected by private transaction.[168]

Do the words of canon 1927, *"de matrimonio dissolvendo"* exclude transaction in causes involving separation? Transaction, strictly speaking, is not admitted in cases of separation [169] but transaction in the broad sense,[170] or what is known as friendly agreement (*compositio amicabilis*),[171] may take place between the parties in those cases permitted by law and in the manner legally prescribed.[172] Likewise, compromise through arbitration has no place in matrimonial causes concerning the dissolution of the bond or separation: [173] but transaction and compromise are possible in other matrimonial causes, such as espousals [174] and settlements in matters of temporal goods.[175]

---

[160] Canons 1925-1932.

[161] Canon 1927.

[162] Canon 1930. Cf. Austrian Instruction, §200—*Coll. Lacen.*, V, 1310.

[163] DeBecker, *De Sponsalibus et Matrimonio,* p. 448 in note; Wernz-Vidal, *Ius Canonicum,* V, n. 693, note 31; VI, n. 668.

[164] Lega, *De Iudiciis Ecclesiasticis,* I, n. 10.

[165] C. 11, X, *de transact.*, I, 36.

[166] De Smet, *De Sponsalibus et Matrimonio,* n. 310 sq.

[167] Canon 1119.

[168] Cf. Noval, *De Iudiciis,* n. 725.

[169] Wernz-Vidal, *Ius Canonicum,* V, 693, note 31; DeBecker, *De Sponsalibus et Matrimonio,* p. 448 in note.

[170] Lega, *De Iudiciis Ecclesiasticis,* I, n. 6.

[171] Lega, *De Iudiciis Ecclesiasticis,* I, n. 10; Wernz-Vidal, *Ius Canonicum,* VI, n. 668; Noval, *De Iudiciis,* n. 725.

[172] Canons 1128-1132.

[173] Canon 1930; Wernz-Vidal, *Ius Canonicum,* VI, n. 681: V, n. 693, note 31; Lega, *De Iudiciis Ecclesiasticis,* I, n. 22.

[174] Austrian Instruction, §4—*Coll. Lacen.*, V, 1286.

[175] Austrian Instruction, §244—*Coll. Lacen.*, V, 1314.

Canon 1965 considers only matrimonial causes affecting the bond and then not only that litigation may be avoided but that the invalid marriage may be convalidated. Defect of consent, lack of substantial form, and invalidity due to the presence of diriment impediments from which the Church is wont to dispense, cover the cases mentioned. The obligation placed upon the judge is a grave one [176] and, considering the character of matrimony, is neither unbefitting a judge nor one which he should regularly entrust to another.[177] When a cause is brought to the attention of the diocesan curia it is generally too late to effect a reconciliation and a convalidation. Confessors and pastors have a better opportunity to adjust the matter. In this they should act prudently and cautiously. Only when they have exhausted their powers of persuasion should recourse to the ecclesiastical court be suggested.[178] If there is a defect in consent the judge will strive to have the consent renewed in the proper fashion.[179] Lack of substantial form [180] can be remedied by simple convalidation.[181] If the invalidity of the marriage arises from a diriment impediment from which the Church can and does dispense: disparity of cult, crime, consanguinity in the collateral line beyond the first degree, affinity (except in the right line, marriage having been consummated),[182] public honesty, and spiritual relationship, dispensation should be sought and the marriage convalidated simply.[183] It is to be noted that radical sanation (*sanatio in radice*) is not mentioned in canon 1965 as a method of convalidating the invalid bond. When a marriage case has been brought to the officials a radical sanation is not to be hoped for in view of the rights of the parties and the possibility that the matrimonial consent may have been withdrawn.

---

[176] Farrugia, *De Matrimonio et Causis Matrimonialibus,* n. 360; Cerato, *De Matrimonio,* n. 167.

[177] Cf. canon 1925 §3. Bassibey, *Le Mariage,* p. 132.

[178] DeBecker, *De Sponsalibus et Matrimonio,* p. 361, in note; S. C. de Sacr., Instr., of 1923, n. 10 §1—*AAS,* XV (1923), 389.

[179] Canon 1136.

[180] Canons 1094-1099.

[181] Canon 1137.

[182] Cf. canon 1045.

[183] Canons 1133-1135.

CHAPTER VI

The Documentary Process

The seventh chapter of Title XX in Book IV of the Code treats of certain matrimonial cases which are excepted from the normal judicial procedure. This simplified method of deciding marriage cases of evident nullity, a process of comparatively recent origin, is a section of importance in discussing the matrimonial competence of the diocesan curia. Discussion of these excepted cases will be divided into two parts considering:

Art. 1. The *nature* of the jurisdiction employed in these cases;

Art. 2. The consequent *interpretation* of the canons.

Art. 1. Is the Power of the Ordinary in These Excepted Cases Basically Judicial or Administrative?

It is certain that the cases grouped under this chapter of the Code are excluded from the solemnities of strictly judicial processes as outlined for trials in general (Canons 1552-1924) and for matrimonial trials in particular (Canons 1960-1989). Further, no one will deny that the method or mode or treating these excepted cases resembles administrative procedure. The real question lies, however, in the intimate nature of the authority employed by the Ordinary in deciding these cases—is it basically a *judicial* power or an *administrative* authority? The phrases "administrative process" or "administrative declaration" describe the method but do they define the nature of the jurisdiction? Processes in cases for a dispensation in a ratified but non-consummated marriage are, by method, judicial and yet the Instruction of the Sacred Congregation of the Sacraments indicates that they should rather be termed administrative processes in view of the power which finally disposes of the matter.[1]

[1] S. C. de Sacr., Instr., 1923, proem.,—*AAS*, XV (1923), 389.

It will be essayed to show that the use of the word "administrative" in connection with these excepted cases is misleading as to the *nature* of the authority employed since the power exercised in canon 1990 is *fundamentally judicial.* This will be done by a detailed examination of:

§1. The historical evidences in the development of the process;
§2. A consideration of the opinions of authors who treat this matter;
§3. The captions or inscriptions;
§4. The words of the canons, themselves;
§5. The special process in marriage cases where there is lack of proper form;
§6. A particular response of the Pontifical Commission for the Authentic Interpretation of the Code.

§1. *The historical evidences in the development of the process*—Although the proximate source of the new process is found in the Holy Office decree of June 5, 1889,[2] the earliest indications of a brief, or expeditious, form of treating matrimonial cases are found in the introduction of the summary judicial process by Clement V in the fourteenth century. Matrimonial causes, even as other causes, had been conducted with all the legal formality of the solemn trial. Once Alexander III had made inroads in legal exactions,[3] the way lay open for Clement V to inaugurate the new summary judicial process by his Constitutions "Dispendiosam"[4] and "Saepe."[5] The former was intended to terminate delay in certain trials, including matrimonial causes, by giving less attention to the solemnities of the judicial process.[6] When an explanation of the clause ". . .

[2] *Fontes,* n. 1118.

[3] C. 6, X, *de iudiciis,* II, 1.

[4] C. 2, *de iudiciis,* II, 1, in Clem.

[5] C. 2, *de verb. signif.,* V, 11, in Clem.

[6] "Dispendiosam prorogationem litium (quam interdum ex subtili ordinis juduciarii observatione causarum docet experientia provenire) restringere in subscriptis casibus cupientes, statuimus: ut in causis . . . super matrimoniis vel usuris, et eas quoquomodo tangentibus, ventilandis, procedi valeat de cetero simpliciter et de plano ac sine strepitu iudicii et figura, volentes non solum ad futura negotia, sed etiam ad praesentia, et adhuc etiam per appellationem pendentia hoc extendi."—C. 2, *de iudiciis,* II, 1, in Clem.

simpliciter et de plano ac sine strepitu et figura iudicii procedi mandamus . . ." was asked, Clement showed in the Constitution "Saepe" that it meant the avoiding of delay by dispensing with the minutiae of forensic procedure without sacrificing necessary proofs or precluding legitimate defense.[7] Though this summary procedure was urged, it was not forbidden, should the parties agree, to observe, in whole or in part, the solemn formalities of a trial; nor would such action render the process null or even voidable. A summary judgment was not the omission of all legal formality but of some *determined* accidental requirements. Neither was it an administrative process.

When, in 1741, Benedict XIV gave to the Church his celebrated Constitution "Dei miseratione"[8] as the standard law for all future matrimonial causes, he provided a sure but not an expeditious treatment for cases of nullity. Insistence was placed on the need of two conformable sentences before the invalidity of the marriage bond was juridically admitted. Authorities disagreed as to whether or not the new legislation abolished the summary judicial procedure in matrimonial causes.[9] But one thing was beyond doubt. Two conformable sentences of nullity were always necessary whether the invalidity was patent or not.[10] The Constitution met the needs of the times and yet marriage causes could occur where the insistence on two sentences would cause a needless loss of time and expense as when the invalidity of the bond was notoriously evident.

Between the promulgation of the Benedictine Constitution and the Holy Office decree of June 5, 1889, a gradual but effec-

---

[7] C. 2, *de verb. signif.*, V, 11, in Clem.

[8] *Fontes*, n. 318.

[9] Bouix, *De Iudiciis Ecclesiasticis,* II, p. 445, admitted that the question was not definitely settled in the Constitution, yet remarked that for all practical purposes the summary process should not be used lest the entire proceeding be assailed as irregular. Feije, *De Impedimentis et Dispensationibus Matrimonialibus,* n. 593, held that the summary process might be employed as long as the prescriptions of the Benedictine constitution were observed. This latter opinion was preferred. Cf. Austrian Instruction, n. 193 sq.; cf. Wernz, *Ius Decretalium,* IV, n. 747, note 88; Lega, *De Iudiciis Ecclesiasticis,* II, n. 361.

[10] ". . . nolentes omnino, ut ullo in casu Matrimonii vinculum dissolutum censeatur, nisi duo iudicata, vel resolutiones, aut Sententiae penitus similes, et conformes, a quibus neque Pars, neque Defensor Matrimonii crediderit appellandum, emanaverint." Const., *Dei miseratione,* §14—*Fontes,* n. 318.

tive weakening of the rigor of matrimonial procedure was taking place in cases of obvious invalidity. Benedict XIV, himself, allowed the nullity of a marriage to stand after one sentence only had been given by the Sacred Congregation of the Council and granted the parties freedom to remarry.[11] The previous year he had allowed the Sacred Congregation of the Council to accept the judicial testimony of a witness who had responded to proposed articles but not to any interrogations.[12] In 1788 the Sacred Council disregarded the prescriptions of the Benedictine Constitution in a case of evident nullity when a bishop, in proposing the matter to Rome, observed that the case would never be terminated if it had to be subjected to the usual procedure.[13] In all these cases it was the Holy See that considered the advisability of disregarding the Benedictine regulations when the burdensome prescriptions of the law did not contribute to the establishment of the truth of the case. Soon, however, indults were granted to various bishops allowing them in certain cases to omit some formalities of the customary process.

On November 13, 1793, the bishop of Agria sought enlightenment of the Holy See as how to proceed in the cases of those people who, when a first marriage had been dissolved by the sentence of a civil court or a non-Catholic consistory, were desirous of contracting a second alliance. The instruction of the Holy Office, under the date of August 28, 1794, explained to the bishop that the sentences of civil and non-Catholic tribunals carried no authority in the eyes of the Church. The bishop must examine each case to determine whether a diriment canonical impediment had rendered the prior union invalid. In this judgment (*in huiusmodi iudicio instituendo*) the acts of the other tribunals might be accepted as extrajudicial proofs. In view of the peculiar circumstances which the bishop's query had set forth, the Holy See granted him the quinquennial faculties of proceeding in a summary judgment in the examination of these impediments as often as no other course lay open, yet

---

[11] Benedict XIV, decretum, *Etsi matrimonialis,* Sept. 27, 1755—*Bullarium Benedicti XIV*, III, pars II, p. 287.

[12] Cf. S. C. C., Baren., March 16, May 4, 1754—*Thesaur. Resol. S. C. C.*, t. 18, pp. 25, 33.

[13] S. C. C., Santandrien, Apr. 26, July 12, Aug. 30, 1788—*NRT*, XX (1888), 624.

always with the assistance of the defensor of the bond.[14] The bishop's failure to comprehend the necessity and the sense of this instruction is given as the reason prompting further inquiries of the Holy See in August of 1794.

The reply of the Holy Office given in 1795 recounts the two doubts which had been proposed, viz., that the bishop could not understand the *need* of these special faculties since he thought that all local Ordinaries had the native faculty of judging the validity of marriages according to the prescribed form of ecclesiastical law and further that the bishop failed to understand the genuine sense of the conceded faculties. The Congregation reviewed the regulations of the Benedictine Constitution and expressed amazement at the so-called native faculties of local Ordinaries. Untoward circumstances might permit local Ordinaries to deviate somewhat from the rigor of the normal process which, *per se,* all Ordinaries were obliged to observe unless they enjoyed a special concession from the Holy See. The faculties which had been granted to the Bishop of Agria were explained as permitting him to disregard the prescriptions of the Constitution "Dei miseratione" provided the sense of this papal document was observed in the substantial points of the judgment, namely, that the judicial order and form were observed in some way, omitting the citation and extrajudicial interrogation of the other spouse when prudence and necessity urged. But never were the offices of the defensor of the bond to be omitted. The defensor was to lay his objections candidly before the bishop. Notwithstanding objections raised by the defensor, the bishop of Agria, if he believed the marriage null, could, removing the appeal, proceed to the solution of the matter.[15]

---

[14] ". . . facultatem ad quinquennium tibi impertitur procedendi summarie instituto iudicio in horum impedimentorum examine, quoties aliter fieri nequeat, deputata tamen persona aliqua, qui . . . defensoris Matrimoniorum munere fungatur."—Roskovany, *Matrimonium in Ecclesia Catholica,* I, p. 294. Cf. Bassibey, *Le Mariage,* p. 35.

[15] "En quomodo iuxta apostolicas sanctiones quilibet Ordinarius facultatem nativam habet iudicandi in hisce causis matrimonialibus. Ast quando alicubi tristissimae urgent circumstantiae, ob quas praescripta iudicialis tessera servari nequeat, Ordinariis succurritur epikeia legis, elargiendo nimirum eis extraordinarias facultates recedendi quanto minus fieri possit ab ordine antefacto, quibus quidem facultatibus quilibet Ordinarius, seorsum a speciali S. Sedia concessione, certo certius destituitur . . . dum indultum ei fuit . . . recedere ab enuntiata tessera, modo

The request of the bishop of Sonora, Mexico, in 1848 is seen as another stage in the history of the shorter process which is had today. The bishop found the necessity of two conformable sentences burdensome and detrimental to the common good when the nullity of the marriage was evident. He cited two cases of professed religious in major orders who had publicly contracted marriages which were most clearly invalid, and asked the Sacred Congregation of the Council to declare that in such evident and notorious cases, in which the invalidity of the marriage could in no wise be concealed, the Benedictine regulation, requiring an appeal and two conformable sentences, need not be observed, or if such a declaration already existed, that he be acquainted of it. After discussing the question the Congregation decided that the form demanded by Benedict XIV must be observed though it seemed inclined to make some concession in the matter. The response was *"Negative et ad mentem."* [16] The mind of the consultors did not appear in the Thesaurus with the response but is found in the periodical *La Correspondence de Rome*, where the Congregation, though unwilling to declare that the Benedictine regulations did not hold, apparently heeded the bishop's request by allowing him to send the case for the second sentence to a nearby bishop instead of the distant metropolitan curia or to pass the second sentence himself, being assisted in this second hearing by priests who had taken no part in the first trial and sentence.[17]

---

tamen servet quod iuxta laudati Pontificis sensum ad substantiam pertinet horum iudiciorum, nempe ut, quomodolibet posthabito iudiciali ordine et forma, omissa quoque, si prudentia aut necessitas exigat, citatione seu extraiudiciali interpellatione alterius coniugis, non omittatur saltem deputatio probi hominis scientia iuris canonici praediti, qui rem totam callens validitatem matrimonii pro viribus et quantum honesto fieri potest protueatur, omnia, quae in id conferunt, diligenter persequatur, eidemque Episcopo ingenue aperiat; quodsi haud obstante hoc defensoris opere Episcopus credat matrimonium ei exhibitum esse nullum, possit remota appellatione ad solutionem procedere." S. C. S. Off., response 1795 to the Bishop of Agria—Roskovany, *Matrimonium in Ecclesia Catholica,* I, p. 297.

[16] *Thesaur. Resol. S. C. C.,* Aug. 26, 1848, t. 108, p. 362. Cf. *NRT*, XX (1888), 615.

[17] ". . . de demander à Sa Sainteté un indult, pour autoriser Monseigneur l'Évêque de Sonora à confier la seconde sentence conforme à un Évêque voisin, vu l'éloigement du Métropolitain, ou bien de se réserver cette second sentence, en se faisant assister de quelques prêtres,

Though the Sacred Congregation of the Council, itself, was wont to observe the requirements of the two conformable sentences even in cases of evident nullity [18] (yet the Congregation had previously deviated from the normal procedure in some particular cases), a case of bigamous marriage is reported to have been decided in 1869 by the first tribunal giving the two sentences itself without an appeal to the court of second instance.[19] The obligation of an appeal and a second conformable sentence was not so burdensome at Rome or in those diocesan courts where the metropolitan tribunal was not far distant. But in cases where the court of second instance was remotely situated (*e.g.*, the condition explained by the Bishop of Sonora), which was most frequently the case for metropolitan tribunals for which the Sacred Congregation of the Council was the court of second instance, the rigor of the normal process was burdensome and not at all in the interests of souls.

The practice of the Holy See was ever to insist upon the prescriptions of the Benedictine Constitution though now and then relaxations of the law were given in particular instances. This attitude is further typified in two cases which occurred in France about the year 1887. In that year the Paris Curia treated a case where the marriage was so evidently null by reason of the diriment impediment of consanguinity that the defensor offered no objection and appealed the sentence to the Sacred Congregation of the Council merely to fulfill the letter of the law. The case had to await its turn at Rome and after some delay the inevitable conforming sentence was returned. Within a few months a similar case was presented and the Paris Tribunal, hoping to expedite the affair, sent a letter to the Holy See explaining the case and asking permission to have the second sentence passed by a neighboring episcopal curia or some metropolitan court which the Sacred Congregation of the Council might designate unless, as an alternative, the Holy See would admit the first sentence as final in view of the evident nullity of the marriage. This request, which bears a resemblance to

---

qui n'auront pas pris part à la première sentence."—*Correspondence de Rome,* tom I, 2 ed. (1848-1849-1850), p. 33.

[18] *E. g.,* S. C. C., Teatina, July 18, 1765, where a case of a marriage evidently null by reason of bigamy was tried twice.—*Thesarus Resol. S. C. C.,* t. 30, p. 130.

[19] *NRT,* XX (1888), 629.

indult granted the Bishop of Sonora, was denied with the response *"non expedire."* [20] The officials were preparing to dispatch the acts of the cause to Rome but upon hearing of an indult granted the bishop of Fort Wayne [21] asked the Holy See to consider the one sentence as final. This time the request was granted.[22]

The other case is found in the query addressed to the Holy See by a French bishop asking how he would proceed in establishing the freedom to marry in the following case. The wife of a soldier, whose death in battle had been indicated by several sources, wished to remarry. The Holy Office replied, April 27, 1867, that the bishop could permit the woman to contract a second union provided authentic documents and reliable witnesses established summarily and extrajudicially, at least, not only the indications of the soldier-husband's death, as explained in the query, but also indications that the man had the sincere will of returning home and had no reason for remaining away from his family.[23]

In comparing the two cases occurring in the same country and at about the same time it will not be amiss to direct attention to the fact that the Benedictine legislation was not relaxed in the case presented by the Parisian tribunal which concerned the *validity* of an existing marriage while a brief process was tolerated in the other case which turned on the *existence* of the marriage. These cases present two distinct questions as a later response of the Sacred Congregation of the Council was to indicate.[24]

Several rescripts to bishops during the year immediately preceding that in which the Holy Office decree was promulgated, have an important place in the development of the new process. The request, which a Vicar General directed to the Holy See, set forth the following case. A marriage had been

---

[20] *LCC,* XIII (1890), 22.

[21] Mar. 20, 1889—*Fontes,* n. 1114.

[22] S. C. S. Off., Dec. 18, 1889—*LCC,* XIII (1890), 24.

[23] "Dummodo ex authenticis documentis et ex testibus fide dignis saltem summarie et extraiudicialiter constet non solum de iis quae ab Episcopo exponuntur, sed insuper N. N. sincero animo prosequuntum fuisse uxorem et liberos, neque ullam adfuisse causam quare eos deseret, permitti posse Oratrici, ..."—*NRT,* XX (1888), 630. Cf. Bassibey, *Le Mariage,* n. 469.

[24] S. C. C., Dec. 14, 1889—*ASS,* XXII, 553.

contracted by parties who were affected by the impediment of consanguinity. No dispensation had been sought. A civil divorce followed. Now the woman was about to marry civilly. The ecclesiastical authorities found it impossible to observe the normal process as time did not permit and as the people, not appreciating the situation, were fully determined to have the wedding ceremony performed outside the Church rather than postpone it and spend time and money on an ecclesiastical process. Wherefore, the Vicar General requested faculties to examine the case extrajudicially and then pronounce the finding (*de nullitate prioris matrimonii extraiudicialiter cognoscendi, eamque pronunciandi modo de ea constet*). The Holy Office under the date of February 1, 1888, replied that the woman could be permitted to enter the second union provided the existence of the impediment and the failure to obtain a dispensation were established through a process held in the Curia.[25] During the subsequent month of the same year the Holy Office replied to another query from France. A woman had civilly married a man who had already been married. The fact of the man's bigamy was notorious as he had been condemned by a civil court. The woman now wished to remarry yet hesitated to place her case before the ecclesiastical court in view of the expenses and inconveniences. The Vicar General asked that the woman be declared free to remarry without an observance of the form required by the Constitution "Dei miseratione." The Holy Office sent its reply, March 23, 1888, stating that the woman might be given a testimonial of her freedom to marry provided that the impediment of ligamen was proven in a process which was, at least, summary and extrajudicial.[26]

A response of the Holy Office to the Bishop of Angoulême is couched in language practically identical to that which it used in the general decree published nine months later. The Vicar General of the diocese of Angoulême had addressed the Holy See on March 9, 1888, asking for the faculty of pronouncing a

[25] "Dummodo ex processu in Curia faciendo constet de existentia impedimenti, prout in precibus, et nullam obtentam fuisse dispensationem, permitti posse mulieri transitum ad alias nuptias."—*NRT*, XX (1888), 631.

[26] "Quod dummodo ex processu saltem summario et extraiudiciali constet de impedimento ligaminis, detur mulieri documentum libertatis." —*NRT*, XX (1888), 632.

definitive sentence in matrimonial causes of evident nullity without observing the usual regulations, especially those of the Constitution "Dei miseratione" requiring an appeal and second sentence.[27] The widespread evil of civil divorce was leading to many second marriages and the disposal of the numerous cases which were presented to the local curia created a problem if the normal procedure was to be observed. The response bearing the date of September 5, 1888, merits close attention:

> Provided there is question of the impediment of consanguinity, affinity from lawful intercourse, spiritual relationship, ligamen, disparity of cult (unless the point concerns the validity of a baptism, which matter must always be presented to the Holy See) and clandestinity; and further provided that from authentic documents or witnesses worthy of faith, certainty is clearly established concerning the existence of the impediment and the lack of a dispensation or sanation; the faculty is granted of proceeding to a definitive sentence without an appeal, omitting the form of the Benedictine Constitution *Dei miseratione,* but with the active assistance of the defender of the bond in each case.[28]

In the United States some non-Catholics, who had civilly married and later been civilly divorced, were converted to the faith. At the time of their conversion they had already remarried or intended to remarry. Were the first marriages valid

---

[27] ". . . pro facultate ferendi definitivam sententiam in matrimonialibus causis, omissis solemnitatibus a iure praescriptis, praesertim a Constitutione *Dei miseratione,* quando de nullitate matrimonii certo constet, . . ." S. C. S. Off., Sept. 5, 1888—*NRT,* XXVI (1894), 26.

[28] "Dummodo agatur de impedimentis consanguinitatis, affinitatis ex copula licita, cognationis spiritualis, ligaminis, disparitatis cultus (dummodo non agatur de valore baptismi forsitan collati, quo in casu semper recurrendum erit ad Sanctam Sedem), et clandestinitatis; atque ex authenticis documentis vel ex testibus fide dignis certo omnino constet de existentia impedimenti, et de dispensatione aut sanatione super eo non concessa, supplicandum Sanctissimo pro facultati procedendi ad sententiam definitivam absque appellatione, non forma Benedictinae Constitutionis Dei miseratione, adhibito tamen et audito in singulis casibus matrimonialis vinculi Defensore.

Eadem die et feria.

Facta de his omnibus Smo. D. N. Leone PP. XIII relatione, Eadem Sanctitas Sua resolutionem Emum. Patrum approbavit et benigne concessit petitam facultatem."—*NRT,* XX (1888), 633; XXVI (1894), 26.

as contracts or as Sacraments? The ecclesiastical authorities had been asked to examine the former marriages to ascertain the freedom of the converts to contract the second union. The bishop of Fort Wayne, Indiana, asked the Holy Office: "Granting that documents and certain proofs (admitted by the episcopal curia and the defensor) show the certain nullity of the first marriage due to the impediment of ligamen or disparity of cult, was there need of an appeal by the defensor and the judgment of the court of second instance as prescribed by the Benedictine regulations in cases of the invalidity of marriages contracted in the Church (*in facie Ecclesiae*): or would it suffice that the first union be clearly shown as absolutely invalid, so that the court of second instance need not be approached?" The reply came that the case need not be appealed provided that by a process, at least extrajudicial, the invalidity of the first marriage due to a pre-existing diriment impediment, was clearly proven.[29]

The Holy Office on the fifth of June in 1889 issued a general decree allowing that where the existence of the impediment of disparity of cult, ligamen (the first spouse still living), consanguinity, affinity from lawful intercourse, spiritual relationship, or the impediment of clandestinity (non-observance of the form prescribed by the decree Tametsi in places where it was in force by reason of publication or custom), could be proven by certain and authentic documents, or lacking these, by certain arguments, adduced to show that these impediments had existed and were not dispensed from, then the Ordinary, omitting the solemnities required by the Constitution *Dei miseratione,* with the intervention of the defender of the bond, could declare the marriage *invalid and a second sentence was unnecessary.*[30]

---

[29] "Posito tamen quod ex documentis et probationibus certis a curia episcopali et a defensore matrimonii admissis, constet primum matrimonium vel propter bigamiam alterius partis, vel propter cultus disparitatem fuisse certe nullum, requiritne appellatio defensoris et iudicium in secunda instantia a Benedicto XIV praescriptum in casu de nullitate matrimonii in facie Ecclesiae initi? An sufficit certe constare primum matrimonium fuisse absolute nullum, ita ut nulla requiratur secunda instantia et iudicium? Resp. Dummodo per processum saltem extraiudicialem certo constet de nullitate matrimonii ob praeexistens dirimens impedimentum evidenter comprobatum: Negative." S. C. S. Off., March 20, 1889—*Fontes,* n. 1114. Cf. *AER,* V (1891), 388.

[30] "Quando agitur de impedimento disparitatis cultus, et evidenter constat unam partem esse baptizatam, et alteram non fuisse baptizatam; quando agitur de impedimento ligaminis, et certo constat primum coniu-

At last after the way had been prepared by a number of particular concessions the rigor of the procedure demanded by the Constitution *Dei miseratione* of Benedict XIV, had been mitigated by a general decree. Some of the documents playing a part in effecting the change have been noticed. No doubt there are many more which by reason of their particular nature will be found only in diocesan archives or in local periodicals of those years between 1741 and 1889. Among the documents which have been seen, the rescript to the Bishop of Angoulême on September 5, 1888, expresses the mind of the Holy Office at a period some nine months before the general decree was issued. The similarities and divergencies in the two documents—the one a particular dispensation, the other a general dispensation—are worthy of attention.

Both enumerate the same six impediments. Cases of disparity of cult were restricted to those where the consideration hinged on the fact of baptism. Both rescripts indicate this, albeit in different expressions. The particular response mentions the "impediment of clandestinity" while the later decree explains it as applying to cases where the decree *Tametsi* was in force either by direct promulgation or by customary observance. The parity placed on the testimony of documents and that of worthy witnesses in the earlier letter is lessened by the general rescript which subordinates the testimony of witnesses to that of the documents without doing away altogether with oral testimony. The defender of the bond is ranked an important personage in both documents. The particular rescript mentions the lack of a dispensation or a sanation. That a sanation is not recounted in the general decree is not to be wondered since a dispensation is the ordinary method of removing canonical incapacities. The real distinction is seen in the

---

gem esse legitimum et adhuc vivere; quando denique agitur de consanguinitate aut affinitate ex copula licita, aut etiam de cognatione spirituali, vel de impedimento clandestinitatis in locis ubi decretum Trident. Tametsi publicatum est, vel uti tale diu observatur, dummodo ex certo et authentico documento, vel, in huius defectu, ex certis argumentis evidenter constet de existentia hiuismodi impedimentorum super quibus Ecclesiae auctoritate dispensatum non fuerit; hisce in casibus, praetermissis solemnitatibus in Constitutione Apostolica Dei miseratione requisitis, matrimonium poterit ab Ordinariis declari nullum, cum interventu tamen defensoris vinculi matrimonialis, quin opus sit secunda sententia." S. C. S. Off., June 5, 1889—*Fontes,* n. 1118.

conclusions of both rescripts. The reply to the Bishop of Angoulême allowed the bishop to give the final sentence, the necessity of an appeal being removed (*ad sententiam definitivam absque appellatione*). The general decree stated that Ordinaries can declare (the word declare seemingly indicates the *finality* of the *one* sentence) the marriage invalid. The general decree did not say, however, that appeal was removed. Indeed it never mentioned the word *appeal.* But it did say that a second sentence (evidently the first was considered a judicial act) was not necessary.[31]

The general decree of June 5, 1889, did not distinguish cases where the question concerned the *existence* of the marriage (permission to pass to second nuptials on the supposed death of the former spouse) and those wherein the *validity* of the marriage was the point at issue. In the replies to particular queries the Holy Office had shown itself more lenient in allowing extrajudicial procedure in the former cases than in the latter.[32] Most of the cases which have been cited were those in which the validity of an existing union was questioned and the particular concessions relieved the Ordinaries from the necessity of an appeal and a second sentence. It was in this sense that the new decree was received, so that should the defensor conscientiously believe the marriage valid he could and should appeal.[33] This notion is borne out by the response to the query of the Bishop of Breslau, given by the Sacred Congregation of the Council on December 14, 1889, which declared that the process to establish the freedom of a person whose spouse was supposedly deceased might be effected in an extrajudicial manner and without the presence of the defensor of the bond.[34]

The history of the new process from the decree of 1889 up

[31] ". . . ab Ordinariis *declarari* nullum, cum interventu tamen defensoris vinculi matrimonialis, quin opus sit secunda sententia." S. C. S. Off., decree, June 5, 1889—*Fontes*, n. 1118.

[32] Case of existence of marriage, cf. S. C. S. Off., April 27, 1887—*NRT*, XX (1888), 630, which is rather in derogation of Holy Office instructions of Aug. 21, 1670 (*Fontes*, n. 742), and of Feb. 24, 1847 (*Fontes*, n. 900), than of the Benedictine Constitution *Dei miseratione* which considered the validity of an existing marriage.

[33] *LCC*, XIII (1890), 223. Peries, *Procédure Canonique*, n. 128.

[34] *ASS*, XXII, 553. From this it is seen that a parity between cases concerning nullity of the bond and those directed against existence of marriage is unwarranted. Cf. *LCC*, XIII (1890), 20.

to its incorporation into the Code now claims attention. It was inevitable that some doubts as to the employment of the process would arise in the course of time. The Archbishop of Warsaw submitted a question to the Sacred Congregation on November 18, 1893, in which he cited the decree and asked if it were universal in application. The query evidently came within the scope of the Holy Office so that the Sacred Congregation of the Council remitted the matter to that body and received an affirmative response on February 19, 1894, to the question: "Whether the Holy Office decree of June 5, 1889, is general for the universal Church so that in judicial practice it is permissible to omit certain prescriptions of the Benedictine Constitution and terminate the cause by one sentence?" [35]

A point may be noted here. In it may be seen the reason why the "impediment of clandestinity" was omitted when canon 1990 was formulated. Under the decree *Tametsi* there were many possibilities for confusion. It must be recalled that the exemption of one party to the marriage from the form prescribed in the decree *Tametsi* was communicated to a party who was otherwise obliged to observe the definite form.[36] The treatment of marriage cases between Catholics and heretics, civilly contracted, caused concern in the province of Cologne so that the Archbishop addressed the Holy Office in a letter on December 18, 1891, asking how a summary process could be instituted without obeying the prescriptions of the Benedictine Constitution.[37] The Holy Office on July 2, 1892, granted the Archbishop of Cologne and his suffragans the faculty to treat these cases providing the defensor was present and that by extrajudicial acts and other possible means, clear and conclusive proofs were never lacking.[38] Apparently the question

[35] "An decretum S. O., 5 Iunii 1889 generale pro universa Ecclesia eatenus sit, ut in praxi iudiciali liceat praetermittere quaedam praescripta Const. Benedictinae, causamque una sententia claudere? Affirmative."—*ASS*, XXVII, 142.

[36] Cf. Benedict XIV, *Matrimonia*, Nov. 4, 1741—*Coll.*, n. 1420; Pius VIII, Litt. ap., *Litteris*, Mar. 25, 1830—*Fontes*, n. 482; Cappello, *De Sacramentis*, III, n. 659-4°.

[37] Two dubia were submitted. The one discussed here is the second. "I. Quis sit Ordinarius coram quo processus huiusmodi instituendus sit? II. Qua summaria ratione idem processus instrui valeat praeter normas in Benedictina Constitutione praestitutas?"—*NRT*, XXVI (1894), 36.

[38] "Ad II . . . dummodo numquam deficiat matrimonii defensor, qui munere suo fungatur ad tramites iuris, et extraiudicialibus saltem

was neither asked nor answered with any relation to the decree of 1889. An attempt to interpret this indult in the light of that decree seems unwarranted.[39] So this indult to the province of Cologne is mentioned here to show that it is not introducing the note of an administrative, or extrajudicial, power into the decree of 1889. It has no direct connection with that decree: civil marriage contracts were regarded at the time as empty ceremonies and the declaration of nullity in such cases in those places where the decree *Tametsi* was in force did not demand the observance of the Benedictine Constitution,[40] to say nothing of the prescriptions of the decree of 1889 which was but a general dispensation mitigating the rigors of the Constitution *Dei miseratione.*

By far the most important clue to the nature of the power employed in the process introduced by the decree of 1889 is to be found in the reply accorded the Bishop of Albany by the Holy Office on June 10, 1896. The bishop, citing a local case where the existence of the impediment of disparity of cult had been established through the offices of a layman, having no special delegation for the matter, asked whether not only a summary but also an extrajudicial (administrative) process might be employed in establishing the impediment of disparity of cult. The response distinguishes the prenuptial investigation where the parties are in no wise suspected of being incapacitated by the impediment of ligamen from the establishment of the impediment for the purpose of declaring the nullity of a pre-existing marriage. In the former case the inquiry can be made even extrajudicially and without the necessity of special delegation. In the latter case, which is the point under consideration in this chapter, the Holy Office refers to the response given the Bishop of Fort Wayne, March 20, 1889, and the general decree of June 5, 1889. It then adds that the process can be instituted in a summary and extrajudicial manner (*modo*), omitting the requisite solemnities of the Benedictine Constitution *providing, however, that the judicial form is always*

actis atque omni alio quo fieri poterit modo suppleatur, ita ut numquam desint clarae concludentes probationes."—*NRT,* XXVI (1894), 24.

[39] Cf. *NRT,* XXVI (1894), 36.

[40] *NRT,* XX (1888), 621; XXVI (1894), 25. Cf. S. C. S. Off., to Paris, April 6, 1895—Bassibey, *Le Mariage,* p. 75.

observed in substantial matters, and the intervention of the defender of the bond is had: if proof of the existing impediment is clearly established, the Ordinary can proceed to pronounce a *sentence* of nullity.[41]

This particular response, coming as it does after the decree of 1889 and in a way clarifying it, indicates that the new process is not strictly administrative as is the usual investigation of the freedom to marry (*status liber*). Though the query implies that those asking the question distinguished between a summary (judicial) and an extrajudicial (administrative) process, the reply allows the use of a summary and extrajudicial method (*modo*). Whether this means a combined summary judicial and extrajudicial manner or, on the other hand, a summary extrajudicial method is not clear. Yet one thing is certain. The process is *substantially judicial* as the form of a judgment is required as far as essentials are concerned (*semper requiritur forma iudicii, quoad substantialia*). Further the response states that the Ordinary can pronounce *sentence* of nullity.

Early in the present century several French bishops inquired of the Holy Office as to the application of the brief process in cases of clandestinity involving the absence of the proper pastor, or the properly delegated priest, at the marriage of those people who were held to observe the regulations of the decree *Tametsi* but who contracted marriage outside their proper residence in places where the provisions of the Tridentine decree did not apply. To their queries whether the defensor could refrain from an appeal in these cases; whether the solemn procedure could be omitted when it was known that the parties went away "*in fraudem legis*"; whether the defensor was ex-

---

[41] "Si vero agatur de investigando impedimento disparitatis cultus ad effectum declarandi nullitatem vinculi praeexistentis, quo contrahere volentes sunt innodati, licet, uti iam ab anno 1889 sub die 20 Martii, et iterum sub die 5 Iunii statuit haec ipsa S. Officii Congregatio, procedi possit praetermissis solemnitatibus in Constitutione *Dei miseratione* requisitis, modo summario et extraiudiciali; semper tamen forma iudicialis quoad substantialia servari debet, cum interventu defensoris vinculi matrimonialis; et, si evidenter de impedimenti existentia constet, Ordinarius procedere potest ad proferendam nullitatis sententiam. Planum est ex iis deducere quod in hoc secundo casu semper requiritur forma iudicii, quoad substantialia, nec non interventus defensoris vinculi matrimonialis; quod profecto praestari a nemine poterit, nisi prius habita speciali ac regulari delegatione."—*Fontes,* n. 1180.

cused from appealing when the first trial, held with all the requisite solemnities, proved beyond a doubt the invalidity of the marriage due to lack of proper form; whether the curtailed process was applicable when the marriage ceremony had taken place before a non-Catholic minister or a civil magistrate: the Holy Office referred to the decree of 1889 and insisted that the brief method applied only in cases where the existence of the impediment was certain and evident and, if certitude was not obtainable, the defensor had the obligation of appealing to the court of second instance.[42] A few years later the Holy Office in answer to a dubium admitted that the new process could be employed where the invalid granting of a dispensation from the impediment of disparity of cult was established, without the need of bringing each case to the Holy See for a definitive *sentence.*[43] This terminates a survey of the development of the new process bringing the matter within the time when the codification of canon law was under way. In the reorganization of the Roman Curia Pius X tried to effect the distinction in ecclesiastical authority between judicial and administrative power,[44] by designating the competence of the various Roman Congregations as administrative and that of the Tribunals as judicial.[45] The distinction, usually based on the character of the organization handling the matter or the form of the process, was not exactly established at the Roman Curia and when it passed into the Code the limitations were less recognizable.[46]

The history of the new procedure thwarts any attempt to project the opinion that administrative power is fundamentally operative in these canons on excepted cases. There are several matrimonial proceedings that are rightly termed administrative and which are by nature not judicial. The history just sketched has indicated some. The process observed in the prenuptial investigation of the freedom to marry (*status liber*) is administrative by nature:[47] the process establishing the freedom to

---

[42] S. C. S. Off., March 27, 1901—*Fontes,* n. 1251.

[43] S. C. S. Off., June 21, 1912—*Fontes,* n. 1293.

[44] Const. *Sapienti Consilio,* June 29, 1908—*Fontes,* n. 682. Monin, *De Curia Romana,* p. 176.

[45] Cf. Maroto, *Institutiones Iuris Canonici,* II, p. 259.

[46] Biccari, "Ricorsi alla Santa Sede,"—*Perfice Munus,* II (1927), 908.

[47] Canons 1019-1034. S. C. S. Off., June 10, 1896—*Fontes,* n. 1180. Cf. Cappello, *De Sacramentis,* III, nn. 147-3; 158.

marry in the event of the alleged death of the former spouse (a question concerning the *existence* of a marriage) is administrative by nature:[48] the procedure in declaring a marriage null by reason of the absence of due form, as expressed in the decision of the Pontifical Commission for the Authentic Interpretation of the Code October 16, 1919, is administrative by nature and the history just traced indicated the inclination of the process toward that character.[49] But there is no historical justification for an opinion that administrative power is operative in these excepted cases where the question concerns the *validity* of existing marriages or for denying that the process is fundamentally a judicial procedure. The word "administrative" may be the unhappy expression describing the manner used in these cases but it must not be confused with the fundamental nature of the authority involved. Authors[50] agree that the decree of 1889 merely did away with necessity of an appeal and a second sentence in cases of evident nullity though the usual procedure, solemn judicial or as was more usual summary judicial[51] manner was employed. The Code merged the two forms of judgments and as a consequence the term "summary" does not mean the same now as previously when it designated a summary judicial process. Today the term is rather applied to administrative processes.[52] To insist that the fundamental basis of the process has been completely changed is an assumption entirely unwarranted.[53]

§2. *A survey of the views of authors on the nature of these excepted cases*—As the proposition of this chapter is a determination of the fundamental authority, or power, employed in these excepted cases, it is well to consider what modern commentators believe to be the nature of the power employed in canon 1990.

---

[48] Cf. Canons 1142, 1069 §2, 1053. S. C. S. Off., Apr. 27, 1887—*NRT*, XX (1888), 630. Cf. Desmet, *De Sponsalibus et Matrimonio*, nn. 564, 702-c.

[49] S. C. S. Off., indult to Archbishop of Cologne, July 2, 1892—*NRT*, XXVII (1894), 24.

[50] Cappello, *De Sacramentis*, III (edit. 1927), n. 893; Wernz-Vidal, *Ius Canonicum*, V, n. 704; *LCC*, XIII (1890), 224.

[51] Wernz, *Ius Decretalium*, IV, n. 747, note 88.

[52] Noval, *De Iudiciis*, n. 35. Roberti, *De Processibus*, I, p. 26, note 1, marks the application as improper.

[53] Cf. Can. 6 nn. 3°, 4°.

Most authors consider the power as administrative but do not strive to establish their statements. Some entitle a paragraph "administrative declaration" and merely state that these are cases in which it is permitted to proceed in a *simple manner*, or as it is called "administrative." Nothing is mentioned as to the nature of the power,[54] except perhaps to say that no judicial process is necessary.[55] De Smet remarks that the Ordinary proceeds in a manner rather administrative:[56] Cappello notes that today the faculty of proceeding administratively is granted:[57] Lanier declares that the process is not strictly judicial but is administrative procedure which reduces itself to the bare essentials,[58] yet this author, unlike some others,[59] admits the difficulty of finding the first declaration being termed a sentence by canon 1992 yet likens it to a simple declaration.[60] Vlaming states that canon 1990 remits any solemnities previously recounted in the Code even those which belong to the judicial order generally; that this procedure is administrative and use is made only of those proofs and *formalities* which are required and suffice to give certitude as to the existence of the non-dispensed impediments. The author is not convincing for in attempting examples he immediately falls into judicial terminology speaking of the *actor* proposing the case and of the Ordinary giving a written *sentence* of the nullity. Further he allows the defensor of the bond to put questions to the parties in the presence of a *tribunal* which is either permanently erected in the diocese or has been specially constituted for this purpose.[61] Surely a process administrative by nature does not allow such procedure.

Vermeersch-Creusen mention the dispute as to the nature

---

[54] Cerato, *De Matrimonio,* n. 169.

[55] Chelodi, *Ius Matrimoniale,* n. 180; Farrugia, *De Matrimonio et Causis Matrimonialibus,* nn. 164-A, 379; Wernz-Vidal, *Ius Canonicum,* V, n. 704. Cf. *Ephemerides Theologicae Lovanienses,* I (1924), 578.

[56] *De Sponsalibus et Matrimonio,* n. 702.

[57] *De Sacramentis,* III (ed. 1923), n. 892.

[58] *Guide Pratique de la Procédure Matrimoniale,* p. 2.

[59] E. g., Cappello, *De Sacramentis,* III, n. 891; Wernz-Vidal, *Ius Canonicum,* V, n. 704; Chelodi, *Ius Matrimoniale,* n. 180; who transpose the word *sentence* of Canon 1992 into *declaration.*

[60] Lanier, *Guide Pratique de la Procédure Matrimoniale,* p. 5. Yet in another place (p. 2) he terms the declaration *judicial* (déclarer juridiquement).

[61] Vlaming, *Praelectiones Iuris Matrimonii,* n. 803.

of the authority used in the process and admit that the opinion of Noval, who holds that the power is judicial, is probable. Yet Vermeersch-Creusen incline to the view that the power is administrative by stressing the word "extrajudicial" in the Holy Office decree of June 10, 1896, while overlooking the warning in the same decree that the process should be substantially judicial. Nevertheless, the *Epitome* allows oral testimony in this administrative process.[62]

Some other authors hold the view that the power in canon 1990 is really judicial. While Roberti does not treat this section directly there are indications in the first volume of his treatise *"De Processibus"* that he favors the opinion that the power is judicial. In remarking that a distinction between judicial and administrative authority is often drawn from the organization exercising the power or the form of the process, he states that the form of a process is no certain indication as that the form of a process may be restricted in a process which is truly judicial as happens in the documental process under canon 1990.[63] Blat holds that the process is judicial with the practical consequence that the vicar general is incompetent in these cases.[64] Noval defends the judicial nature of the process and advances reasons for his stand. While solemnities are omitted certain requirements such as the intervention of the Ordinary, the citation of the parties, the presence of the defensor and the provision for an appeal, provide all the essential elements to a judicial hearing. And while the procedure may be very special the requisites for a trial are had and the process is truly judicial and not administrative. Stress is laid on the word *sentence* in canon 1992 and for confirmation a comparison is instituted with the process admitted for the declaration of nullity in marriages null for lack of form as provided for in a response of the Pontifical Commission for

[62] *Epitome,* III, n. 297. Cf. *Periodica,* XIII (1925), p. (212).

[63] "Nec formae processuales cum disceptatione in contradictorio magis perfectum discrimen statuunt inter potestatem iudicialem et administrativam. Reapse formae processuales possunt in processu vere iudiciali coarctari, ut fit in processu documentali (c. 1990 ss.)."—Roberti, *De Processibus,* I, p. 67: cf. also p. 162. [In a personal communication Roberti has expressed his opinion that this process has a judicial character.]

[64] Blat, *Commentarium,* IV, n. 551.

the Interpretation of the Code in 1919.[65] This view is acceptable and, by a deeper examination and further development of details, further arguments will be adduced to prove that the power in the documental process is truly judicial.

§3. *An examination of the captions or inscriptions.*—A review of the captions of the different divisions of the Fourth Book may add to an intelligent understanding of the nature of the power exercised in deciding these excepted cases. The Code asserts[66] that ecclesiastical laws are to be understood according to the proper signification of the words considered in their text and context. The captions are to be scrutinized in the light of their *historical development* and *present arrangement.* While these inscriptions have not the force of law and do not form the context, properly speaking, to the section under consideration, for the context is composed of other canons, nevertheless the captions furnish authentic indications of the context. *"A rubro ad nigrum valet illatio,"* is an old saying.[67]

When the present Fourth Book of the codified law was submitted to the bishops in the draft of 1914 it was headed: "Book Five. On Ecclesiastical Trials" and divided into four parts, *viz.,* "I. On Trials in General; II. On Special Trials; on the criminal trial; matrimonial trial; trial of religious profession; the cause of Saints; III. On Administrative Processes; IV. On the Dismissal of Religious."[68] A revised draft in 1916 presented the following rubrics: "Book IV. On Processes" with three divisions, "I. On Trials; II. On Administrative Processes; III. On Causes of Beatification and Canonization." When the Code appeared the present arrangement was to be found. The placing of the second section in the last part with the change of caption from "On Administrative Processes" to the present wording is to be remarked.[69] Why was the substitution made? The question is proposed not because the canons under con-

---

[65] Noval, *De Iudiciis,* n. 873.

[66] Can. 18.

[67] Cf. Maroto, *Institutiones Iuris Canonici,* I, p. 155.

[68] Liber V. De Iudiciis Ecclesiasticis. I. de iudiciis in genere; II. de iudiciis specialibus; de iudicio criminali; matrimoniali et professionis religiosae; de causa sanctorum; III. de processibus administrativis; IV. de dimissione religiosorum.—*Il Monitore Ecclesiastico,* III (1921), 16.

[69] *Il Monitore Ecclesiastico,* III (1921), 16. Roberti, *De Processibus,* I, p. 26.

sideration were directly affected but that a comprehension of the term "administrative process," which is commonly applied to those processes in the third part of the fourth book, might be obtained.[70] It will readily be admitted that there is no division of power in the Church such as there is in civil government, if the sources of authority, the pope and the bishop, are considered. There is no necessity for a division for each possesses the plenitude of power—legislative, judicial, administrative, and coactive; the one, for the entire Church, the other, for his respective diocese. But what of the power when it is exercised by the different branches of the Roman Curia or by the Vicar-General or the Official? It is commonly considered that a division of ecclesiastical power into administrative authority and judicial authority is practical in these cases.[71]

In the present arrangement, the Fourth Book is entitled "On Processes" which, being a wide term, can include all types of procedure whether judicial or non-judicial.[72] Three distinct parts make up the book: "I. On Trials (*De Iudiciis*); II. On the Causes of the Beatification of the Servants of God and the Canonization of the Blessed; III. On the Manner of Proceeding in Despatching Certain Affairs or in Applying Penal Sanctions." The first part treats judicial processes wherein questions are settled after a cognition and definition according to legal prescriptions.[73] The third part treats of non-judicial (or as commonly expressed today, administrative) processes. Whether that term administrative is happily applied to all processes in the third part is left to the discussion of authorities on that section. The concern here is to show that it does not exactly designate the power employed in canons 1990-1993. In that third part of Book IV are found terms commonly accepted as non-judicial in character. For example, the process is *summary* (Can. 2142), being terminated by a *decree* against which the legal remedy is a *recourse* to the Holy See (Can. 2146 §1) and this does not generally suspend the execution of the decision (Cans., 2146 §3; 2156; 1601).

The chapter on excepted matrimonial cases is found to be

[70] Cf. Roberti, *De Processibus*, I, pp. 26, 101, 102.
[71] Cf. canons 259, 1601; 368, 1573.
[72] Noval, *De Iudiciis*, nn. 1, 5.
[73] Canon 1552. Cf. Dig. VI, 2, 12.

qualified by the several captions: Book IV. On Processes; Part I. On Trials; Section II. On the Peculiar Norms Observable in Some Certain Trials; Title XX. On Matrimonial Causes. The last or seventh chapter of this twentieth title is that about which the discussion revolves. The term "cause" is more restrictive than the word "case" and designates a matter or question submitted to judgment.[74] Indications are that the entire twentieth title deals with matrimonial causes. Can the caption of the seventh chapter support the opinion that the fundamental nature of the authority used in deciding these excepted cases is not judicial? The caption of the chapter reads "On cases excepted from the regulations heretofore laid down" (*de casibus exceptis a regulis hucusque traditis*). How deeply is the axe of exception laid to the judicial treatment of these cases? While the caption says *cases* and not *causes*, how can a *generic* word (case) coming in a subdivision restrict a *specific* term (cause) used in the grand division?[75] Indeed the cases mentioned are not excepted from all the previously related regulations. The exception indicated in the inscription is better understood in the light of the words of the first canon which have the force of law and the canon speaks of "omitting the solemnities thus far recounted."[76] The exemption is to be looked for in the accidental rather than the essential points of a trial. While the Code merged the solemn and the summary judicial processes into the present single judicial trial containing parts of both old proceedings, the exemption in the cases under consideration is seen as an omission of those parts of the present normal trial which have been taken over from the old solemn process giving a process that might be described as "summary judicial" and qualified by the term documentary. Moreover, the first canon of the chapter explicitly mentions some judicial regulations such as the citation of the parties and the presence of the defensor who is a judicial personage.

The examination of the context affords ample indications that the nature of the power in these excepted cases is funda-

---

[74] "Causa est res, seu ius deductum in iudicium."—Vives, *Compendium Iuris Canonici*, p. 409. Cf. Dig. L, 5, 8 §5. Gaius, *Institutes*, IV, §15, §53.

[75] Cf. Reg. 34, R. J. in VI°.

[76] ". . . praetermissis solemnitatibus hucusque recensitis . . ."—canon 1990.

mentally judicial. If the process were truly non-judicial or administrative in nature, its logical position would be in the third part of the Fourth Book. If the opinion is offered that these canons have been so placed in the general treatment of matrimonial causes to emphasize the exception,[77] the perusal of the captions does not mark the distinction as clearly as the fundamental difference between the judicial and administrative power demands. All the inscriptions favor the fundamentally judicial nature of the process and it remains for the proposers of the administrative manner with the implication that the process is not judicial to dislodge the favored opinion.[78]

§4. *An examination of the canons, themselves*—What indications of the nature of the authority employed are found in the canons of this chapter? Words are to be understood in their proper signification in the text.[79] The three canons shall be examined *separately* and the *general tenor* of the chapter tested in order to further an understanding of the character of the power involved.

In canon 1990 three words are found upon which the opposing theory might be rested, *viz.*, cases (*casibus*), Ordinaries (*Ordinariis*), and (*declarare*). Yet all three are ambiguous if distinctive terms are desired. A case can include, as has been seen, a judicial *cause* or an administrative (non-judicial) case; the Ordinary (i. e., the residential bishop or one in similar position) [80] having the plenitude of authority, is invested with both judicial and administrative power; and "declare" may mean either a pronouncement of a sentence (judicial) or the publication of a decree (administrative). Indeed, the word "declare" is used in the decree of 1889 where it means a judicial sentence which terminates the cause.[81] In that document the word "declare" appears to have been used instead of the phrase "pronounce sentence" to indicate that this sentence is not merely the first of two sentences but definitive or final in itself.[82] A cursory comparison of canon 1990 with canon 1986, which

---

[77] Cf. Vlaming, *Praelectiones Iuris Matrimonii*, n. 803.

[78] *Il Monitore Ecclesiastico*, III (1921), 277.

[79] Can. 18.

[80] Cf. can. 198 §1.

[81] S. C. S. Off., June 5, 1889—*Fontes*, n. 1118.

[82] Cf. canons 1868 §1, 1987.

certainly regulates a *judicial* matter, reveals the use of the word "declare" (nullitatem declaraverit) in both canons.

The indications favorable to the opinion that the power is fundamentally judicial are more numerous and convincing. The fact that documents are the only type of testimony explicitly admitted by the canon is not derogatory to the judicial nature of the process. Documentary evidence has an important and well recognized place in trials.[83] The argumentative part of a trial, or judgment,[84] may be restricted to a consideration of documentary evidence without destroying the essential elements of a trial.[85] All the essential elements of a trial are found in this canon (1990) whether they are enumerated as three: (1) citation of parties; (2) proof; (3) defense;[86] or four: (1) the object of controversy (nullity of marriage); (2) passive subjects (cited parties): (3) active subject (Ordinary): (4) legitimate form (proof by document and defense by Defender of the bond).[87] Citation is a judicial act and not a mere notification.[88] The canon allows the omission of previously mentioned *solemnities* but not of essential regulations. The presence of the defender of the marriage bond is required. This is strongly indicative that the authority deciding the matter is judicial, for the defensor is characteristically a judicial personage.[89] The defensor is employed by reason of *special* direction in processes preliminary to seeking a dispensation in a ratified but non-consummated marriage case, fundamentally an administrative procedure.[90]

If the process in excepted cases is not judicial by nature and the presence of the defender of the bond is insisted upon, a difficulty is found. The defensor is *not obliged to furnish the oath of office.* By canon 1621 the officials in a judicial process are required to take an oath of office but what is to happen in an administrative process? A defensor who has

[83] Cf. Canons 1812-1824.

[84] Canon 1552 describes rather than defines a trial (*iudicium*) as of two parts: a legitimate discussion and definition (*legitima disceptatio et definitio*).

[85] Roberti, *De Processibus,* I, pp. 56, 67.

[86] Lega, *De Iudiciis Ecclesiasticis,* I, n. 48: II, n. 361.

[87] Noval, *De Iudiciis,* n. 16.

[88] Cf. cans. 1712, 1715. Wernz-Vidal, *Ius Canonicum,* VI, n. 382.

[89] Can. 1586, 1968—2°, 1969—2°.

[90] Canon 1967: S. C. de Sacr., Instr. 1923, nn. 27-29.

been in office will have already furnished the oath but what if this is the defensor's first case? In seeking to avoid this difficulty it has been stated that although the matter is not properly judicial (therefore administrative, or non-judicial) and cannot come under the canon mentioned (Can. 1621) yet the parity of the cause, the mind of the legislator, and *the very nature of the thing*, undoubtedly demand that the defensor take the oath of office.[91] Indeed, the very nature of the matter demands that the oath be taken. If the process is judicial the difficulty vanishes. Further, as has been stated, the process held for a ratified non-consummated marriage is basically administrative. The defensor acts in such a case and takes the oath of office because the Instruction of 1923 (§19) expressly places the obligation and does this without any reference to canon 1621, whereas in other cases of parity between this process and judicial processes, canons, judicial by nature, are given as references.

Passing to canon 1991, a phrase may be found there which seems to indicate the administrative nature of the process, *viz.*, declaration (hanc declarationem). Just as the term "declare" used in the previous canon is ambiguous so also is the word "declaration" which refers to it. But the action of the defensor in "provoking" the case to the judge of second instance is nothing more than an appeal in the true sense of the term.[92] If the power in these excepted cases is administrative this action of the defensor would be a recourse against a decree.[93] An appeal suspends the sentence:[94] a recourse against a decree does not generally hinder the execution of the decree.[95] Behold an obstacle to the opinion that the authority is administrative. What general prescription of law prevents the parties to the case from accepting the declaration and remarrying immediately? The canonical principle is that a recourse is *in devolutivo tantum* unless it is expressly allowed as *in suspensivo.*

[91] "Causae enim non est proprie iudicialis: . . . manifestata enim est, ex paritate causae (!), means legislatoris, et fere natura rei postulatur ut . . . iuramentum detur."—*Periodica,* XIII (1925), p. (212).

[92] Dig. XLIX, 1, 1 §2: XLIX, 2, 1. Canons 1879, 1986.

[93] Cf. canons 345, 647 §2, n. 4, 1340 §3, 1395 §2, 1428 §3, 1601, 2146 §1, 2153 §1, 2194.

[94] Canon 1869 §2.

[95] Canon 2146 §3.

Whereas, if the power is judicial, an appeal suspends the first sentence and the parties cannot act upon it. Moreover, the very inclusion of canon 1991 allowing for the event of prudent doubt on the part of the defensor, indicates that the process is judicial since there is always a possibility of a serious controversy (*disceptatio*). Otherwise the case is provoked from the Ordinary (exercising administrative power) to the *judge* of the second instance and not to the Ordinary, as such. But a judge *per se* enjoys no administrative power. Does the character of the process undergo a fundamental change while being provoked from the Ordinary to the judge? Here is a difficulty if the process is fundamentally administrative. There is no difficulty if the authority is judicial. The same word "provoke" (*provocare*) is found in canons 1986 and 1991 and in both defines the very same action of the defensor in bringing the cause to the court of second instance.

Canon 1992, the last canon of the chapter, allows the *judge* of the next instance to *discern* in the same manner as did the Ordinary who first treated the question, whether the *sentence* is to be confirmed or whether the *cause* should be subjected to the ordinary trial. The only word in this canon which could favor the administrative nature of the process is the term *discern*. But what strength has this when the canon explicitly states that the declaration of the Ordinary in the first canon of the chapter was a *sentence?* A sentence is a legitimate pronouncement whereby a judge defines a cause proposed by litigants and treated in a judicial manner.[96] The term "declaration" apparently was used in canon 1990 to show that the sentence there was *per se* definitive or final; for, as has been noted, in the ordinary matrimonial process the sentence of the first court is not sufficient but two conformable sentences must be had.[97] Authors in writing of this canon stress the term *discern* which is an ambiguous word and entirely overlook, nay even transpose, the technical word "sentence" (*sententiam*) which the canon contains into the word "declaration" (*declarationem*).[98] If the sentence is not upheld, then the cause (*causa*)

[96] Can. 1868 §1. Cf. can. 1552 §2—1°.

[97] Canons 1986, 1987; Cf. Benedict XIV, Const., *Dei miseratione*, §14—*Fontes*, n. 318.

[98] *E.g.*, Chelodi, *Ius Matrimoniale*, n. 180; Cappello, *De Sacramentis III*, n. 891; Wernz-Vidal, *Ius Canonicum*, n. 704.

is sent to the tribunal in the place where the matter was first tried to be subjected to the normal judicial process. But note that the matter which the second judge *discerns* is called in the very words of the canon a *cause*. This is another indication that the entire process is fundamentally judicial of an extraordinary type as the solemnities of the normal matrimonial trial are omitted.

Therefore the text of these three canons furnish many indications that the process is by nature judicial. Proposers of the opposing doctrine will find meager basis in the wording of the canons to support their claims.

§5. *A consideration of the present process used in cases null by reason of lack of form*—In the recasting of the old legislation, the Code omits mention of clandestinity as found in the Holy Office decree of June 5, 1889. Could marriages null by reason of the lack of due form be treated under the process detailed in canon 1990? A dubium was proposed to the Pontifical Commission for the Authentic Interpretation of the Code asking whether the Ordinary, omitting the solemnities of the Constitution *Dei miseratione*, could declare null those marriages of Catholics (even apostates) contracted without observance of the due form (i. e., civilly or before a non-Catholic minister), provided the intervention of the defender of the bond was had, so that there was no necessity of a second sentence? The very formulation of the dubium indicates that the solemnities omitted in canon 1990 are chiefly those formerly required by the Constitution *Dei miseratione* and still required in the normal judicial matrimonial trial, the need of an appeal and a second conformable sentence.

The response to the doubt remarked that the cases mentioned required *no judicial process* or *intervention of the defensor* but were to be settled by the Ordinary himself, or by the parish priest after consultation with the Ordinary, in the investigation prior to a new marriage which is made along the lines indicated in canon 1019 sq.[99]

---

[99] "Utrum Ordinarius, praetermissis iuris solemnitatibus in Constitutione Apostolica *Dei miseratione* requisitis, matrimonium possit declarare nullum cum interventu tamen defensoris vinculi matrimonialis, quin opus sit secunda sententia, hisce in casibus, nempe:

1. Si duo catholici, in loco certe antehac obnoxio cap. *Tametsi* Conc. Tridentini, vel post Decretum *Ne Temere,* matrimonium civile tantum

What does the response indicate as to the nature of the process employed in canon 1990? Certain cases of marriages null for want of form [100] require no judicial process or intervention of the defender of the bond. The dubium had been centered about the application of canon 1990 to such cases. In the contrary sense, then, the process in canon 1990 in which the offices of the Ordinary, alone, without the intervention of the defensor, are of no avail and in which an administrative investigation (can. 1019 sq.), conducted without a previous *citation* of the parties to the case and an allowance for defense, is not permissible, must be *judicial* by nature.[101] The question implies that the process in canon 1990 is administrative with the addition of the defensor while the response intimates that the process in canon 1990 is judicial even prescinding from the presence of the defensor.

The response is best understood after a view of the history of the brief process. Returning to the historical development of the process in these excepted cases it will be instructive to look for the reasons why the marriages null for want of form are not included in canon 1990. The decree of June 5, 1889, enumerated six *impediments*, one being the absence of form as required by the decree "Tametsi." Apparently all six impediments were on an equal basis. But even before this decree of 1889 there can be noticed a tendency to single out marriages

inierunt, omisso ritu ecclesiastico, et, obtento civili divortio, novum in Ecclesia inire student matrimonium vel novum matrimonium, civiliter initum, in foro ecclesiastico convalidare.

2. Aut catholica pars, quae cum acatholica, spretis Ecclesiae legibus, in templo sectae protestanticae (in loco certe antehac obnoxio cap. *Tametsi* Conc. Tridentini, et ubi Benedictina declaratio extensa non est, vel post Decretum *Ne Temere*) matrimonium contraxit, obtento civili divortio, in facie Ecclesiae novum matrimonium cum catholico consorte inire vult.

3. Aut apostatae a fide catholica, qui in apostasia civiliter vel ritu alieno se iunxerunt, obtento civili divortio, poenitentes ad Ecclesiam redire et cum parte catholica alteras nuptias in Ecclesia celebrare desiderant.

Resp: Casus supra memorati nullum iudicialem processum requirunt aut interventum defensoris vinculi, sed resolvendi sunt ab Ordinario ipso, vel a parocho, consulto Ordinario, in praevia investigatione ad matrimonii celebrationem, de qua in can. 1019 et seqq." Pontif. Comm. Inter. Cod., Oct. 16, 1919, ad 17—*AAS*, XI (1919), 479.

[100] Cf. can. 1094 sq. N. B. The response considers only those marriages not contracted *in facie Ecclesiae*, i.e. civilly or before a non-Catholic minister.

[101] Noval, *De Iudiciis*, n. 873.

null for want of form from other cases of nullity.[102] Especially in the matter of civil marriages was there to be noted the tendency to admit extrajudicial proofs.[103] After the general decree a distinction is seen in the indult granted to the Archbishop of Cologne in which extrajudicial acts were admitted in cases of marriages of mixed religion civilly contracted.[104] The perfection of the application of the Tridentine decree "*Tametsi*" by the decree "*Ne temere*" in 1907 was sufficient to detach cases null for lack of form from the same basis as the other impediments recounted in the decree of 1889. The presumption was that these unions were not even marriages or that the very *existence* of a marriage (aside from any question of the validity of the union) was questionable. These cases were approaching the type of process used in the presumption of the death of a former spouse where no defender of the bond was required because the existence of the marriage was in question.[105] The lack of form came to be considered no longer an impediment, strictly speaking, as it had been designated in the decree of 1889 (i.e., an incapacity in the person) but rather a qualification necessarily demanded in the external manifestation of the matrimonial consent.

The absence of a requisite external act admits easier proof than the incapacity inherent in the parties who observe the required form. Is it to be wondered, then, that the one process becomes truly administrative while the other remains what it was in the decree of 1889? [106]

§6. *A particular response of the Pontifical Commission for the Authentic Interpretation of the Code*—In the year 1922 a member of the archdiocesan curia of Paris who had been both vicar general and official resigned the former office and, continuing in the capacity of official, decided matrimonial cases of evident nullity by virtue of canon 1990. His competence in these excepted cases was challenged by the defensor.[107] Ad-

[102] Cf. *NRT,* XX (1888), 621.

[103] Cf. e.g. S. C. S. Off., Mar. 23, 1888—*NRT,* XX (1888), 632.

[104] S. C. S. Off., July 2, 1892—*NRT,* XXVI (1894), 24.

[105] S. C. C., Dec. 14, 1889—*ASS,* XXII, 553.

[106] Absence of form admits an administrative process but a defect in the proper form, i.e., ceremony before an unqualified priest as witness, must be treated according to the *normal* process for it does not come under canon 1990.

[107] " . . . étant Official de la Curie de Paris, mais ayant cessé à cette

vice was sought from the Pontifical Commission for the Authentic Interpretation of the Code in a letter dated October 23, 1922. The series of questions submitted at the time is reproduced here. Apparently they had been formulated with the notion that the power utilized in canon 1990 was administrative by nature.

I.

1. Quum can. 1990 Ordinario potestatem faciat declarandi de plano nullitatem in hisce casibus, an Officialis servet facultatem diiudicandi, servato iuris ordine, huiusmodi casus qui illi delati fuerint?

Et quatenus affirmative:

2. An lata ab Officiali sententia nullitatis, teneatur Defensor vinculi ad interponendam appellationem ex officio, etsi pateat nullitatem matrimonii esse evidentem?

3. An saltem, introducta causa coram Tribunali, possit aut etiam debeat Officialis, statim ac adverterit nullitatem esse evidentem, acta causae, in quocumque statu inveniantur, tradere Ordinario qui evidentem nullitatem declaret absque solemnitatibus?

Et quatenus affirmative:

4. An Defensor vinculi, eo quod causa iudicialiter incepta fuerit, possit aut debeat huiusmodi traditioni se opponere, et deinde, lata ab Ordinario sententia appellationem ex officio necessario interponere?

5. An verba quibus utitur canon 1990 "ex certo et authentico documento" intelligenda sint strictu sensu et excludant omnem testimonialem probationem, ita ut, semel auditis testibus, sententia ab Ordinario ferri iam non possit?

II.[108]

1. Quum canon 1990 de clandestinitate taceat, et tamen afferantur adhuc nonnullae causae nullitatis ob defectum formae Tridentinae (quoad coniugia ante Decretum "Ne temere")

épouye d'étre Vicáire Général pour me consacrer exclusivement aux causes judiciaires, le droit m'a été contesté dijuger sommairement d'aprés le Canon 1990 les causes de nullité de mariage évidente."

[108] The entire set of questions is related here. This second section deals with marriage null for lack of form.

adhuc vigeat hac de re disciplina Codici anterior, iuxta Decretum Sancti Officii 5 iunii 1889, ita ut nullitatem evidentem ex capite clandestinitatis declarare possit Officìalis, nec tamen Defensor Vinculi appellare debeat ex officio?

2. An saltem, uti in praecedentibus questionibus, Officialis possit aut etiam debeat, quum nullitas matrimonii "ex certo documento" aut in huius defectu "ex certis argumentis," iuxta Decreti verba, evidens evadit, actae causae Ordinario tradere ad nullitataem declarandum, quin defensor vinculi appellationem interponere teneatur?

The Commission rearranged the questions and the President replied in two separate responses under the dates of December 19, 1923, and May 5, 1924:

Cum dubia circa causas matrimoniales quae proposuisti ad hanc Commissionem, quadam aequivocatione laborant, visum est ea posse reformari, prout sequitur:

1°—Utrum in casibus de quibus in Canone 1990, necesse sit ut loci Ordinarius per se evidentem matrimonii nullitatem declaret an id possit ipsemet Officialis?

2°—Utrum in iisdem casibus Ordinarius possit procedere ad ordinariam tramitem iuris?

3°—Cum Canon 1990 de clandestinitate taceat et tamen afferuntur adhuc nonnullae causae nullitatis ob defectum formae Tridentinae, (quoad coniugia ante decretum Ne Temere) utrum vigere de hac re disciplina Codici anterior iuxta decretum Sancti Officii, 5 Iunii 1889, ita ut nullitatem evidentem ex capite clandestinitatis declarare possit Officialis nec tamen Defensor Vinculi appellare debeat ex officio?

4°—An per iudicem secundae instantiae, de quo Can. 1991, intelligi debeat Ordinarius Dioecesis ad appellationem designatae aut Officialis, aut Tribunal Collegiale huius Dioecesis?

Porro hisce dubiis, infrascriptus Emus Commissionis Praeses respondit:

Ad 1 am. Negative ad partem Iam; affirmative ad secundam salvo praescripto Canonis 1573 §2.

Ad 2 am. Negative et serventur Can. 1990-1991.

Ad 3 am. Faveat orator significare utrum in Curia Parisiensi pendeant causae nullitatis matrimonii ob defectum formae Tridentinae quoad coniugia contracta ante decretum Ne Temere, an dubium sit tantum doctrinale.

Ad 4 am. Est Metropolita, vel loci Ordinarius ad appellationem designatus ad normam Can. 1594 §1 et §2, firma hoc quoque in casu responsione at Iam.

Quae dum Tibi, Reverendissime Domine, significo, cuncta bona a Deo deprecor.

Sign. Petrus Card. Gasparri, Praesses,
A Card. Sincero, Pro Secretarius.

The second reply which dealt with the matter of clandestinity was given in a letter of May 5, 1924:

Acceptis tuis informationibus die 29 elapsi Februarii modo ad propositum a te dubium "an vi Canonis 1990 Codicis Iuris Canonici possit Ordinarius declarare via administrativa et summaria evidentem ex capite clandestinitatis nullitatem matrimoniorum quae ante decretum 'Ne Temere' celebrata fuerunt" respondere censeo: "Negative, nisi agatur de illis matrimoniis clandestinis quibus etiam figura, ut aiunt, matrimonii deficiat et de quibus in responsis huius Pontificiae Commissionis sub die 16 Octobris 119 n. 17, Acta S. Sedis Volum. XI, pag. 479.

Ceterum quemadmodum ex citatis tuis litteris deprehendetur hoc genus causae matrimonialis in dies fiunt rariores.

Interim, quo par est, obsequio me profiteor,

Addictissimum in Domino.

Sign. Petrus Card. Gasparri.
J. Bruno, Secretarius.

From the facts it can be gathered that the questions submitted to the Commission were addressed under the impression that the authority employed in these excepted cases was administrative. Yet no strict distinction between judicial and administrative power was kept in view for in the first series of queries the first question implies that the power in canon 1990 is judicial, while the third question hints that the authority may be administrative. The fourth and fifth questions confirm these indications. The response with its rearranged questions gives all indications that the power in these excepted cases is judicial. Any reference to the Vicar General which would suggest an administrative characteristic is carefully omitted. The references which are made all pertain to the canons on judicial procedure in general from which the Vicar General is excluded. The reply to the first question gives the strongest indications of the judicial character of the proceedings, the second that there is a difference in degree not in kind from the normal matrimonial trial, and the fourth that the case in the court of second instance is a truly judicial concern.

From what has been said the word "administrative"—whether used to define the nature of the process in the excepted cases or to describe the mode of procedure—is in the former case erroneous and in the latter misleading. How should the special process be designated? Prior to the Code there were two processes truly judicial in nature—the solemn and the summary. These have been merged into one process by the Code.[109] Today the term "summary process" has come to be applied, either correctly or incorrectly,[110] to the non-judicial or administrative cases considered in the third part of the fourth book of the Code. Consequently, this use (or abuse) precludes the use of the term "summary" in connection with canon 1990. The process has been termed "The Summary Trial." The terms of "Special Matrimonial Trial" or better "The Documental Process"[111] are preferable. However a name will not change the nature of the process; but any name which is applied to this special form of process should indicate the judicial character of the authority that is being exercised.

Art. II. The Consequent Interpretation of These Canons

§1. *A notion of the documents used.* The ordinary judicial process admits two kinds of testimony—oral and documentary.[112] In the extraordinary matrimonial process the evidence is restricted to documentary proof. Since the documents have been confected at a period prior to the introduction of the case (tempus non suspecta) when no prudent suspicion would be cast on their reliability, this kind of testimony is known as pre-

---

[109] Cf. Roberti, *De Processibus*, I, pp. 9, 14.

[110] Cf. Roberti, *De Processibus*, I, p. 26; Vermeersch-Creusen, *Epitome*, III, n. 4.

[111] Cf. Roberti, *De Processibus*, I, p. 67.

[112] Canon 1812.

constituted or approved proof (*probatio probata*).[113] The terms document,[114] instrument,[115] and writings [116] are often used indiscriminately.[117] Yet an instrument may be considered a broad term designating any proof and including document as a species.[118] A document is a written instrument or means of proof and has been defined as a writing confected to constitute a future proof of some fact [119] (which is the purpose of public documents) or better as a writing from which a fact can be proven.[120] This later definition is more acceptable as it includes even private writings or documents. It does not demand that the document be confected with the sole intention that a future means of proof is being provided.[121] As canon 1990 demands the use of "certain and authentic documents which suffer no contradiction or exception" a general notion of the different kinds of documents will aid in arriving at an understanding of the canon. Documents may be divided into:

1. *Public*—a written instrument or certification confected by a public person (in virtue of his office) with the due legal solemnities.[122]
   a. *Ecclesiastical*—confected by a legitimate ecclesiastical official.[123]
   b. *Civil*—performed by a civil official.[124]

Private—any writing of a private person.[125]

---

[113] Cf. Wernz-Vidal, *Ius Canonicum*, VI, n. 506; Lega, *De Iudiciis Ecclesiasticis*, I, n. 512.

[114] Cf. canon 1813 §1.

[115] Cf. captions of Chapter V and articles I and II in this section of the Code.

[116] Cf. canon 1815.

[117] Cf. Noval, *De Iudiciis*, n. 541; Wernz-Vidal, *Ius Canonicum*, VI, n. 507.

[118] Cf. Bouix, *De Iudiciis Ecclesiasticis*, I, p. 320; Lega, *De Iudiciis Ecclesiasticis*, I, n. 507.

[119] "Scriptura ad constituendam alicuius rei futuram probationem confecta."—Lega, *De Iudiciis Ecclesiasticis*, I, n. 507. Cf. canon 56.

[120] "Quaevis scriptura ex qua factum comprobari possit."—Noval, *De Iudiciis*, n. 541.

[121] Cf. Wernz-Vidal, *Ius Canonicum*, VI, n. 507, note 4; Vermeersch-Creusen, *Epitome*, III, n. 198.

[122] Cf. canon 1813.

[123] Cf. canon 1813 §1.

[124] Cf. canon 1813 §2.

[125] Cf. canon 1813 §3.

a. *Authentic*—recognized directly or indirectly by public authority as true and genuine.[126]

b. *Purely private*—enjoys no public recognition.[127]

2. *Original*—the very writing itself.

Transcript (example or copy)—a copy of the original.

Certified (authenticated or attested) copy—a copy of the original with the attestation of a public personage that the copy conforms to the original.[128]

3. *Genuine*—confected by the one whose name it bears.

Apocryphal—writer unknown.

Spurious—counterfeit; not proceeding from the true source.

4. *Legitimate* (legal)—fulfilling solemnities of the law.

Illegitimate—confected by an incompetent person[129] or in an improper manner.

5. *Integral*—entire or complete.

Defective (vitiated)—containing some flaw as erasure, addition, etc.[130]

Canon 1990 demands that the documents be certain (i.e. dependable and relatively indisputable)[131] and authentic (i.e. of approved authority). The documents employed need not be public documents but even certain and authentic private documents can be used. Public documents, of course, provide the best proof. Whether ecclesiastical or civil, public documents are recognized as trustworthy in those matters which are directly and principally affirmed in them[132] and are presumed genuine until the contrary is established by evident arguments.[133] This is a simple presumption of law.[134] Public ecclesiastical documents include the acts confected by the pope, Roman curia, and Ordinaries in authentic form while in the

[126] Cf. Lega, *De Iudiciis Ecclesiasticis,* I, n. 514; Noval, *De Iudiciis,* n. 551. E.g. bank check, promissory note, receipt, will, contract, etc.

[127] *E.g.* letters, annotations, etc. Cf. Bassibey, *Le Mariage,* p. 357.

[128] Cf. canon 1813 §1-4°.

[129] E.g. cf. canon 374 §2.

[130] Cf. canon 1818.

[131] Canon 1991 allows for prudent doubt on the part of the defensor that the existence of the impediment may not be certain.

[132] Canon 1816.

[133] Canon 1814.

[134] Cf. canons 1825 §2, 1826.

exercise of their work, as well as authentic attestations of these same acts given by these officials or their notaries; instruments executed by ecclesiastical notaries; ecclesiastical judicial acts; inscriptions of baptism, confirmation, ordination, religious profession, marriage, and death, which are kept in the registers of a Curia, parish, or religious institute, and written attestations drawn from these records and confected by the parish priest, Ordinary, or ecclesiastical notary, or authentic copies of them.[135] Public civil documents are judged according to the common usage of the country.[136] These would include birth certificates, marriage licenses and records, certificates of death, burial permits, judicial acts and sworn statements witnessed by a notary or public official.

Private documents may be sources for establishing facts. Private writings [137] which the public law recognized directly or indirectly as true have a standing in judicial matters.[138] These may be termed authentic private documents [139] which will generally be signed writings drawn up with some regard for form such as a will. These are practically akin to public documents.[140] Private documents not recognized by public authority do not constitute approved proofs but lend a proof which must be substantiated (*probatio probanda*).[141] The value of these documents is restricted. If they are acknowledged by the party or recognized by the judge, they furnish proof *against* the author of them or the subscriber, or such persons as receive benefits from them.[142] Such writings are considered as an extrajudicial confession [143] but of themselves they have no proving force against any other persons than the three classes mentioned above.[144] There does not seem to be the insistence on the di-

---

135 Canon 1813 §1. Cf. Lega, *De Iudiciis Ecclesiasticis,* I, n. 515.

136 Canon 1813 §2.

137 Canon 1813 §3.

138 Cf. canon 1817. Lega, *De Iudiciis Ecclesiasticis,* I, n. 513.

139 Cf. Bouix, *De Iudiciis Ecclesiasticis,* I, p. 322; Bassibey, *Le Mariage,* p. 349.

140 Cf. canon 1813 §2. Cf. canons 779, 1019 §2.

141 Cf. Lega, *De Iudiciis Ecclesiasticis,* I, n. 513; Bouix, *De Iudiciis Ecclesiasticis,* I, p. 323.

142 E.g. the record of the birth of parents may enter in the matrimonial case of their children in respect to impediment of consanguinity.

143 Canon 1753.

144 Canon 1817.

vision of private documents into signed and unsigned[145] as formerly.[146] However, an unsigned document would not have much legal value.

How are these documents to be presented and recognized? The original documents or authentic copies are to be presented[147] so that the judge[148] and defensor[149] may examine them. It is within the defensor's power to demand the original writings,[150] though the authentic copy will usually suffice unless the faithfulness of the transcript is questioned. In such an event the judge is the one who decides whether the document whence the copy was drawn is to be presented.[151] If the production of the original source is impossible or difficult then the judge may direct that other steps be taken to establish the faithfulness of the authentic copy.[152]

In this process documents provide the principal and basic proof. At times the testimony of witnesses may be helpful in arriving at a better understanding of the documents produced. In this event the testimony of persons does not seem contrary to the regulations of the Code as long as this type of proof is secondary and does not supply in the points where documents can and should be had. For those who claim that the power in this process is administrative, a difficulty appears when oral testimony is admitted. There is no incongruity in having oral testimony in a process which is by nature judicial. Prior to the Code the use of evident arguments in the defect of documents was possible.[153] The Code omits mention of the use of certain arguments in defect of documents. Does this absolutely forbid any other proof except documentary or does it make documentary proof the principal source of testimony and allow oral testimony a secondary role? The latter opinion seems more

---

[145] Cf. ". . . adversus auctorem vel subscriptorem . . ."—canon 1817.

[146] Cf. Lega, *De Iudiciis Ecclesiasticis,* I, n. 516.

[147] Canon 1819.

[148] Canon 1820.

[149] Canons 1820, 1968—2°, 1969—1°.

[150] Canon 1969—2°.

[151] Canon 1821 §1.

[152] Canon 1821 §2.

[153] ". . . dummodo ex certo et authentico documento, vel in huius defectu, ex certis argumentis evidenter constet de existentia huiusmodi impedimentorum super quibus Ecclesiae auctoritate dispensatum non fuerit." S. C. S. Off., June 5, 1889—*Fontes,* n. 1118.

logical. Documents can bear witness to the fact that some act had taken place but how can a document certify that an action or an event never transpired? How, for instance, can the non-reception of baptism by the one party in a case of disparity of cult be proven from authentic and certain sources? Could any document be expected in this case? The non-baptism of the one party would have to be established by testimony concerning the religious affiliation and character of the parents, indications that the child may or may not have been baptized at an early age, and other bits of indirect proofs upon which the presumption of the non-baptism may be based. The best testimony that could be had would be restricted to an oath or a written deposition of competent witnesses that to their knowledge the person had never been baptized. Moreover, are certain and authentic *documents* testifying to the non-issuance of a dispensation to be expected?[154] The only way the absence of a dispensation can be ascertained is by lack of any record of such a dispensation having been granted as ascertained from a search of authentic registers. This negative *argument* should be supported by further testimonies that the marriage was never convalidated. Testimony other than that of documents[155] is apparently demanded in the process. But this is secondary in points where documents are obtainable while on other points it is the only proof possible. The letter of the law could be fulfilled by having such testimony reduced to writing and subscribed before an ecclesiastical notary.

§2. *The impediments considered*—The impediments include the five impediments recounted in the Holy Office decree of 1889[156] with the addition of the impediments arising from orders and solemn vow of chastity. The lack of proper form is omitted for it is no longer considered an "impediment" and a special process is now provided for in such cases. The impediments mentioned are all such as are public in nature.[157] These are enumerated as the impediment of disparity of cult, holy orders, solemn vow, ligamen, consanguinity, affinity, and spir-

[154] Cf. Noval, *De Iudiciis,* n. 873.

[155] Cf. Vermeersch-Creusen, *Epitome,* III, n. 296: *Gregorianum,* VII (1926), 142.

[156] *Fontes,* n. 1118.

[157] Canon 1037. Cf. Chelodi, *Ius Matrimoniale,* p. 31; Wernz-Vidal, *Ius Canonicum,* V, p. 167.

itual relationship. The impediment of age [158] is not mentioned among the impediments in canon 1990. Possibly this is due to the fact that such an event would be rare. However, since the existence of the impediment could be established from baptismal records, since the granting of a dispensation in this matter would be most rare a marriage invalid by reason of the impediment of age is apparently included under the process in canon 1990.[159]

Considering these impediments individually the first to claim attention is that of disparity of cult.[160] Apparently the scope is confined to cases where there is a question of the fact of baptism. A matter of the invalidity of a baptism which had been conferred would scarcely be admitted into the class of marriages evidently invalid.[161] The baptism of the one party in the Catholic Church [162] can be established from the parochial records [163] but documents recording the testimony of a person by virtue of canon 779 should not be accepted unless, perhaps, it had been given at a time prior to the marriage ceremony. The non-baptism of the other party would have to be established in a series of negative proofs from which oral testimony reduced to some documentary form does not seem excluded. Extreme care must be exercised in the matter of sworn statements. Today the sanctity of an oath is widely disrespected. In the civil courts an affidavit is considered as "the most miserable species of evidence." [164] The officials in the curia must prudently weigh evidences of this nature and consider it only as the last recourse.

Documentary evidence of the impediment of Holy Orders [165]

---

[158] Canon 1067 §1.

[159] Cf. Vermeersch-Creusen, *Epitome,* III, n. 296; Lanier, *Guide Pratique de la Procédure Matrimoniale,* p. 6; Wernz-Vidal, *Ius Canonicum,* V, n. 705, note 56; Bassibey, *Le Mariage,* p. 352.

[160] Canon 1070.

[161] ". . . disparitatis cultus (dummodo non agatur de valore baptismi forsitan collati, quo in casu semper recurrendum erit ad Sanctam Sedem) . . ." S. C. S. Off., to Bishop of Angoulême, Sept. 5, 1888—*NRT,* XX (1888), 633; XXVI (1894), 26. Cf. also S. C. S. Off., to Bishop of Albany, June 10, 1896, where it was a question of the fact of baptism.—*Fontes,* n. 1180.

[162] Canon 1070 §1.

[163] Canons 470, 777.

[164] Moore, *A Treatise on Facts,* II, p. 1094.

[165] Canon 1072.

may be sought in the case of a secular cleric in the diocesan archives in the place of ordination[166] and in the curial archives of the proper Ordinary.[167] It may be ascertained from the document which is to be given the cleric, himself,[168] or even from the annotation added to the baptismal record of the cleric.[169] For the religious in holy orders documents would be sought in the same manner except that a record would be retained in the register of the institute rather than in any diocesan archive of a local Ordinary.[170] The existence of the solemn vow of chastity which would nullify a marriage[171] (including the special force given the simple vows of the Jesuits) may be established from the parochial baptismal register[172] and the records of the religious institute.[173] In the impediment of ligamen it must be recalled that any prior marriage is generally considered as valid until the contrary is proven.[174] The fact that one of the parties had been previously married would be revealed from such sources as the matrimonial register in the place where the previous ceremony had taken place[175] or from the baptismal record of the party,[176] or, in the case of a marriage of conscience, from the diocesan records of the place where the ceremony had been performed.[177] Where marriage had been contracted in virtue of canon 1098 then the testimony of those who witnessed the marriage would have to be sought. The existence of the impediment of consanguinity[178] would be established by a comparison of baptismal entries[179] and marriage records.[180] Even civil documents may help materially in this question. Affinity likewise may be gathered from a perusal of the baptismal and marriage

---

[166] Canon 1010 §1.
[167] Canon 1010 §2.
[168] Canon 1010 §2.
[169] Canons 470 §1, 1011.
[170] Canons 1010, 1011.
[171] Can. 579, 1073.
[172] Canon 470 §2.
[173] Canon 576 §2.
[174] Canon 1014.
[175] Canon 1103.
[176] Canon 470 §2.
[177] Canon 1107.
[178] Canons 96, 1076.
[179] Canon 777.
[180] Canon 1103. Cf. Bassibey, *Le Mariage*, p. 352.

registers: [181] the impediment of spiritual relationship arising on the occasion of baptism [182] can be known from the baptismal register.[183] The existence of the impediments lends itself to easier proqf than the non-existence of any dispensation from these impediments.

§3. *The absence of a dispensation*—Obviously there can never be a dispensation from the impediment of ligamen. However, it is possible that the first marriage was invalid,[184] but this would be in itself a matrimonial case. Again it is possible in the cases of disparity of cult and ligamen that the impediments have ceased either because the person had been baptized in the meantime or the spouse to the first marriage had died. In such events a valid marriage was possible after the impediments had ceased and there is the possibility that the marriage may have been convalidated.[185] In the impediments of holy orders and solemn vow the dispensation would rather have been given from the obligation of the respective states directly than for the purpose of marriage. These cases would be rare. In the impediments more frequently encountered—disparity of cult, consanguinity, affinity, and spiritual relationship—a record of the granting of a dispensation should be revealed in a search of the archives in those dioceses through which it could have possibly been granted.[186] It may even be hinted in annotations in the parochial matrimonial record.[187] Proof in the absence of any record of a dispensation or of a later sanation of the marriage is negative in character. The circumstances of the marriage ceremony, the character of the parties, and the condition of their married life may add other evidences to establish a moral certitude that a dispensation or sanation was never sought.

§4. *The solemnities omitted*—When certain and authentic documents show that these impediments existed and it is equally certain that a dispensation was never granted, then the brief form of a matrimonial process is possible. This dispenses with

[181] Canons 77, 1077, 777, 1103.
[182] Canons 768, 1079.
[183] Canon 777.
[184] Cf. canon 1069 §2.
[185] Cf. canon 1133 sq.
[186] Cf. canons 56, 375, 1046, 1047.
[187] Canons 470, 1103.

the necessity of a collegiate tribunal of at least three judges: [188] a formal accusation: [189] the necessity of any other evidence than documentary testimony to establish the existence of the impediments: [190] the publication of the process: [191] the appeal *ex officio* by the defensor: [192] and consequently the necessity of a second conformable sentence.[193]

If the documentary process is judicial, what is to be said of the juridical capacity required in the actor? No formal accusation is necessary.[194] But as a judicial concern the process must have been introduced by someone. Nothing prevents the Ordinary from acting *ex officio* and directing the Promoter of Justice to institute proceedings.[195] Yet an occasion of this kind would be beyond the ordinary course of events.

As a judicial process the matter would demand an actor. A non-Catholic could not validly act in these processes: [196] and Catholics who wittingly contracted an invalid marriage, have no juridical right to accuse this marriage.[197] But all the impediments enumerated in canon 1990 are impediments not only public by nature [198] but even public in fact. The very requirements that the existence of the impediments be established from certain and authentic documents, indicate that the impediments are in fact public.[199] Since the impediments are by nature public, the Promoter of Justice is capable of accusing the marriage.[200] Prior to the Code any Catholic could accuse a marriage null by reason of a public impediment.[201] By the Code this capacity was restricted to the Promoter of Justice who for the public good could *ex officio* accuse a marriage invalid by

[188] Canons 1576 §1—1°, 1966.

[189] Canons 1970, 1971. Cf. S. C. S. Off., June 20, 1883—*Fontes*, n. 1076.

[190] Canon 1974.

[191] Canon 1983.

[192] Canon 1986.

[193] Canon 1987.

[194] Cf. canons 1706, 1970, 1990.

[195] Cf. Noval, *De Iudiciis*, n. 849.

[196] Cf. S. C. S. Off., Jan. 27, 1928, ad 1—*AAS*, XX (1928), 75.

[197] Canon 1971 §1—n. 1. Cf. Pontif. Comm. Inter. Cod., Mar. 12, 1929, ad 5—*AAS*, XXI (1929), 171.

[198] Publica natura sua, *i.e.* quia resultant ex facto de se publico.

[199] Cf. Chelodi, *Ius Matrimoniale*, p. 31; Wernz-Vidal, *Ius Canonicum*, V, p. 167; Vermeersch-Creusen, *Epitome*, III, n. 286.

[200] Canon 1971 §1—n. 2.

[201] Cf. S. C. S. Off., June 20, 1883—*Fontes*, n. 1079; Austrian Instruction, §115; Bassibey, *Le Mariage*, n. 186.

reason of an impediment public *natura sua.*[202] Should the Promoter act in the cases included under canon 1990? If the public good demands, he can and should act *ex officio:* otherwise he should not institute proceedings.

§5. *What the process comprises*—In this brief process all judicial formality is not omitted but it is reduced to the bare essentials. The Ordinary, when the parties have been cited, can, with the intervention of the defensor, declare the marriage invalid. The Ordinary in this case acts with judicial power. Hence the term includes not only the bishop but even the Official who enjoys ordinary power in judicial matters, but not the Vicar General.[203] It is possible that the role of judge in these cases can be filled by a delegated judge.[204] The proper Ordinary is determined even as in the formal judicial process.[205] The Ordinary who might be competent in establishing the freedom to marry may become competent in these cases by reason of connected causes. Where the brief method is possible it is a matter of justice that it be employed so that time and expense will be saved. If in the course of a normal trial, the judges find that the case is one of evident nullity, the matter should be settled at once by canon 1990.

The parties to the invalidly contracted marriage are to be cited. Citation is a judicial act and the ordinary regulations respecting citation are to be observed: [206] unless the parties freely present themselves to the Ordinary.[207] One citation is sufficient [208] and if the defendant in the case does not accept the summons he is considered as legitimately cited.[209]

The Ordinary, or the judge, declares the marriage invalid. This declaration is a sentence.[210] Being a sentence the legal requirements must be observed.[211] The judge having moral certitude based on the evidence submitted pronounces sen-

[202] Canon 1971 §1—n. 2. Cf. Noval, *De Iudiciis,* n. 834.

[203] Canon 1573 §1. Cf. *supra,* Pont. Comm. Inter. Cod., to Paris, Dec. 19, 1923.

[204] Canon 199 §1.

[205] Canon 1964.

[206] Canon 1712 sqq.

[207] Canon 1711 §2.

[208] Canon 1714.

[209] Canon 1718.

[210] Canon 1992.

[211] Cf. canons 1868-1877.

tence.[212] After an invocation of the Divine Name the sentence should make mention of the judge, the parties, and the defensor. It should also state the case briefly and show the basis of the sentence. After this it concludes with the date and place and the signatures of the judge and notary.[213]

The presence of the defensor is required in the process. He takes an active role and his presence is necessary for the validity of the action.[214] Should the defensor prudently consider the existence of the invalidating impediment uncertain or that a dispensation had probably convalidated the marriage, he is obliged to appeal the case to the judge of the second instance.[215] Warning of this appeal is to be given to the judge who pronounced the sentence within ten days[216] and the appeal must be made before the court of second instance within a month.[217] The acts of the case[218] are to be transmitted to the other court[219] with the notation that the matter is one of the excepted cases. By this appeal the sentence of the first Ordinary is suspended.[220] Consequently, the parties cannot accept the first sentence and enter a second union. They must await the decision of the judge to whom the case was appealed.

The judge of the second instance, whether of the Metropolitan curia or of the court specially designated for appeals from a metropolitan court,[221] accepts the acts of the case. The parties do not have to appear. The judge together with the defensor of that curia reviews the acts along the lines delineated in canon 1990 to determine whether the first sentence is to be upheld or whether the matter remains doubtful and should be submitted to the normal matrimonial trial.[222] In such an event the case is returned that it might be tried before the collegiate tribunal in the curia of the original diocese.[223]

---

[212] Canons 1869, 1872.
[213] Canon 1874.
[214] Canon 1587.
[215] Cf. Canons 1991, 1986.
[216] Canon 1881.
[217] Canon 1883.
[218] Canon 1642.
[219] Canon 1644.
[220] Canon 1889.
[221] Canon 1594.
[222] Canons 1960 sqq.
[223] Cf. canons 1572, 1576 §1—1°.

If, following the regulation of canon 1992, the matter is sent back to the first curia, the Ordinary who initially decided the case by virtue of canon 1990 is not incompetent to act as one of the judges in the tribunal in the customary process.[224] The juridical principle that a judge who sees a cause in one grade is absolutely incompetent to judge the same cause in another grade,[225] is not thereby violated. The Ordinary in rehearing the case is not judging it in another grade but in the first, or same, grade. This is not contrary to law.[226]

---

[224] Can. 1576 §1—1°.

[225] Can. 1571.

[226] Noval, *De Iudiciis,* n. 105; Roberti, *De Processibus,* I, p. 151; Lega, *De Iudiciis Ecclesiasticis,* I, n. 325. Cf. can. 1893, 1897 §2.

BIBLIOGRAPHY

SOURCES

Acta Apostolicae Sedis (*AAS*), Romae, 1909–

Acta Sanctae Sedis (*ASS*), 41 vols., Romae, 1865–1908.

Acta et Decreta Concilii Provincialis Mechliniensis IV, Mechliniae, 1923.

Canones et Decreta Concilii Tridentini, 19 ed., Taurini, 1913.

Codex Iuris Canonici Pii X Pontificis Maximi iussu digestu Benedicti Papae XV auctoritate promulgatus, Romae, 1918.

Codicis Iuris Canonici Fontes, 4 vols., Romae, 1923–1926.

Collectanea Sacrae Congregationis de Propaganda Fide (*Coll.*) 2 vols., Romae, 1907.

Collectio Lacensis, Acta et Decreta Sacrorum Conciliorum Recentiorum (*Coll. Lacen.*), 7 vols., Friburgi Br., 1870-1890.

Concilia Germaniae, Hartzheim, 11 vols., Coloniae Augustae Agrippinensium, 1760.

Concilia Magnae Britanniae et Hiberniae, Wilkins, 3 vols., London, 1737.

Concilii Plenarii Baltimorensis II, Acta et Decreta, Baltimore, 1894.

Concilii Plenarii Baltimorensis III, Acta et Decreta, Baltimore, 1884.

Corpus Iuris Canonici, 2 vols., Lipsiae, 1922.

Corpus Iuris Civilis, Berolini, 1922.

Denzinger-Bannwart, *Enchiridion Symbolorum Definitionum et Declarationum de Rebus Fidei et Morum*, 14–15 ed., Friburgi Br., 1922.

Mansi, *Sacrorum Conciliorum Nova et Amplissima Collectio*, 51 vols., Paris, 1901–1919.

Regulae Servandae in Iudiciis apud S. Romanae Rotae Tribunal, Romae, 1910.

Regulae Servandae in Iudiciis apud Supremum Signaturae Apostolicae Tribunal, Romae, 1912.

Regulae Servandae in Processibus super Matrimonio Rato et Non Consummato, etc., Romae, 1923.

Raccolta di Concordati su Materie Ecclesiastiche tra la Santa Sede e Le Autorita Civili, Romae, 1919.

Roskovany, *Matrimonium in Ecclesia Catholica Potestati Ecclesiasticae Subjectum: cum amplissima collectione monumentorum et literatura*, 4 vols., Pestini-Nitriae, 1870–1882.

Roskovany, *Monumenta Catholica pro Independentia Potestatis Ecclesiasticae ab Imperio Civili*, 13 vols., Quinque-Ecclesiis, Pestini, Nitriae, 1847–1879.

Sacrae Romanae Rotae Decisiones seu Sententiae, 9 vols., Romae, 1912–

SS. D. N. Leonis Papae XIII, Allocutiones, Epistolae, Constitutiones, etc., 6 vols., Brugis, 1900.

Theodosiani Libri XVI cum Constitutionibus Sirmondianis, Berolini, 1905.
Thesaurus Resolutionum Sacrae Congregationis Concilii, 167 vols., Romae, 1718–1908.

WORKS OF REFERENCE

Aertnys-Damen, *Theologia Moralis,* 11 ed., 2 vols., Taurini, 1928.
Aichner, Compendium Iuris Ecclesiastici, 9 ed., Brixinae, 1900.
Allies, *The Life of Pope Pius the Seventh,* London, 1875.
Artaud, *Histoire du Pape Pie VII,* 2 ed., 2 vols., Paris, 1837.
Augustine, *A Commentary on Canon Law,* 3 ed., 7 vols., St. Louis, 1923.
Ayrinhac, *Marriage Legislation in the New Code of Canon Law,* New York, 1918.
Bachofen, *Summa Iuris Ecclesiastici Publici,* Romae, 1910.
Badii, *Institutiones Iuris Canonici,* 2 vols., Florentiae, 1921.
Balmez, *European Civilization: Protestantism and Catholicism Compared,* 6 ed., Baltimore, 1859.
Bargilliat, *Praelectiones Iuris Canonici,* 2 vols., Paris, 1915.
Bassibey, *Le Mariage devant les Tribunaux Ecclesiastiques,* Paris, 1899.
Bellarmine, *Omnia Opera,* 8 vols., Naples, 1858.
Benedict XIV, *Opera Omnia,* 17 vols., Prati, 1839-1847.
Benedict XIV, *De Synodo Dioecesana,* 2 ed., 2 vols., Parmae, 1764.
Bernardus Papiensis, *Summa Decretalium,* ed. Laspreyres, Ratisbon, 1840.
Billot, *De Ecclesiae Sacramentis,* 2 vols., Romae, 1908.
Billuart, *Summa S. Thomae hodiernis academiarum moribus accommodata, sive Cursus Theologiae,* Trajecti ad Mosam, 1770.
Blat, *Commentarium Textus Codicis Iuris Canonici,* Liber IV, De Processibus, Romae, 1927.
Bouix, *De Iudiciis Ecclesiasticis,* 3 ed., 2 vols., Paris, 1883.
Bouuaert-Simenon, *Manuale Iuris Canonici,* 2 ed., Gandae et Leodii, 1926.
Brouwer, *De Iure Connubiorum Libri Duo,* 2 ed., Delphis, 1714.
Burke, *Competence in Ecclesiastical Tribunals,* Washington, 1922.
Calvin, *Institutiones Christianae Religionis,* Berolini, 1834.
Cappello, *De Curia Romana,* Romae, 1911.
Cappello, *Summa Iuris Publici Ecclesiastici,* Romae, 1923.
Cappello, *Tractatus Canonico-Moralis de Sacramentis,* Taurini, 3 vols., 1923: vol. III (1927).
Catharius, *De Foro Competenti,* Romae, 1648.
Catholic Encyclopedia, 15 vols., New York, 1917.
Cavagnis, *Institutiones Iuris Publici Ecclesiastici,* 3 vols., Romae, 1896.
Cavagnis, *Della Natura di Societa Giuridica e Publica Competente alla Chiesa,* Roma, 1887.
Cerato, *Matrimonium a Codice I. C. integre desumptum,* 4 ed., Patavii, 1927.
Chelodi, *Ius Matrimoniale,* 3 ed., Trent, 1921.
Chelodi, *Ius de Personis,* Trent, 1925.
Cicognani, *Commentarium ad Librum I Codicis,* Romae, 1925.
Cicognani, *Ius Canonicum,* Romae, 1925.

Cimetier, *Pour Étudier le Code de Droit Canonique,* Paris, 1927.
Cocchi, *Commentarium in Codicem Iuris Canonici,* 7 vols., Turin, 1925–1927.
Coglioli, *Manuale delle Fonti del Diritto Romano,* Torino, 1911.
Coronata, *Ius Publicum Ecclesiasticum,* Taurini, 1924.
Corpus Scriptorum Ecclesiasticorum Latinorum, Tempsky, Vienna, 1866–
D'Annibale, *Summula Theologiae Moralis,* 2 ed., Mediolani, 1881.
De Angelis, *Praelectiones Iuris Canonici,* 5 vols., Romae, 1908.
De Augustinis, *De Re Sacramentaria Praelectiones Scholastico-Dogmaticae,* 2 vols., Romae, 1887.
De Becker, *De Sponsalibus et Matrimonio,* Bruxellis, 1896.
Department of Commerce, Bureau of Census, *Special Reports, Marriage and Divorce,* part I, Washington, 1909.
De Oliva, *Tractatus de Foro Ecclesiae,* Coloniae Allobrogum, 1733.
De Smet, *De Sponsalibus et Matrimonio,* 4 ed., Brugis, 1927.
De Smet, *Praxis Matrimonialis,* 3 ed., Brugis, 1920.
De Urrutigoyti, *Tractatus de Competentiis Iurisdictionis,* Lugduni, 1667.
Devoti, *Institutiones Canonicae,* Leodii, 1883.
Devoti, *Ius Canonicum Universum Publicum et Privatum,* 3 vols., Romae, 1837.
Duchesne, *The Early History of the Christian Church,* trans., New York, 1912.
Dugan, *The Judiciary Department of the Diocesan Curia,* Washington, 1925.
Esmein, *Le Mariage en Droit Canonique,* 2 vols., Paris, 1891.
Farrugia, *De Matrimonio et Causis Matrimonialibus,* Taurini, 1924.
Ferraris, *Prompta Bibliotheca Canonica,* 9 vols., Romae, 1885–1892.
Feije, *De Impedimentis et Dispensationibus Matrimonialibus,* 3 ed., Louvain, 1885.
Funk, *Didascalia et Constitutiones Apostolorum,* Paderbornae, 1905.
Funk, *A Manual of Church History,* trans., 2 vols., London, 1910.
Gallemart, *Sacrosanctum Concilium Tridentinum,* Augusta Vindelicorum, 1781.
Gasparri, *Tractatus Canonicus de Matrimonio,* 3 ed., Paris, 1904.
Graesse-Benedict, *Orbis Latinus oder Verzeichnis der Wichtigsten Lateinischen Orts-und Landernamen,* Berlin, 1909.
Grisar, *Luther,* 2 vols., St. Louis, 1913.
Guizot, *The History of Civilization, trans. Hazlitt,* 2 vols., London, 1856.
Hurter, *Theologiae Dogmaticae Compendium,* 6 ed., 3 vols., Oeniponte, 1889.
Hefele, *Conciliengeschichte,* 2 ed., 9 vols., Freiburg Br., 1873–1890.
Jomini, *Life of Napoleon,* trans. Halleck, 4 vols., New York, 1864.
Jungmann, *Dissertationes in Historiam Ecclesiasticam,* 7 vols., Ratisbon, 1880.
Keezer, *The Law of Marriage and Divorce,* Boston, 1906.
Keyserling, *The Book of Marriage,* New York, 1926.
Lanier, *Guide Practique de Procédure Matrimoniale,* Paris, 1927.
Lapide, *Commentaria in Omnes Divi Pauli Epistolas,* Antwerp, 1635.

Laurentius, *Tractatus de Iudice Suspecto,* Venetiis, 1607.
Lefebre, *L'Histoire du Droit Matrimonial Francais,* Paris, 1900.
Lega, *Praelectiones in Textum Iuris Canonici de Iudiciis Ecclesiasticis,* 2 vols., Romae, 1898.
Lehmkuhl, *Theologia Moralis,* 2 vols., Friburg Br., 1888.
Lehr, *Traite Elementaire de Droit Civil Germanique,* 2 vols., Paris, 1892.
Leo XIII, *The Great Encyclical Letters of Pope Leo XIII,* ed. Wynne, New York, 1903.
Lightfoot, *The Apostolic Fathers,* London, 1893.
Mackenzie, *Studies in Roman law,* London, 1862.
Maine, *The Early History of Institutions,* New York, 1888.
Mansella, *De Impedimentis Matrimonium Dirimentibus ac de Processu Iudiciali,* Romae, 1881.
Maroto, *Institutiones Iuris Canonici,* 2 vols., Matriti, 1919.
Martin, *The Roman Curia as it now exists,* New York, 1913.
May, *Marriage Laws and Decisions in the United States,* New York, 1929.
Migne, *Encyclopedie Theologique,* 50 vols., Paris, 1846.
Migne, *Patrologia Graeca,* 161 vols., Paris, 1858–1864.
Migne, *Patrologia Latina,* 221 vols., Paris, 1847–1870.
Mombert, *A History of Charles the Great,* New York, 1888.
Monin, *De Curia Romana,* Louvain, 1912.
Moore, *A Treatise on Facts, or the Weight and Value of Evidence,* 2 vols., New York, 1908.
Noval, *Commentarium Codicis Iuris Canonici, Liber IV De Processibus, Pars I De Iudiciis,* Romae, 1920.
Noldin, *Summa Theologiae Moralis,* 3 vols., Oeniponte, 1923.
Ojetti, *De Romana Curia,* Romae, 1910.
Pallavicini, *Istoria del Concilio di Trento,* 4 vols., Romae, 1833.
Peries, *Code de Procedure dans les Causes Matrimoniales,* Paris, 1894.
Perrone, *De Matrimonio Christiano Libri Tres,* 3 vols., Leodii, 1861.
Pesch, *Praelectiones Dogmaticae,* 9 vols., Friburgi Br., 1920.
Pignatelli, *Consultationes Canonicae,* 11 vols., Coloniae Allobrogum, 1700.
Pighi, *De Sacramento Matrimonii,* Veronae, 1919.
Pollock-Maitland, *History of English Law,* 2 vols., Boston, 1895.
Reiffenstuel, *Ius Canonicum Universum,* Venice, 1735.
Richmond-Hall, *Marriage and the State,* New York, 1929.
Ringrose, *Marriage and Divorce Laws of the World,* New York, 1911.
Roberti, *De Processibus,* vol. I, Romae, 1926.
Richter, *Canones et Decreta Concilii Tridentini,* Lipsiae, 1853.
Rupert, *Des Lois Civiles Concernant Les Mariages Des Christiens,* trans. from Italian, Paris, 1853.
Ryan-Millar, *The State and the Church,* New York, 1922.
Sabetti-Barrett, *Compendium Theologiae Moralis,* New York, 1929.
Sanchez, *De Matrimonio,* Lugduni, 1679.
Santi, *Praelectiones Iuris Canonici,* 2 vols., Ratisbon, 1892.
Sarpi, *Histoire du Concile de Trente,* Amsterdam, 1783.
Sasse, *Institutiones Theologicae de Sacramentis Ecclesiae,* 2 vols., Friburgi Br., 1898.

Schaff-Wace, *Nicene and Post Nicene Fathers,* 2 series, New York, 1905.
Schmalzgrueber, *Ius Ecclesiasticum Universum,* 6 vols., Romae, 1843–1845.
Sebastianelli, *De Iudiciis Ecclesiasticis,* Romae, 1906.
Shahan, *An Outline of Church History,* New York, n.d.
Sherman, *Roman Law in the Modern World,* 2 ed., 3 vols., New York, 1924.
Smith, *The Marriage Process in the United States,* New York, 1893.
Smith, *Church and State in the Middle Ages,* Oxford, 1913.
Stockton, *Marriage, Civil and Ecclesiastical,* Buffalo, 1912.
Tanquerey, *Synopsis Theologiae Dogmaticae,* 3 vols., Romae, 1921.
Telch, *Epitome Theologiae Moralis,* 6 ed., Oeniponte, 1924.
Theologia Dogmatica, Polemica, Scholastica, et Moralis, RR. Patrum Societatis Jesu, 3 ed., 10 vols., Paris, 1880.
Thomas Aquinas, St., *Summa Theologica,* 6 vols., Taurini, 1917.
Thomassinus, *Vetus et Nova Ecclesiae Disciplina,* Mogontiaci, 1787.
Tiffany, *Handbook of the Law of Persons and Domestic Relations,* 2 ed., St. Paul, 1909.
Vermeersch-Creusen, *Epitome Iuris Canonici,* 3 ed., 3 vols., Mechliniae-Romae, I, II (1927), III (1928).
Vives, *Compendium Iuris Canonici,* 4 ed., Romae, 1905.
Vlaming, *Praelectiones Iuris Matrimonii,* 3 ed., 2 vols., Bussum, 1921.
Waterworth, *Canons and Decree of Trent,* London, 1848.
Wernz, *Ius Decretalium,* 6 vols., Prati, 1911.
Wernz-Vidal, *Ius Canonicum,* 3 vols., Romae, 1923–1927.
Westermarck, *The History of Human Marriage,* 5 ed. rewritten, 3 vols., New York, 1922.
Zitelli, *Apparatus Iuris Ecclesiastici,* 3 ed., Romae, 1903.

PERIODICALS

American Ecclesiastical Review (*AER*), Philadelphia, 1889–
Analecta Iuris Pontificii, Roma, 1855–1890.
Apollinaris, Roma, 1928–
Archiv für katholisches Kirchenrecht (*AfkK*), Mainz, 1885–
Catholic Historical Review, Washington, 1920–
La Correspondence de Rome, Liege, 2nd ed., vol. I (1848–1850).
Ephemerides Theologicae Lovaniensis (*ETL*), Louvain-Brugis, 1924–
Gregorianum, Commentarii de Re Theologica et Philosophica, Roma, 1920–
Il Monitore Ecclesiastico, Romae, 1888–
Ius Pontificium, Roma, 1921–
Le Canoniste Contemporain (*LCC*), Paris, 1878–
Nouvelle Revue Theologique (*NRT*), Paris, 1869–
Perfice Munus, Torino, 1925–
Periodica, de Re Canonica et Morali, Romae et Brugis, 1905–

Universitas Catholica Americae

WASHINGTON, D. C.

FACULTAS IURIS CANONICI

1929

No. 53

DEUS LUX MEA

TITULI

QUOS

AD DOCTORATUS GRADUM

IN

IURE CANONICO

APUD UNIVERSITATEM CATHOLICAM AMERICAE

CONSEQUENDUM

PUBLICE PROPUGNABIT

THOMAS HENRICUS KAY

SACERDOS DIOECESIS ALBANENSIS

IURIS CANONICI LICENTIATUS

HORA XI A. M. DIE XXIV MAII MCMXXIX

TITULI

DE IURE CANONICO

I.	De Dissertatione.	
II.	De Historia Iuris Canonici.	
III.	De Ratione inter Ecclesiam et Statum.	
IV.	Canones 1–7	De Ambitu Codicis.
V.	Canones 8–24	De Legibus Ecclesiasticis.
VI.	Canones 25–30	De Consuetudine.
VII.	Canones 31–35	De Temporis Supputatione.
VIII.	Canones 36–62	De Rescriptis.
IX.	Canones 63–79	De Privilegiis.
X.	Canones 80–86	De Dispensationibus.
XI.	Canones 356–362	De Synodo Dioecesana.
XII.	Canones 363–390	De Curia Dioecesana.
XIII.	Canones 423–428	De Consultoribus Dioecesanis.
XIV.	Canones 451–478	De Parochis et Vicariis Paroecialibus.
XV.	Canones 479–486	De Ecclesiarum Rectoribus.
XVI.	Canones 487–498	De Notione Religionis, et de Erectione et Suppressione Religionis, Provinciae, Domus.
XVII.	Canones 499–537	De Religionum Regimine.
XVIII.	Canones 538–586	De Admissione in Religionem.
XIX.	Canones 587–591	De Ratione Studiorum in Religionibus Clericalibus.
XX.	Canones 592–631	De Obligationibus et Privilegiis Religiosorum.
XXI.	Canones 632–672	De Transitu ad Aliam Religionem, de Egressu e Religione, et de Dimissione Religiosorum.
XXII.	Canones 673–681	De Societatibus in Communi Viventium Sine Votis.
XXIII.	Canones 726–730	De Simonia.
XXIV.	Canones 951–991	De Ministro et Subjecto Sacrae Ordinationis.
XXV.	Canones 1094–1103	De Forma Celebrationis Matrimonii.
XXVI.	Canones 1104–1109	De Matrimonio Conscientiae et de Tempore et Loco Celebrationis Matrimonii.
XXVII.	Canones 1110–1117	De Matrimonii Effectibus.
XXVIII.	Canones 1118–1141	De Separatione Coniugum et de Matrimonii Convalidatione.
XXIX.	Canones 1552–1568	De Notione Iudicii et de Foro Competenti.

Tituli

XXX.	Canones 1569–1607	De Variis Tribunalium Gradibus et Speciebus.
XXXI.	Canones 1608–1645	De Disciplina in Tribunalibus Servanda.
XXXII.	Canones 1646–1666	De Partibus in Causa.
XXXIII.	Canones 1667–1705	De Actionibus et Exceptionibus.
XXXIV.	Canones 1706–1725	De Causae Introductione.
XXXV.	Canones 1726–1731	De Litis Contestatione.
XXXVI.	Canones 1742–1746	De Interrogationibus Partibus in Iudicio Faciendis.
XXXVII.	Canones 1960–1992	De Causis Matrimonialibus.
XXXVIII.	Canones 1993–1998	De Causis Contra Sacram Ordinationem.
XXXIX.	Canones 2195–2198	De Natura Delicti Eiusque Divisione.
XL.	Canones 2199–2211	De Imputabilitate Delicti, de Causis Aggravantibus vel Minuentibus, et de Iuridicis Delicti Effectibus.
XLI.	Canones 2212–2213	De Conatu Delicti.
XLII.	Canones 2214–2240	De Poenis in Genere.
XLIII.	Canones 2241–2285	De Poenis Medicinalibus seu de Censuris.
XLIV.	Canones 2286–2305	De Poenis Vindicativis.
XLV.	Canones 2306–1213	De Remediis Poenalibus et Poenitentiis.

DE IURE ROMANO

XLVI. The periods of Roman Law.
XLVII. Personality.
XLVIII. Slavery.
XLIX. Citizenship.
L. The Roman family.
LI. Exheredatio.
LII. Praeteritio.
LIII. Omissio.
LIV. Classes of Heirs.
LV. Institution and substitution of heirs.
LVI. Legacies.
LVII. Fideicommissa.
LVIII. Intestate succession.
LIX. General principles of obligation.
LX. Contracts.

Vidit Facultas:

PHILIPPUS BERNARDINI, S.T.D., J.U.D., Decanus.
LUDOVICUS H. MOTRY, S.T.D., J.C.D., a Secretis.
VALENTINUS T. SCHAAF, O.F.M., J.C.D.
FRANCISCUS J. LARDONE, S.T.D., J.U.D.

Vidit Rector Magnificus Universitatis:

JACOBUS HUGO RYAN, Ph.D., S.T.D.

VITA

Thomas Henry Kay, born at Green Island, New York, on April 16, 1902, attended the James Heatly School of that place, was graduated from the Troy High School in 1919, and entered Holy Cross College, Worcester, Mass., with the class of 1923. Preparation for the priesthood was made at St. Joseph's Seminary, Dunwoodie, N. Y., and priesthood conferred at Albany, N. Y., on June 11, 1927. Later, a course in Canon Law was pursued at the Catholic University in Washington.

www.ingramcontent.com/pod-product-compliance
Lightning Source LLC
LaVergne TN
LVHW050226080826
844660LV00012B/481

* 9 7 8 0 8 1 3 2 2 2 4 2 4 *